Also by Dr. Michael Price

17 Days That Changed America

How to Manage Money Like a Minister

Murder on the Disoriented Express

Backfill

That Season That Was

Everyone Has A Story

The Vietnam Conflict,
One Ohio County,
and 11 Untold Stories

Dr. Michael Price

Deep Indigo Books
Indigo Sea Press
302 Ricks Drive
Winston-Salem, NC 27103

This book is a work of non-fiction as diligently researched by the author. All events, individuals, dates and settings are solely part of the author's processes.

For information regarding bulk purchases of this book, digital purchase and special discounts, please contact the publisher at indigoseapress@gmail.com

Manufactured in the United States of America
ISBN 978-1-63066-586-9

With Gratitude

As I write these words, a familiar phrase keeps running through my mind…"it takes a village." Now, I know what you're thinking.

You're thinking that there's more to the phrase than those four words, and you're right. The complete sentence reads, "It takes a village to raise a child." But while there is some uncertainty about where those epic words originated, on the African continent or among Native Americans, there is no ambiguity behind its meaning. It takes a group effort by a number of individuals, each making a specific contribution, that produces success. More, there is an intimate interconnectedness among these individuals, and it's that connection that is most valuable.

It literally took a village for me to write this book. In this case, it was several individuals who grew up in the village of Beallsville, Ohio, and the surrounding townships that comprise Monroe County. Specifically, it was the brothers and sisters, friends, and schoolmates of the eleven young men from the county who sacrificed their lives in Vietnam for the principles of freedom and democracy that allowed me into their homes and into their hearts. And in those intimate and sometimes painful conversations, I learned a great deal about these young men, including where they lived, where they went to school, and how their unexpected passing affected those around them. Memories were the common thread that keeps the families and friends of these eleven sons from one of the poorest counties in Ohio alive and connected. For some, it's all they have remaining of their loved ones who gave so much and received so little. Indeed, none of what follows would have been possible without their recollections.

With sincere gratitude and endless thanksgivings, I say thank you to…

My sister-in-law, Barbara Price, who grew up in Beallsville and still lives in the area. She was among the first to pique my interest in writing such a book. Moreover, her own recollections of what it was like to hear about the deaths of those she had known growing up made this book more than a collection of stories to me. Her insights and reflections added context to this work and feeling to each word on the pages.

Deep appreciation also goes to Vietnam veterans and brothers Bryan and Bill Beisel. Not only did these two men serve in Southeast Asia, but they grew up and attended school with two of the deceased soldiers, Dwight Ball and Steven Janeda. Beyond the depth and breadth of knowing countless things about Monroe County, the military knowledge of these two men proved invaluable in writing this book. The two of them should write a book themselves! And lest I forget, equally valuable was Bryan's wife, Susan, who was in high school with one of the eleven soldiers that died in Vietnam, William "Bobby" Lucas.

I am also deeply indebted to Debbie Ball, the wife of Dwight Ball, who allowed me to read countless letters from her husband. Through those letters and our conversations on the telephone, I gained insight into what it was like to live and love and suddenly lose.

A profound and sincere note of gratitude also goes out to the siblings of Bobby Lucas, including sister Toni Kanzigg and brothers Clint and Wade Lucas; the family members of Charles Schnegg, brothers Roger and Fred; and to the only living sibling of Dwight Ball, Ms. Helen Wykoff. Although it's been nearly six decades since they received the news of their family's loss, these siblings' memories are still vivid.

I am also thankful for all those that I encountered during my early days of research, including Army veteran Danny Kuhn, who was kind enough to quit what he was doing at home and talk with me at the VFW in Beallsville; the members of the VFW in Fly, Ohio, who not only provided me with encouraging words but empowered me with countless rounds of beer; and to those on the staff at Wayne National Forest in

Monroe County, including Kelly Miller and Kyle Morrow, whose knowledge of the area and keen insights made me sound more competent than I am.

And speaking of making me sound smarter than I am, a meaningful thank you goes out to my proofreader, Deb Miller. She continues to prove that nothing, not even the best grammar software on the market, can best the human eye when reviewing a manuscript. In every sense of the word, she is par excellence.

Dr. Mike Simpson and the good folks at Indigo Sea Press in Winston-Salem, North Carolina, continue to be my "go-to" publishing company. This will be the sixth time I've had the honor of working with Mike and his staff to get a book published, and each time they've treated me with respect and reverence. For that, I am and will be forever grateful and appreciative.

I also want to express my gratitude and thanksgiving to my wife, Betty. Although her memory has been shortened to minutes, her inspiration and love as a wife and friend will remain with me forever.

Above all, I thank all those who responded to the call for military service in Southeast Asia and around the world during one of this country's most challenging times. You stepped up when others may have stepped away, and finally…decades later…you're receiving a small portion of the enormous gratitude you deserve. And for the families of those 58,000 names that appear on *The Wall*, your loved one's sacrifice will not be forgotten. This book is written and dedicated to them "…On behalf of a grateful nation…"

Dr. Michael Price

Introduction

(Washington) The Department of Defense has released a list of soldiers killed last week in Vietnam. Included among the list is Army Pfc. Brian Cooper, who died of wounds suffered as he attempted to save the life of three fellow soldiers in his company after they began receiving enemy fire while on patrol. Also injured in the effort to save his fellow soldiers was Bruce Williams of Montgomery, Alabama. Williams was awarded the Bronze Star for his bravery. Cooper was 19 years old.

According to additional information, Pfc. Cooper was born on January 11, 1949. After graduating high school, he was conscripted/drafted into the military and completed his basic training at Fort Lee, Virginia. Following advanced training, he was deployed to Vietnam in June 1968. Cooper died four months shy of his 20th birthday. Among the loves of his life are his 1959 Chevrolet El Camino which remains in the family driveway. Standing over his flag-draped coffin bearing the American flag, the minister at Cooper's funeral is reported to have said these words:

"We live in confusing times, times of change and times of disagreement. There are those...who willsay that Brian Cooper was a man who died defending his country, and there are those who will say that he was a child that died in vain! We must have faith that none of God's children die in vain! But through allthe change there is one thing that remains constant, and eternal, and can never die, and that is the human soul."

Pfc. Cooper is survived by his parents, Mr. and Mrs. (Evelyn) Cooper, and a younger sister, Gwendolyn "Winnie" Cooper, age 7.

1

Truth be told, one will not find Brian Cooper's name among the more than 58,000 names engraved on the granite stone of the Vietnam Veterans Memorial...*The Wall*...in Washington, DC., because the Brian Cooper, in this case, never existed. Instead, he was a fictitious character that made a cameo appearance on the ABC hit show of the 1980s, *The Wonder Years*.

Following his introduction in the opening episode that aired on Wednesday evening, January 31, 1988, the mention of Cooper's name is limited. Brian Cooper had been entirely written out of the script by the midway point of the show's first tv season. Whatever one may feel about the award-winning show or the series' initial airing topic, one must credit the show's writers because they captured the true essence of the heartbreak that would eventually find its way into countless homes in America. It's safe to say that everybody in this country knew someone who had lost their life or was missing in action in the Vietnam conflict. I count myself as one of those individuals.

Robert Agar, known by many in my hometown as Bobby, lived two houses down from my family. He was the oldest member of a blended family and had several siblings. According to the *Coffelt Database of Vietnam Casualties*, he was born near the end of October 1948. Following graduation from Magnolia High School in New Martinsville, West Virginia, in 1966, he joined the Marine Reserves and completed basic training at Parris Island, South Carolina. He arrived in Vietnam the day after Christmas, 1966, and was assigned as a rifleman to Company A, 1st Battalion, 4th Marine Regiment, 3rd Marine Division, which was operating in Thua Thien Province, located below the demilitarized zone that divided North and South Vietnam. According to the casualty report, Cpl. Agar was killed just after sunset on October 29,

1967, one day after his 19th birthday, as a result of *"...fragmentation wounds to the body from a hostile grenade while engaged in action against hostile enemy" (Coffelt Database of Vietnam Casualties).* He was one of nearly a dozen soldiers killed that day near Camp Evans in Phong Dien District, Thua Thien Province.

The Marines killed alongside Agar that day in Thua Thien Province included Lance Cpl. William Dykes, of Kingsport, Tennessee, who was six days away from celebrating his 21st birthday, and Lance Cpl. Larry Havers, of Allegany, New York. He celebrated his 21st birthday fifteen days earlier. Also killed was Lance Cpl. Edwin Kahkonen, 18, of Augusta, Maine, one of ten soldiers from Augusta to lose their lives in Vietnam, and Cpl. Bristol Robertson, 19, of Roxbury, Massachusetts. Robertson arrived in Thua Thien Province one day before Kahkonen on July 23, 1967.

Other Marines died alongside Agar, including Pvt. Michael Lauer, 19, of Allentown, Pennsylvania, who began his tour of duty eight days before his passing. Also killed was Pvt. James Preziosi, 20, of Commack, New York, a Purple Heart recipient and the son of a single parent, and Pvt. John Yager, 19, of Granada Hills, California. He was one of over 5,000 soldiers from California to be killed or considered missing in Southeast Asia.

Agar's military records indicate that at the time of his passing, he received a monthly base pay of $168.60, plus Hostile Fire Pay of $65 and Foreign Duty Pay of $13. He is buried at Northview Cemetery in New Martinsville, West Virginia, and was posthumously awarded the Purple Heart.

But while Cpl. Agar may have been the first casualty reported to be from New Martinsville, he was not the last soldier from the town or Wetzel County to lose his life in Vietnam. The first to lose his life from the county was Marine Lance Cpl. John Darrell Smith, 21, of Hundred. Lance Cpl. Smith was wounded from small arms fire in Quang Nam

Province on May 21, 1966, and died two weeks later. Agar would follow nearly sixteen months later. During the next three years, the town of New Martinsville would lose Army Lt. Howard Crothers, 26, in May 1968, Marine Pvt. Brian Long, 23, a week before Thanksgiving 1969, and Army Pfc. Ronal Williams, 20, in the early months of 1970. In realistic terms, that's one life lost each year from a county with less than 20,000 citizens! The deaths of these five soldiers, and nearly seven hundred more statewide, would bestow upon the state of West Virginia the dubious honor of being the state to lose the most soldiers per capita during the Vietnam conflict.

However, this number of lost lives in the Vietnam conflict pales compared to the county immediately to the west and across the Ohio River from Wetzel County...Monroe County, Ohio. Strikingly, Monroe County, the second least populated of the state's eighty-eight counties, lost eleven soldiers in Southeast Asia between 1965 and 1971. The similarities in the lives of these eleven are quite apparent.

Several of the young men from Monroe County who lost their lives in Vietnam came from large families in which they were the oldest of the children, and many were blended families. Additionally, two soldiers were cousins, and they died one month apart, while two other Monroe County soldiers were medics. While two of the soldiers passed away on a Sunday and two others on a Thursday, the same funeral home took care of the needs of several of the families of these fallen soldiers. At the same time, it is reported that one preacher may have officiated at as many as three or more of the burials. While most of these soldiers were under six feet tall, and several participated in high school sports, three were married at the time of their passing, and the remaining eight were single. Two soldiers were known to have left their homeplace and either worked or were educated out of the county immediately before entering military service. Six soldiers attended the same high school, Beallsville High School, while three others attended River High School in Hannibal, Ohio. Last but not least, many of these soldiers had relatives who served in the military, and nearly all eleven were conscripted/drafted. Subsequently, their path to the military was not from pressure but from patriotism and duty to country.

In contrast, are the location and cause of death of these eleven young men as each saw their life come to a sudden end in a place thousands of miles away from their home. Seven soldiers died from small arms fire, and two were reportedly killed by friendly fire. Two soldiers, one a Marine, were killed in the hotbed of military action, Quang Nam Province, while two others died in the central highlands of South Vietnam. In addition, one Army soldier was wounded and later died as the result of a landmine, while another was killed attending to the medical needs of others. Lastly, the oldest of the eleven soldiers was 32 years old. Conversely, the average age of the remaining soldiers was just over 20 years old.

To fully understand the lives of these eleven soldiers before their deployment to Vietnam and the sorrowful facts behind their passing, one must go beyond what the local and regional newspapers may have said about them. And I did exactly that!

I began my preliminary research in the summer of 2022 with a general internet search for each of the eleven soldiers. Unfortunately, this avenue provided me little information since it had been over a half-century since the last of these soldiers passed away in 1971. Next, I delved deeper into the lives of these 11 sons of Monroe County by referencing three online sources: the *Coffelt Database of Vietnam Casualties*, *The Wall of Faces*, and the *Virtual Wall*. These three websites proved invaluable sources for a soldier's date and place of birth, branch and rank in the military, date and location of death in Vietnam, and any awards the soldier may have received. In addition, I paid strict attention to any posts from family members or other soldiers who may have served with one of the Monroe County soldiers in basic training, advanced training, or in Vietnam. I especially noted those who had left an email address on their posting and planned to follow up. These three sources provided me essential facts about each soldier and a firm foundation on which to build.

In the late summer of 2022, I continued my research using an online newspaper website called *newspaperarchives.com*. This source provided me with additional details about each soldier's life that may have appeared in any U.S. newspaper, from the day the soldier was born until the day they met their untimely death. The newspapers I used extensively include regional and local newspapers such as the *Daily Jeffersonian* (Cambridge, Ohio), whose circulation includes Monroe County, and the *Woodsfield* (Ohio) *Beacon*. However, I quickly discovered countless errors in my newspaper searches, especially in the spelling of the soldier's last name. When confronted with this, I referred to the website *Findagrave.com* for the correct spelling…the name and spelling that appears on the soldier's tombstone. In another printed error, one newspaper reported that several of the eleven soldiers from Monroe County were in the Marines. Wrong! There was only one. The fact that the soldier's obituary commonly listed the parents as Mr. and Mrs. and did not give the mother's first name also made research challenging.

During this same period, I accessed online county tax records for the names and addresses of living relatives I had "gleaned" from reading obituaries. Much of the information regarding Monroe County and the history of the county's townships comes from *Hardesty's History of Monroe County, Ohio* (1882), *Caldwell's Atlas of Monroe County, Ohio* (1898), *Howe's Historical Collection of Ohio* (1907) and the online source *Ohio Genealogy Express*.

Following the preliminary research, I felt I was ready to take the last, and most valuable, step in my research...visiting the area where these eleven young men were raised, went to school, and where many lived their abbreviated lives. This research segment proved easy and convenient since I was born and grew up a few miles east of Monroe County in Wetzel County, West Virginia. More, I was familiar with the county, having competed in sports against athletes from several of the county high schools.

For over a week in the fall of 2022, I traveled the roads, ridges, hills, and valleys of Monroe County, including north and south State Route 7, the longest state route in Ohio. Additionally, I drove north and south on Route 26 and east and west on county roads like Route 800, Route 556, Route 145, and along one of America's most scenic roads, County Road 78. Along the way, I passed through towns and villages with historical names like Berne, Hannibal, and Malaga and biblical ones like Antioch (the ancient city in Asia Minor where the early followers of Jesus were first called Christians), Bethel (the site in the Old Testament where Jacob slept and dreamed of angels going up and down a ladder between heaven and earth), Sardis (one of the seven churches of Asia mentioned by John of Patmos in the Book of Revelation), and Jerusalem (considered by Christians to be one of the world's most holy cities). In all, I racked up nearly 250 miles on my rental car navigating county roads and tracking down leads.

Beyond stopping in towns like Woodsfield, New Matamoras, and Beallsville, I stopped and talked with people involved in the Office of Veteran's Affairs, county administration, and local businesses. Most valuable were the countless Vietnam veterans I met at the local VFW and

American Legions in Beallsville and Duffy, Ohio. While few wanted to talk about their time in Vietnam, most were more than willing to share their experiences in the military, like basic training and beyond.

The most valuable parts of my research came following my return from Monroe County when I spoke on the phone with several family members about their deceased siblings and spouses. Many of my questions about their brother or husband were answered, and most were open about the pain they felt when they heard the news about their family's loss. Some said they still miss their loved ones, even today…nearly six decades later. The ones I spoke to remember where they were when they received the tragic news, who was with them, and how they reacted. Even more appreciated, some allowed me to read letters from their loved ones who had served in Vietnam. Naturally, I could not contact some families because there were no living relatives, bad health, or declining memory, which is a collective loss. Other family members did not wish to speak to me at all. I understand and respect their decision.

As the calendar turned into a new year, I was ready to begin writing.

I am no more a professional writer than I am a highly-educated military historian. However, I feel that three decades of researching and writing sermons and writing five books on a variety of topics has equipped me with the skill to write a book on such a delicate subject. From the beginning, my goal was to write a book that is well-researched, easily read, and informative, and at the same time, sympathetic and respectful to those eleven families that lost a son, husband, or father in the Vietnam conflict. The reader will notice early on that the work has limited citations and few, if any, footnotes.

Footnotes and citations add pages to the book, and extra pages mean the book will cost more. As I have noted in all my works: "if you want to know where I located a particular piece of information found in the work, call or write me. I'll be glad to help." This said, the book unfolds in this manner.

In *Chapter One*, I provide a brief history of Monroe County, Ohio, to provide context to what follows. The pages in this chapter deal with the seven townships where ten of the soldiers grew up, and the communities where they lived, including Beallsville, Brownsville, Clarington, Lewisville, New Matamoras, Sardis, and Woodsfield. One soldier lived in Belmont County, Ohio, but attended school in Monroe County. For the purpose of clarity, a soldier from Monroe County is defined as one who: (a) was born and raised in the county, (b) attended school in the county, or (c) graduated from one of the four county schools at the time such as Beallsville High School, River High School. Skyvue High School or Woodsfield High School. To fully understand as much as possible about these soldiers, one needs to know where these 11 soldiers grew up and were educated.

Chapter Two explores how hundreds of thousands of young men came to be in the military, especially what was termed the "selective service process" or conscription/draft. Much of the information presented in this chapter comes from two sources: *Rough Draft: Cold War Military Manpower Policy and the Origins of Vietnam-Era Draft Resistance*, by Amy Rutenberg (2019), and *Channeling*, the monthly newsletter of the Selective Service System, published from January 1961 thru December 1969.

The contents of *Chapter Three* trace America's military involvement in Southeast Asia, the policies that warranted our involvement, and the actions that dictated the American military response, beginning immediately after World War II and ending with the passing of the last of the Monroe County soldiers to die in the region (1971). Along the way, I share the names and the heart-wrenching stories of some of the 58,000 soldiers from across the U.S. who left families and loved ones to further the cause of democracy in a remote and seemingly unheard part of the world. Included in the list is the story of Army E5 Michael May, 21, of Vassar, Michigan, an Infantry Operations and Intelligence Specialist, who, if the post is correct, is one of the nearly one thousand soldiers who died on their first day of military service in the Vietnam conflict. I also touch on the story of Army Cpl. Edward Cervantez, who was a batboy for the Chicago White Sox before losing his life in Phu Yen Province in 1968. Additionally, I highlight the extraordinary lives of the eight nurses and sixteen chaplains that died in the conflict prior to Easter 1971. After all, *Everyone Has a Story*.

The focus of *Chapter Four* is directly on the lives of the eleven soldiers of Monroe County, how and where they lived and grew up, and how and where they died, albeit sometimes graphic and in detail. The stories are arranged chronologically by the date of the soldier's death, beginning with Staff Sgt. Glenn McCammon (1965), followed by Army Pfc. Jack Pittman and Marine Pvt. Duane Greenlee (1966), Army Cpl. Charles Schnegg (1967), SP4 Richard Rucker and Army Staff Sgt. James Ravencraft (1968), Navy HM3 William "Bobby" Lucas (1969), Army Cpl. Dwight Ball and Army SP4 Steven Janeda (1970), and Army SP4 Phillip Brandon and Army Medic Dale Hood (1971).

The last chapter, *Chapter Five*, concludes with some general thoughts.

Throughout, I endeavored to keep my views and opinions absent and any opinions or views of family members or former soldiers to a minimum. Sadly, I could not mention the backstory of every one of the over 58,000 who lost their lives in Southeast Asia, and I am deeply sorrowful. I am equally apologetic for any misspelled names, dates of death, or mislocated states, cities, or towns these young soldiers may have called home. It was not intentional, and I ask your forgiveness for the error. Moreover, I did the best I could with the information available.

Granted, there may have been other books written on the subject at hand, but those only skimmed the surface of the lives of these eleven young men. This work is unique, however, because it delves deeper into the similarities of their young lives and the differences that brought about their unfortunate deaths. Every soldier that served in Vietnam and mentioned in this work has a back story, and these eleven young men from the second least populated county in Ohio are no different. Consequently, this book cannot, and should not, be read in one sitting. The stories within my work are too rich, too moving, and too emotional to race through to merely get to the end. Moreover, each chapter lays a foundation for the chapter that follows it. Lastly, it is worth mentioning that the names, dates, locations, etc., are noted as if they are relative to the time of the Vietnam conflict and not years afterward. In other words, read this work as if it were the years of American involvement in Southeast Asia. However, I must warn you that some stories I share of lost lives in Southeast Asia are graphic and disturbing. War is hell; ask anyone who's been there.

When all the reading is done, I wanted my readers to hear the most complete story to date and to know as much about the eleven young men from Monroe County, Ohio, as I do. But, above all, I wanted my readers to know that these soldiers, along with their families, gave so much, and that the sacrifice of these young men of Monroe County will not be forgotten. The story of these young men, from birth to death, men who gave so much, needs…no, it demands…to be told!

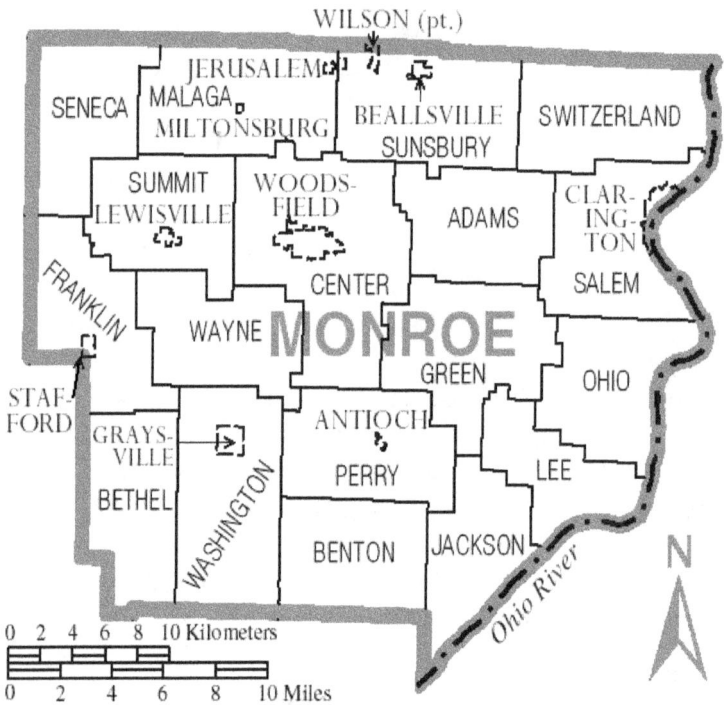

WILSON (pt.)

SENECA

JERUSALEM

MALAGA
MILTONSBURG

BEALLSVILLE
SUNSBURY

SWITZERLAND

SUMMIT
LEWISVILLE

WOODS-
FIELD

ADAMS

CLAR-
ING-
TON

FRANKLIN

CENTER

SALEM

WAYNE

MONROE

GREEN

OHIO

STAF-
FORD

GRAYS-
VILLE

ANTIOCH

LEE

BETHEL

WASHINGTON

PERRY

BENTON

JACKSON

Ohio River

N

0   2   4   6   8   10 Kilometers

0   2   4   6   8   10 Miles

Chapter I

Paraphrasing the words of the late historian and noted American author David McCullough as found in his epic work entitled *"The Pioneers: The Heroic Story of the Settlers Who Brought the American Ideal West"* (2019), the years immediately following the signing of the Treaty of Paris in 1783 brought an official end to the American Revolution while opening vast amounts of land west of the Allegheny mountains in Pennsylvania and north and west of Virginia. The opening of this land nearly doubled the size of the original thirteen colonies. Naturally, these almost 275,000 square miles of land were void of roads, organized settlements, or schools. However, this did not stop those who intended to begin a new life in a new land. Immigrants from Europe, willing to sacrifice "life and limb" for a chance to settle and make a new home, would land on the east coast of America, and then travel west through Maryland, Pennsylvania, and Virginia.

It is believed that the first group of unorganized settlers may have come to the lands west of the Ohio River from nearby Sistersville, West Virginia. Crossing the river via a ferry, they found the soil rich, the hunting of animals abundant, and a wealth of timber for building. As more and more settlers came into the unbroken wilderness, they moved north and west. Many of these early settlers were considered squatters with no legal land rights. Nevertheless, their process of acquiring land was common. First, they would choose a piece of land to their liking…bottom or flatlands…usually near a water source like a stream or creek. Next, they would build and begin farming the land. Before long, they would call it their own.

In the mid-1780s, the newly established Congress of the Colonies began to draw up plans for the organized settlement of this Northwest Territory, as it came to be called. The general blueprint for the Northwest (Land) Ordinance of 1787 was an effort to lay out rules for the admission of new states and define the state's form and structure of government. Additionally, the ordinance included a bill of rights granting civil liberties to residents, the freedom of worship, the prohibition of slavery, and a fourth segment that deemed the establishment of schools in time. Beyond this, the decree endeavored to establish the legal basis of land ownership.

To legally own land in this vast territory that stretched from the Ohio River to the great lakes, a person could purchase land directly from the government or a land company that would buy up thousands of acres of land and then sell it to settlers. The proceeds from selling this land would pay the debt incurred by the new government during the Revolutionary War. A territorial government soon followed. Despite the government's best intentions to arrange for an orderly acquisition of land by settlers, squatting still occurred in countless areas of the new territory. A name for the new land soon caught on...the Ohio Country...named after the great river that formed a natural boundary to the east. The Native Americans referred to the river as the "O-Y-O."

In a short time, a group of New Englanders calling themselves the Ohio Company would purchase a large swatch of the new land in the southeastern part of the new territory. The original intentions of the company were to buy over one million acres. However, they could only raise enough money to buy approximately three-quarters of a million acres, some portions of it along the west bank of the Ohio River. Their piece of land would begin where the mouth of the Muskingum River meets the Ohio River and stretch north and west. The Ohio Company would later petition the new government to donate land directly to the north of the company's land as a buffer between settlers and Native Americans, and they did.

With the initial land purchase complete, it was time for surveyors to begin platting out a section of the new territory.

After crossing the Alleghenies on foot, a government survey team boarded boats and headed north on the Youghiogheny River to begin their arduous task of platting the newly purchased piece of land. When their boats met the waters of the Monongahela River, they headed north, eventually arriving in Pittsburgh and the headwaters of the Ohio River. The group then headed south on the river, passing Wheeling, (West) Virginia, and countless other settlements that dotted the east side of the river. Eventually, the weary travelers tied up on the western side of the river and to the north of the Muskingum River. It was here that the task of mapping out the vast territory known as the Northwest Territory would begin. Their plan for platting the land was well laid out.

Settlements would be placed within townships, each measuring around six square miles. Except for townships whose eastern boundaries lay along the irregular shore of the west coast of the Ohio River, township boundaries would run north and south and intersect by lines running east and west. Following, townships would be subdivided into sections of 640 acres each. The first tract to be surveyed began in the southcentral area of the new lands and ran north along the west bank of the Ohio River for approximately one hundred miles. The surveyed tract purchased by the Ohio Company would then move west for about 50 miles and finally south for another hundred miles. Finally, the parcels would be numbered.

In July of 1788, the new territorial governor, Major General Arthur St. Clair, issued a proclamation establishing the county of Washington, named after Revolutionary War General George Washington. The Ohio River would form the eastern boundary of the territory. At the same time, the Scioto River would stand as the southern and western boundary. Finally, the northern terminal point of the territory would be Lake Erie. Before long, cabins begin to appear around the original landing site, then trading posts and stores. It is said that before long, the settlement had a population of over 130 men, women, and children.

By the end of 1788, a name was chosen for the settlement. It would be named after the French queen, Marie Antoinette, or simply Marietta.

―――――――――

When the Northwest Territory split into two sections in the late 18th century, the Ohio territory boasted several counties with names that reflected revolutionary heroes, colonial patriots, and familiar landscapes. The list includes Hamilton County, organized in 1790, and Adams County, organized seven years later in 1797. Hamilton County and Adams County are located along the Ohio River in the new territory's southern regions.

In a short time, a fourth county had been formed from Washington County. Located across the Ohio River from newly formed Brooke County, (West) Virginia, Jefferson County was organized in the late summer of 1797 and named after then-vice-president Thomas Jefferson. Laid out by surveyors, it would eventually number fourteen townships and over four hundred square miles. Following Ross County, located in the southcentral part of the newly settled territory and organized in 1798, came Trumbull, Clermont, and Fairfield counties three years later. Ross County, located in the southcentral part of the territory, is named for U.S. Senator James Ross of Pennsylvania.

In contrast, Trumbull County, located in the northeast part of the territory near the western border of Pennsylvania, is named for Gov. Jonathan Trumbull of Connecticut. Located east of Hamilton County, Clermont County measures over four hundred square miles and derives its name from the French term for "clear mountain." Fairfield County is located near the center of the Ohio territory.

In 1801, land would be taken from Washington County, the oldest county in the original Northwest Territory, and one of the newest counties, Jefferson County, to create Belmont County, located to the immediate south of Jefferson County. By the time Ohio was admitted as the seventeenth state to the union on March 1, 1803, no less than eight counties had been birthed from lands derived from the first county organized in the territory, Washington County. More importantly, any provisions laid out in the Northwest Ordinance of 1787 were dissolved.

Lured by good reports sent back home by others who had settled in the lands immediately west of the Ohio River, new travelers found large amounts of unclaimed lands. Subsequently, some settlers chose not to continue their journey downstream on the Ohio River toward Marietta. Instead, they stopped along the western shores of the river south of Wheeling and in the northern areas of inland Washington County. The ancestorial names of these early settlers would include German and Swiss ones like Fankhauser and Tschappat. Before long, a second wave of European immigrants would follow. It is believed that the original intent of the second wave of German and Swiss immigrants was to settle further south, near the confluence of the Kanawha River and the Ohio River. Instead, they stopped north of Marietta to settle. As a result, the area between Jefferson and Belmont counties and Marietta soon began to be populated with people of similar ancestry.

A few months before James Madison was inaugurated to

serve a second term as president in March 1813, the number of Ohio counties had grown to over forty. This includes Muskingum County, formed in 1804 from parts of Washington and Fairfield counties. Six years later, Guernsey County, in the eastern part of the state, was formed from lands in Belmont and Muskingum counties. Finally, on January 29, 1813, with land taken from the neighboring counties of Belmont and Washington, Monroe County, located in the eastern part of the state along the Ohio River, was officially organized and recognized as Ohio's forty-fourth county.

The eighteen townships that would eventually comprise Monroe County have an equally rich history.

Center Township, as the name implies, is found near the geographical center of Monroe County. Most likely, the first settlers were squatters and may have arrived in the area near where Sunfish Creek empties into the Ohio River. The settlers then followed the county's largest creek inland until they found a suitable ground to settle. With a land size measuring nearly forty-two square miles, Center Township is surrounded by Sunsbury, Adams, Green, Perry, Wayne, Summit, and Malaga townships. As the county seat, the site of the county's first agricultural fair, and the only city in America with this name, Woodsfield was surveyed in 1812, founded a year later, chosen as the county seat in 1814, and incorporated in 1835. The first of eleven soldiers from Monroe County to die in Vietnam, *Staff Sgt. Glenn McCammon*, was born in Woodsfield and attended school there.

As the county's second most populated township and third largest in square miles, *Sunsbury Township* is believed to have been settled in the early months of the summer of 1819. The township is located in extreme north central Monroe County. It is bordered by two Belmont County townships to the north,

Washington and Wayne, Switzerland Township to the immediate east, Adams and Green Townships to the southeast, Center Township to the southwest, and Malaga Township to the west. The township's most populated community, Beallsville, is named after Citizen Beall, who is credited with organizing the community in 1824. Beallsville was incorporated in 1850 and is the home to one of the county's four high schools. Five soldiers that attended Beallsville High School died in Vietnam, including *Pfc. Jack Pittman, Pvt. Duane Greenlee, HM3 William "Bobby" Lucas, SP4 Richard Rucker*, and *SP4 Phillip Brandon.*

Located in the extreme northeast part of Monroe County and extending west, *Switzerland Township* lies immediately south of two Belmont County, Ohio, townships: Washington and York. It is also bordered by the Ohio River to its immediate east, Salem Township to its south, Adams Township to its southwest, and Sunsbury Township to its immediate west. The township was first settled in 1819 by German and Swiss settlers that landed at the mouth of the township's largest waterway, Captina Creek. Organized in early 1827, it may lay claim to being one of the county's first townships to do so. Although the township covers nearly 30 square miles, the population density is one of the lowest in the county at just over fifteen people per square mile. Considering that the area was initially settled by immigrant dairy farmers, the early economy of the township centered on the cheese and dairy industry. Although he lived across the Switzerland Township line in Belmont County, *Cpl. Charles Schnegg*, the fourth of the Monroe County soldiers to die in Vietnam, attended Beallsville High School.

Nestled to the immediate south of Switzerland Township along the Ohio River, *Salem Township* is another area within Monroe County initially settled by German and Swiss immigrants. Organized between 1815 and 1819, the township's eastern border is the west bank of the Ohio River and immediately west of Marshall County, (West) Virginia. With Switzerland Township to the immediate north, Ohio Township to the south, a small section of Green Township to the southwest, and Adams Township directly west, Salem Township, once possibly the largest in size, measures approximately 30 square miles. The first settlers are believed to have been squatters that floated down the Ohio River from Pittsburgh on flatboats in the waning years of the 18th century. Landing near where Sunfish Creek empties into the Ohio River, the settlers then followed the county's largest creek inland until they found a suitable piece of ground on which to settle. Like their European relatives to the north in Switzerland Township, this area of the county is a large producer of dairy products like cheese. In one year alone (1881), it is believed that local farmers in the township manufactured nearly forty-five tons of cheese. The township's largest community, Clarington, was laid out by David Pierson in 1822, who named the village after his daughter, Clarinda. *Staff Sgt. James Ravencraft*, the sixth soldier from Monroe County to be killed in Vietnam, was raised in Clarington.

With Lee Township to the south and Green Township to the west, a few miles south of Salem Township lies *Ohio Township*. The township's eastern border hugs the west bank of the Ohio River, and New Martinsville, (West) Virginia, is a short distance across the river. As the township's first settlers, German and Swiss immigrants may have predated the first surveys in the area by a few years since records indicate that the township was not organized until the fall of 1818. With a population density of over 35 people per square mile and spread out over approximately twenty-three square miles, it is considered by some to be one of the most densely populated townships in Monroe County. Originally called Baresville, the township's largest community is Hannibal. It's home to one of Monroe County's two largest employers: aluminum manufacturer Ormet Corporation and its processing and shipping plant, Consolidated Aluminum Corporation (Conalco). North American Coal Company is the county's other significant source of employment. The township is home to another of the county high schools, River High School. The eighth soldier to pass away in Vietnam, *Cpl. Dwight Ball* attended RHS before his military deployment.

Benton Township, in far southcentral Monroe County, was the last township to be established by county commissioners. The township was organized in the late spring of 1851 from land acquired following the establishment of the last of Ohio's eighty-eight counties, Noble County. To the immediate east of Benton Township is Jackson Township, Monroe County's oldest township, to the south are the Washington County townships of Grandview and Ludlow, and to the west and north lies Washington and Perry Townships, respectively. Despite the presence of families in the area in the early 1800s as they trekked north and west from the territory's first permanent settlement in Marietta, it would be almost another half-century before Benton Township was established, organized, and incorporated. The township is the least populated township among the county's eighteen townships, while Brownsville is considered the largest community in the township. There are over fifty other towns or cities in the U.S. named Brownsville, five alone in the state of Ohio. Still, there is only one Brownsville in Benton Township, Monroe County, Ohio, whose location sits on County Road 12. It was the home of *SP4 Steven Janeda*, a graduate of River High School and the tenth soldier from Monroe County to die in Vietnam.

As the only township in the state with this name, *Summit Township* is the last of the eighteen Monroe County townships to lose a soldier in Vietnam. Located in the far west of the county, the township is bordered by five municipalities, including Malaga Township to the north, Center Township to the east, Wayne Township to the southeast, Franklin to the southwest, and Seneca Township to the northwest. The township was organized less than a year before the founding of Benton Township, and it is widely believed that the name Summit may have been chosen because the township sits on one of the highest points in the county, nearly 1,250 feet above sea level. Lewisville, the most populated community in the township, is located approximately 10 miles west of the county seat of Woodsfield and lies at the intersection of County Routes 145 and 78. The latter route is better known by locals as the Shenandoah Trail, which runs through the Wayne National Forest. While there exists over a dozen communities in the U.S. named Lewisville, the most significant loss in Vietnam for Lewisville, Ohio, was Army *Medical Corpsman Dale Hood.*

To date, this chapter's focus has been on the seven townships that lost a soldier in Vietnam, including the townships of Benton, Center, Ohio, Salem, Summit, Sunsbury, and Switzerland. However, the remaining townships in the county are worth highlighting because they offer further context into the lives of these eleven fallen sons of Monroe County. While the information shared about these remaining eleven townships may seem truncated, the history behind their settling, organization, and incorporation is equally as compelling as the previous seven townships. The list of these remaining townships is addressed in alphabetic order to not give semblance to any rank or importance.

Reportedly, *Adams Township* did not have its first settlers until the early 1800s, and it would be another quarter-century until its full incorporation in 1826. Comprising nearly 23 square miles and a population of just over six hundred, the township is bounded by Sunsbury Township to the north and west, Switzerland Township to the northeast, Salem Township to the immediate east, Green Township to the south, and

Center Township to the west. One of the earliest communities in Adams Township to be laid out was Jamestown in the mid-1830s. However, the community's name was later changed to Cameron, after its neighbor across the Ohio River, Cameron, (West) Virginia.

Located in the far southwest part of the county, *Bethel Township* was first settled around 1817 but was not incorporated for another fifteen years. It is the second least populated township in the county and contains nearly twenty-five square miles of land. The township is bordered by Washington Township directly to the east, parts of Washington County to the south, Elk Township (Noble County) to the west, and Franklin Township to its north. Before the establishment of Noble County in 1851, Elk Township was part of Monroe County. As it stands, there are three townships in Ohio named Bethel Township. Sycamore Valley, this Benton Township's most populated community, sits in the northern part of the township along County Road 260.

Bordered by no less than seven other townships, *Green Township* is located in central Monroe County and immediately south of Adams Township. Although it ranks near the top in land size, approximately 28 square miles, it ranks near the bottom in population, with about sixteen people per square mile. The township is believed to have been settled around 1815 and organized nearly a decade later, in 1824. According to historical records, the township's first schoolteacher was

> "...compelled to sign an article that on Christmas or New Year's day, he would treat the scholars (students) to gingercakes (sp.), cider and apples, or they would bar him out of the school house, or, if he got in first, they would smoke him out. If he still refused to sign the article, they would take him to the nearest creek, and dunk him" (Hardesty, pg. 218).

23

There are eleven other Green townships statewide, but the one in Monroe County may be the oldest on the list.

Franklin Township is the second of three townships in far west Monroe County that borders Noble County. Positioned clockwise, the township is surrounded by Seneca, Summit, Wayne, Washington, and Bethel townships, respectively, and the Noble County townships of Elk, Marion, and Stock to the relative west. While the first settlers arrived in 1805 or 1806, the township's most populated community, Stafford, was not laid out until nearly three decades later. The community is located along County Road 12, approximately ten miles west of the county seat of Woodsfield. As one might expect, no less than twenty townships in Ohio bear the same name as the Franklin Township found in Monroe County. Most likely named for the city in Switzerland, many township residents receive mail at the Bern(e) Post Office.

It was in *Jackson Township* that the first settlements in Monroe County were made in the late 1700s. However, the township was not organized until the summer of 1819. As the first township in the county, the remaining townships received their land from the lands of Jackson Township. Measuring nearly 20 square miles, the Ohio River forms the township's eastern border, with Benton and Perry Townships to its west, Green Township to its north, Lee Township to its northeast, and Grandview Township, Washington County, to its south. With such a famous name, it is no wonder that Jackson Township in Monroe County shares its name with nearly forty other townships across Ohio. Because of its location in the southeastern part of the county, residents in Jackson Township have the furthest distance to travel to the county seat, Woodsfield. From New Matamoras in southern Jackson Township to Woodsfield, it is around 25 miles of winding roads.

It is said that *Lee Township*, organized a few years after the end of the Civil War in 1869, may hold the distinction of having some of the earliest settlements in the county. Additionally, the township lays claim to being the only township in the state to have been organized by the Ohio legislature. Similar to its neighbor to the north, Ohio Township, and Jackson Township to the south, the eastern border of Lee Township is formed by the winding waters of the Ohio River. Major Earl Sproat, one of the nearly fifty founding members of the Ohio Company, settled on land in the township. It is widely believed that following his death in the early 1820s, Sproat's land was purchased by James Patton. He is credited with platting Lee Township's largest community, Sardis, in the mid-1840s. Although it is the county's smallest township, measuring just over 17 square miles, it is one of the most densely populated in the county, with nearly sixty people per square mile. The township includes communities with names like Duffy and Fly. George Washington, an investor in the Ohio Company, camped just north of Fly as he surveyed the area in the mid-1750s.

With Somerset and Wayne townships in Belmont County to its north, Sunsbury Township to its relative east, Center Township to its southeast, Summit Township to its south, and Seneca Township to its west, *Malaga Township* was organized in the latter days of 1820. However, the first settlers may have arrived around five years earlier. As one might expect with its proximity to Sunsbury and Switzerland townships, German immigrants comprised much of the early population. Bearing the same name as the township, it is believed that the town of Malaga was platted a few years before the township. Other communities in the township include Miltonsburg and Jerusalem. According to the census of 1840-1880, Malaga and Franklin townships showed the slowest population growth of all Monroe County townships. As the third largest township in size, nearly 30 square miles, and population, Malaga Township is the only township with that name in the U.S.

Recorded to have been organized on December 30, 1823,

Perry Township is another of the Monroe County townships bordered by no less than 6 other townships. In this case, the circular pattern includes Center and Green townships to the north and northeast, Benton and Jackson to the south and southeast, and Washington and Wayne to the southwest and west, respectively. The first settlers seem to have appeared in the early months of 1800. Still, any semblance of permanent settlements did not reportedly happen until 1812. Although the township comprises nearly twenty-five square miles, it takes its place along with Benton, Bethel, and Wayne Townships as one of the least populated townships in Monroe County. Located near the middle of the township is the community of Antioch. Interestingly, the largest church in the area was the Christian Church, which reportedly drew over 100 worshippers weekly. One cannot help but wonder which came first, the organization of the Antioch community or the church's founding, especially since the ancient city of Antioch in Asia Minor was where the followers of Jesus were first called Christians.

Although local historians cite *Seneca Township* as the second settled township in the county, it may have been one of the first townships in the county to have settlers. It is believed that the first settlers to set foot in the future township arrived around 1798. Located in the northwestern part of the county, the township is over twenty-two square miles and is bordered by Somerset Township in Belmont County to the immediate north, Malaga Township to the east, Summit Township to the southeast, and Franklin Township to the south. Three Noble County townships border Seneca Township to the west, including Beaver, Marion, and Stock. Calais is reportedly the first community organized, having been laid out in 1837. Most likely, the township's founders named the township after the Seneca tribe of Native Americans who lived and hunted in the area. In addition to a Seneca Township in Seneca County, Ohio, located in the northcentral part of the state, there is a Seneca Township just across the border in nearby Noble County! While the population of Monroe County reportedly increased nearly two-fold between 1840 and 1880, Seneca Township was the only county township to record a decrease.

The first signs of settlers to *Washington Township* occurred around 1816. Still, the township would not be formally organized until the early summer of 1832. Measuring eight miles from north to south and four miles wide, it is bounded by Wayne Township to the north and Perry and Benton townships to the east and southeast. Additionally, Washington County, the first county organized in the new territory, lies to the south, and Bethel Township to the west. The township shares its prestigious name with over forty other townships in the state. Graysville, the most populated community within the township, is located at the intersection of State Route 26 and County Route 12. The 1880 census records the township's population in excess of 1,800 residents; however, more recent numbers place the population around 500.

The final of Monroe County's eighteen organized townships, *Wayne Township*, is located in the west-central part of the county. Surrounded by Center, Perry, Washington, Franklin, and Summit townships, it is believed that the first organized settlements possibly happened sometime after 1815. The township measures nearly twenty-three square miles, a population of less than four hundred and less than twenty people per square mile. The low population is mainly because the township lies within the Wayne National Forest...the state's only national forest.

Between the 1840 and 1880 censuses, two townships initially part of Monroe County, Elk and Enoch, became townships in Noble County. A third, Union Township, was dissolved entirely from the Monroe County records. These three townships were replaced by four newly formed townships: Benton, Center, Summit, and Lee. Following this change, no more Monroe County townships were added or deleted; subsequently, the final number of townships in the county stands at eighteen.

Despite all that's been written through the years surrounding the history of Monroe County and its eighteen townships, these views pale in comparison to the backstory of the eleven soldiers born and raised in the county.

Center Township and Woodsfield was the place where *Staff Sgt. Glenn McCammon*, the only child of Charles and Mildred McCammon, was raised and attended elementary school. At 32, he is the oldest of the county's soldier sons to die in Vietnam. But those outside the area only know Center Township as the county's largest population and the town as the county seat.

Sunsbury Township, in particular the community of Beallsville, was where *Pfc. Jack Pittman* spent a great deal of his growing up. Attending Beallsville High School where he played football, Pittman not only caught the winning touchdown pass against Woodsfield in the 1963 homecoming game but also had the honor of crowning the homecoming queen at halftime! However, for those residing outside the township, all they may know is that Sunsbury Township is located south of Belmont County, and Beallsville is located at the intersection of Ohio routes 556 and 147.

Those outside of Sunbury Township may only know what they read in the newspaper or see on tv, like it's the only township in Ohio with that name. Others know it as the home of *Pvt. Duane Greenlee*…the only one of the eleven Monroe County soldiers killed in Vietnam to be a Marine and one of the two township soldiers to die in the South Vietnamese province of Quang Nam.

Similarly, those who are only vaguely familiar with

Sunsbury Township may know it as the third largest township in the county land-wise, with a population at the time of the Vietnam conflict of just over 1,300 residents. Even less recognize that *Cpl. Charles Schnegg* and Greenlee rode the same bus to school each day, and Schnegg died one day shy of the day he first entered military service...December 5, 1966 - December 4, 1967.

And likewise, the less-than-avid reader may know that nearly one in four residents of Sunsbury Township has German ancestors. However, less known is that *SP4 Richard Rucker* was another of the Sunsbury Township soldiers who grew up in Beallsville, died during the deadliest month of the Vietnam conflict (May 1968), and was the third member of the Class of 1965 from Beallsville High School to die in Southeast Asia.

Beyond recognizing Salem Township as the location of the county's first settlements, one of the largest producers of dairy products in the region, and the township's largest community, Clarington, named after the daughter of the man who laid out the community, few individuals outside of the area know more. They do not know that *Staff Sgt. James Ravencraft* was a resident of Clarington and was one of three married soldiers from the county to lose his life in Vietnam. He is the only soldier with that last name on the Vietnam Veteran's Memorial Wall, *The Wall*, in Washington, DC.

While most know that Beallsville High School draws students from outside the township, including those from nearby Belmont County, most know little about this particular school. Consequently, most would not recognize the name *HM3 William "Bobby" Lucas*, the fourth graduate of the school to lose his life in military service in Vietnam. As a Navy medic, and known to his family, friends, and schoolmates as Bobby, Lucas died as he attempted to render medical aid to a fallen soldier. He intended to enter the medical field after his term in the service.

29

Many living beyond Monroe County recognize Lee Township for two primary reasons. First, Major Earl Sproat, one of the founding members of the Ohio Company, settled on land there. Additionally, the township is home to one of the county's major employers, Ormet aluminum plant, and its processing and shipping center, Conalco. Beyond that, few know that the township was the home of *SP4 Dwight Ball*. As a student at nearby River High School in Hannibal, Ball was one of five soldiers from the county to receive both the Purple Heart and the Bronze Star for their sacrifice in Southeast Asia, one of two county soldiers to be killed by friendly fire, and was married less than two weeks before he met his untimely death.

As most familiar with the county's history know, Sunsbury Township comprises over 28 square miles and has a population density of nearly fifty people per square mile; only Center, Lee, and Malaga townships rank higher. Conversely, a much smaller number recognizes the name *SP4 Phillip Brandon*. At 19 years, 3 months, and 18 days, he was the youngest of the eleven sons of Monroe to meet an untimely passing. Beyond being the tenth soldier from the county to die in Vietnam, he was the only Monroe County soldier to die in Thua Thien Province.

Outdoor enthusiasts and avid hikers recognize Wayne Township not only because a large portion of Wayne National Forest, the state's lone national forest, is located in the township but a person must travel along many of the township's roads to get to the national forest. Still, many who travel the roads fail to recognize the name *Pfc. Dale Hood*. As a Wayne Township resident, Hood was the last of the county's eleven soldiers to die in Vietnam. More, Hood was one of five county soldiers to die before his 21st birthday, the third Monroe soldier involved in a vehicle-related death in Vietnam, the 2nd medic from the county to die, and the only Wayne Township soldier to die in Quang Tri Province.

———————

It's important to remember what was left behind when these eleven young soldiers, ranging in age from nineteen to thirty-two, responded to the call for military service.

The county's rank near the middle of the state's eighty-eight counties in land size, second to last in total population, and last in people per square mile not only fostered but furthered tight-knit communities. Consequently, these young men left behind almost everyone they had attended school with, socialized with...and even worshiped beside...throughout their young and abbreviated lives.

Beyond the peacefulness of the rolling hills and serenity of the valleys, these same soldiers left behind unique images of the county, including the historic Knowlton (aka Long or Old Camp) Covered Bridge in Washington Township and the Foreaker (aka the Foraker or Weddle) Covered Bridge on Ohio Route 40 near Graysville. Additionally, they left behind the history of the Sistersville Ferry and its crucial role in transporting early settlers across the Ohio River from (West) Virginia into Monroe County. More, they left in their past remembrances of the 20-plus quilt barns that dotted the county's landscape in fourteen of the eighteen townships.

Above all, the eleven soldiers would leave behind families. Three fallen soldiers would leave behind spouses and one with three young children, all under the age of ten. In total, the eleven sons of the county left behind no less than forty siblings, with the majority younger than the soldier himself. All these but fading memories in the soldiers' past.

What lay ahead for these soldiers was in stark contrast to all they had known growing up. Most were leaving Monroe County and their particular township for the first time to complete basic and extended military training. After that, they would find themselves in a politically divided country, thousands of miles away from home, and a country few back home in the county could locate on a map. But, above all, they would find themselves members of an army with a growing presence in Southeast Asia, whose primary directive was to stop the advancement of anti-democratic principles in the region.

However, the process that removed them from Monroe County and into one of the world's hotspots was historical and complicated.

Chapter II

Some historians believe the foundational roots of young men being called to military duty date to pre-biblical times.

The Babylonian Empire of the second century BCE employed a system whereby young men were required to serve in times of war. In return, these individuals were granted land ownership. Despite it being outlawed by the Code of Hammurabi, a collection of rules and legal codes for a just and civil society, hiring substitutes was common. Equally common was the practice of young men leaving their towns to avoid military service. A similar system was popular in the Middle Ages, requiring landowners to provide one male per family for military service.

According to one Ohio newspaper, a reference to conscription/draft is found in the Bible. The first historical mention of young men being called to military service is in the Book of Numbers, and reads that...

> *"The LORD spoke to Moses in the wilderness of Sinai, in the tent of meeting, on the first day of the second month, in the second year after they had come out of the land of Egypt, saying, 'Take a census of the whole congregation of Israelites, in their clans, by ancestral houses, according to the number of names, every male individually, from twenty years old and up, everyone in Israel able to go to war. You and Aaron shall enroll them, company by company....'" (The Daily Jeffersonian, January 18, 1968, pg. 15)*

The first modern conscription, more commonly known as the draft, happened during the French Revolution in the late eighteenth century. Fearing retribution from neighboring European powers for overthrowing the traditional monarchy, France decreed a policy whereby all unmarried, non-disabled young men between 18-25 were to serve in the military.

It is widely believed that the first instances of conscription in the U.S. dates back to the American Revolution. Here, local towns or cities used young men as citizen soldiers to battle British troops on an "as needed" or short-term basis. Even then, a draftee could avoid service by paying an individual as a substitute soldier. A national draft was proposed in 1778 but was unsuccessful because of no consistent standards. The first federally-related draft laws only applied to men serving in the Continental Navy. Later, the framers of the Constitution included the draft in the document to allow for the calling of men between 18 and 45, if needed, stating…

> "…To raise and support Armies, but no Appropriation of Money to that Use shall be for a longer Term than two Years;…To provide for organizing, arming, and disciplining, the Militia, and for governing such Part of them as may be employed in the Service of the United States, reserving to the States respectively, the Appointment of the Officers, and the Authority of training the militia according to the discipline prescribed by Congress…." (Article I, Section 8)

The draft laws were tested at the outset of the U.S. Civil War when the need arose for more troops on both sides of the conflict. As early as 1862, countless enslaved people were freed to replace southern landowners who did not want to fight in the war. In the North, formerly enslaved people enlisted in the Union Army were counted among the draft quotas. Despite the already high number of Union troop volunteers, around ninety percent, draftees, and paid military substitutes, there was a public backlash to mandatory military service in the North.

Stemming from discontent over the inequalities of the draft process during the drawing of names, including the exemption of African-Americans from military service, rioting broke out in New York City on July 11, 1863. Also at the center of the unrest was the widespread practice of wealthy citizens buying their way out of military service for $300. This sum stood in stark contrast to the yearly wages of most workers, around $500.

During the four-day unrest, the rioters, primarily Irish immigrants defying police orders to disperse, attacked businesses, assaulted residents, burned buildings, and damaged the draft headquarters. Rioters also burned an orphanage, but all two hundred children escaped unharmed. Countless soldiers from the Union Army had to be withdrawn from fighting in Gettysburg to quell the rioting, which caused over $2 million in damages. However, the process of drawing names continued the following month. Following the Civil War, the draft was suspended and did not return for over half a century.

———————

In anticipation of America's involvement into WWI, President Woodrow Wilson called for one million volunteers to military service. Unfortunately, the plea drew less than 75,000. Consequently, President Wilson signed the Selective Service Act on May 18, 1917. The act was meant to rectify the contentious issue that developed during the Civil War by being more equitable and consistent.

First, the act required all men between 21-31 to register with the newly created Selective Service System. The law was later modified to include men ages 18-45. Additionally, the act would not allow affluent members of society to avoid military service by "buying" substitute soldiers. Moreover, the act included African-Americans, although they were placed in different units than whites. Lastly, the administration of the draft process was given to local boards in each state. The boards, comprised mainly of citizens from the community, issued draft calls and determined exemptions. At the time, most boards based their decisions solely on class, with the poorest most often chosen because they were the least skilled laborers. The action resulted in nearly twenty-five million registered men, with about three million being inducted. Among those inducted were immigrants to the U.S. However, many were allowed to plead as conscientious objectors to the war. The draft was once more dissolved at the war's end a year later.

The Great Depression resulted in a decrease in the U.S. birthrate and a lessening in the number of eligible men to serve in the military. But while the selective service process continued, it did so at a significantly reduced rate. However, the thought of being drafted seems to have fueled many men to voluntarily sign up to serve in the military rather than leave their fate up to the government. The choice of which branch of the service and the potential training in a given field proved especially attractive. Just as many men decided to avoid the draft by attending college or enrolling in a trade school. Beyond receiving congressional funding in 1934, Army General Lewis Hershey was appointed as the organization's director.

In the years that followed, the U.S. military developed plans in preparation for the next time the draft would be needed by further defining the guidelines and streamlining the process. The new program, introduced in September 1940, was called the Burke-Wadsworth Act or the Selective Training and Service Act. It required young men between 21-35 to register with local draft boards and was the first peacetime draft in U.S. history. The act also limited military service to twelve months; however, the number could be increased if Congress saw the need. Additionally, the military "upped" its standards for its draftees. Those with impairments such as weak eyesight, flat feet, and several teeth missing were excused from service. If a draftee was illiterate or couldn't speak English, they, too, were excused from serving. At one point, the military said they had rejected Superman from serving because he failed his physical. Adding humorously, his x-ray vision caused him to look through the walls of the examination room to the eye chart in the next room. When soldiers were needed to fill the ranks, the Army began offering crash courses in reading and English to qualify men for the draft.

———————

With hostilities growing in Europe and Hitler's growing aggression, Congress passed further legislation that all men between 18-45 were subject to military service. In addition, the law required all men between 18-65 to register for service, limited the number of trained military personnel to less than one million, and conscripted them to twelve months of duty. Men who were fathers and supporting a family were excused from service. The babies of these fathers were called "draft insurance."

Just before the bombing of Pearl Harbor on December 7, 1941, the soldier's term of duty was increased to eighteen months and included men between 18 and 64. Finally, the actual U.S. involvement into WWII increased the period of service to the duration of the war plus six months. The actual implementation of the draft process would fall upon the shoulders of local draft boards. The U.S. Navy and Marines were not initially included in the draft. Strangely, some men between 18 and 40 were excluded from the draft process because the government viewed their jobs as critical to the U.S. economy. It is estimated that between America's full involvement in the war and the end of WWII, the process brought in nearly 200,000 draftees a month.

Despite an effort aimed at equality, there was opposition to the draft procedure during the war. Many African Americans felt discriminated against, while some Japanese and German Americans refused to fight against their own.

In 1945, President Franklin D. Roosevelt called upon Congress to amend contemporary draft laws to include a draft for women who could serve as nurses. As a result, a bill for female conscription passed with House approval. Still, it was never voted on in the Senate because nurse enlistment had risen, and the war soon ended.

When WWII officially ended in September 1945, the draft was again halted, albeit briefly.

———————

The draft was reinstituted by President Truman in 1948 because of the beginnings of the Cold War. Termed the Selective Service Act, the law required all men between 18-26 to register. In June 1951, Pres. Truman signed the Universal Military Training and Service Act to meet the demand for military personnel during the Korean War. The legislation required that men register with the Selective Service at 18, become eligible for the draft at 18 and ½, lowered the physical and mental minimum standards for draftees, and extended the length of service to twenty-four months. Furthermore, the act stated that local draft boards could only take those younger than 18 after it had exhausted men from its 19-and-over pool, that soldiers must have four months of basic training, and affirmed the autonomy of local draft boards to decide deferments rather than issuing hard and fast rules. The act allowed local boards to consider local conditions and situations before determining classifications, including the addition of a deferment for students taking twelve hours or more of college classes.

Two years later, in 1953, President Eisenhower ended the deferment that exempted married men from service. The exception would be for married men that would have caused extreme family hardship in their absence. Eisenhower's actions resulted in an increase of over 200,000 men over the number that volunteered for military service, causing Gen. Hershey to comment that the draft scared men into enlisting.

———————

Conscription...the draft...took place during the 1960s under the legal authority of the peacetime draft because the U.S. never formally declared war on North Vietnam. President Kennedy, who defended the American presence in Southeast Asia, believed in the usefulness of the draft as a motivator for military service, saying that many officers and enlisted men would not have entered the service if not for it. During the first ten years of the U.S. presence in the regional conflict, the draft inducted nearly 1.5 million men, an average of more than 120,000 annually.

Nevertheless, the Vietnam conflict created a new debate over the draft process, including the demographic composition of draft boards, the organization of the boards, the power of the board to decide draftees and to grant student deferments, how board members were appointed and for how long, and the appeal process.

As fighting increased in Southeast Asia in the last half of the 1960s and troop levels increased, General Hershey and the Selective Service System continued to rely on the established pyramid-style structure to fulfill its obligations of supplying men for military service.

———————

At the top of the organization is the main office of the SSS, located in Washington, DC. It is an independent agency within the federal government's Executive Branch, and its director, General Hershey, reports directly to the president. Beyond developing policies, regulations, and guidelines, the agency is expected to provide inductees (men) for military duty. Once each state's quota of inductees is determined by the Department of Defense using projected numbers of enlistees and the number of soldiers from that state or territory already in military service against the number needed and the situation, the variable number is passed on to the next level in the structure, the state or territorial leaders.

The state or territorial headquarters is commonly located in the state's or territory's capital, with oversight by the elected governor or territorial official. Composed mainly of reservists or national guard officers on duty, this second level acts as a conduit to channel any guidance from the national offices through pamphlets, operational bulletins, guidelines, and written policy changes to the next lower level in the organization, local boards.

The local draft board was the judge and jury of the draft process because it administers and executes the main prerogatives of the draft process. The local board's responsibilities include registering, selecting, or rejecting men of military age. Beyond the local board being responsible to the government for seeing that a set number of inductees are provided for military service, it has jurisdiction over a set territory determined by population.

At the time of the Vietnam conflict, there were no less than 4,000 local boards in the U.S. and its territorial possessions. As expected, the number and size of local Selective Service boards varied according to the population of the state or territory. For example, Georgia had over one hundred and sixty local boards, Texas over one hundred and fifty, Missouri nearly one hundred and fifty, California over one hundred and thirty boards, and Virginia approximately one hundred and twenty-five. In 1971, the Buckeye State registered over one hundred local boards among its eighty-eight counties, while

Puerto Rico had no less than eighty local SS boards. As for West Virginia, it operated fifty-four boards or nearly one board per county.

In some cases, there were multiple boards in one city or county. There were no less than seventy local boards in New York City. Similarly, Allegheny County, Pennsylvania, alone had ten boards, and cross-state neighbor Philadelphia County had eight. Texas was no different, where Dallas and Harris (Houston) County recorded at least six. Most of Ohio's multiple boards were in metropolitan areas such as Cincinnati, Cleveland, and Columbus.

Conversely, there were other locations with fewer boards. Delaware logged only five boards, and the territories of Guam and the Virgin Islands, two each. There was only one board for Hinsdale County, Colorado. One of Alaska's four boards was situated in Nome, eleven hundred miles from the state headquarters in Juneau. Moreover, the location of the Nome board was usually only accessible by airplane or dog team for nine months of the year. *(Channeling, Selective Service Newsletter, April 1967, pg. 2)*

Beyond the size of local boards, commonly three to five, the board member's age, composition, and tenure of board members varied little. In general, local boards were all male, primarily veterans, over ninety-six percent white, with an average age near sixty. Further, nearly one in five board members was 70, with almost a dozen over ninety years old. Additionally, over half had served on their board for over 10 years, about one in ten more than twenty years, and nearly two-thirds had served on active military duty. Finally, one in three were college graduates, over two-thirds were considered white collar, and only around fifteen percent were farmers (*In Pursuit of Knowledge: Who Serves When Not all Serve, Report of the National Advisory Commission on Selective Service, February 1967, pg. 19*). One board member, a banker from Kansas City, Kansas, was nearing his 70th birthday and had been a member of his local Selective Service board for nearly thirty years. Another member of the same board was over 80 and a lawyer. A third member was a female and had been on the local board since the early 1940s. It could be that this cross-section of demographics of *"...older, white, male veterans with no special qualifications other than business and political connections..."* was chosen because most others had full-time jobs and a family to support. *(Rutenberg, pg. 167)*

It was not uncommon for some board members to serve a myriad of roles in the community. One local board member in Alabama was his town's mayor, the town attorney, a deacon in his church, president of the local Civitan Club, and chairperson of the county's United Fund. These were in addition to his role as the chairman of the local draft board.

Finally, it was not uncommon for board members to serve until death. On one Georgia board, the combined service of its board members totaled over one hundred and fifty years. Equally common was appointing a family member to replace an outgoing local board member. In 1964, a father retired from one Georgia board and was replaced by his son. A similar thing happened the same year in Maryland and three years later in Texas.

> *"Board members are in a tough spot...They have quotas to fill, but they also have to protect the registrant and keep the community operating as close to normal as possible...They donate their time, supposedly about three hours a day, two days a month...however,...many boards sit down at 3 p.m. and not get up until midnight...Despite this, they stay on for years. Of the 280 board members in Southern California, 36 have served for more than 20 years...."*
> *(The Circleville Herald, January 20, 1966, pg. 10)*

————————

There was little difference among Ohio's one hundred thirty-four local boards and over four hundred board members. Nearly 45% were lawyers, other professionals, public officials, managers, or salaried professionals, while just over 20% were farmers, craftsmen, or service workers.

During the Vietnam conflict, those who served on Monroe County's local Selective Service Board #86 included James W. Booth. He graduated from Washington and Jefferson College, Pennsylvania, and was postmaster in Graysville. Booth, whose father was a former congressman, was appointed to the board in 1950 at age sixty-eight. Charles W. "Billy" Paine, 67, was from Beallsville, and like Booth, he was appointed to the Monroe County draft board in 1950. He was in the gas and oil industry. In 1965, both Booth and Paine received 15-year pins for their presence on the local board.

Also on the local board were Glen Read, Ernest Hulsey, and Mrs. Gerald Cornall. Read, a veteran of WWII, was seventy-two and served on the Monroe County SS board for over a decade. Rather discreetly, and placed among community items, including the announcement of a new area cancer crusade chairman, a local dance, a pancake fundraiser, and the newest Red Cross volunteers, appeared a newspaper article announcing that…

> *"…Glen W. Read, Woodsfield, was named to Monroe County Draft Board by Col. William L. Klore, executive officer of the Selective Service System. Mr. Read fills the vacancy created by the resignation of Earl S. Ward, also of Woodsfield" (The Daily Jeffersonian, March 16, 1965, pg. 12).*

A former postal clerk, Ward was sixty-five when he left the board.

Beyond being an Air Force veteran who served in the Korean War, Hulsey was a former teacher in the county, a retired minister in the Baptist church, and a Monroe County commissioner. At some point during their tenure, both Booth and Hulsey served as chairman of local board #86.

Mrs. Cornall, a former resident of Fly, Ohio, resigned from her position because she moved to Williamstown, West Virginia, before July 1970.

Above all, board members were volunteer residents of the county or city because it was widely believed that locals on SS boards knew the needs of their local communities best. They knew who could be spared for military service and who could not. Who could benefit from military training and who was vital to the local economy. Boards used local knowledge and expertise to make the best judgments on who should be drafted and who should not. In most ways, their localness put a human face on the draft process, despite them receiving no pay and commonly working long hours.

The January 1961 edition of the *Channeling* reports that,

> *"Mrs. Nell G. Roberts, clerk of the Hefferson (sp.) County, Ala, Local Board No. 70, recently registered her 18-year-old grandson, Wallace S. Fulton, Jr." (pg. 3)*

As well, the November 1966 edition of the Selective Service newsletter records that,

> *"...Mrs. Henry Kuykendall, assistant clerk of local board 57 in Oklahoma, registered both her sons in the course of 2 years." (pg. 3)*

According to one newspaper, Ludington, Michigan, resident,

> *"...Bob Rowe registered for the draft this week. He didn't have much choice. Mrs. Clyde C. Rowe, secretary of the local draft board, is his mother." (The Daily Jeffersonian, August 11, 1967, pg. 11)*

A similar article told a similar tale, saying,

> *"...Nelson (Bob) Stats, who turned 18 today, was on hand early Wednesday morning at the Selective Service here to register. Registering him was his mother, Mrs. (Nicholas) Naomi States (sp.), clerk of*

local board 48" (The Daily Jeffersonian, November 29, 1968, pg. 21).

At first glance, it may seem that the job of the local draft board was one without issues. After all, the process, in general, was well laid out by the national offices, and the decentralized administration presumably put the responsibility of meeting quotas on the local boards. Subsequently, the process seemed simple.

Within one month of their eighteenth birthday, males were required to register for the draft, although no reminders were sent from local draft boards. Following the essential registration, the draftee is given a questionnaire about his family status, schooling, medical history, etc. The draftees are given ten days to return the completed form, as it will assist in deciding the draftee's future classification. The failure to register was a crime, and the failure to complete the questionnaire and return it was considered delinquent and may result in immediate reclassification and induction.

Once the questionnaire was completed, the information was forwarded to the selective services' main office in Washington, DC.

In short time, the draftee would receive a letter postmarked "Washington, DC" with an introduction that began "Greetings" (from Uncle Sam). The letter would tell the draftee that he was to board a bus on a specific day, which would take him to an induction center. In addition, the draftee was to bring with them proof of marriage, a birth certificate of any dependent children, and a record of life insurance, if the soldier had insurance. The soldier is also told to notify their employer before the induction date. Finally, the letter states that the soldier is to bring with them enough clean clothes for three days and enough money to cover one month of personal expenses.

Upon arriving at the induction center, the draftee was ushered into a large room, where he would strip down to his underwear and be given a physical. If the draftee failed his test, he was rejected for military service. Those that passed their physical were then taken into another large room, formally inducted into the military, and issued a classification, most commonly 1-A (Available for military service). Other classifications included 1-A-O (Conscientiously opposed to training or military service requiring use of arms), II-D (Deferred, preparing for ministry), III-A (Service deferred to hardships/dependents), and IV-F (Rejected for military service).

Afterward, the new inductees were given a written test to determine their future MOS (military occupational specialty), such as artillery, heavy equipment operator, infantry, radio operator, etc. Within thirty days, the "new" soldier would receive a second government-issued letter telling them to report back to the induction center and details for their upcoming 12 weeks of basic training. Following "boot camp," the soldier would be assigned their advanced orders, most commonly to AIT (advanced infantry training), which meant their next "stop" was Southeast Asia. During this training phase, some deserted their military obligation, and most headed north to Canada.

Those who completed their advanced training had fourteen days to prepare for deployment. When the two weeks were up, the soldiers returned to the centers. There, they were issued a duffle bag full of items, including military-issue underwear, t-shirts, socks, three or four sets of fatigues, two pairs of boots, and a helmet. However, there were no toiletries in the bag, like a toothbrush, soap, or deodorant.

Noticeably absent during the registration through the induction phase was a booklet explaining the general SS process, no address or phone number for the draftee to contact if they had any questions, or even the hours of the local draft board office. To assist in understanding the general process, some newspapers began running columns that sought to answer basic questions that draftees and their families may have.

In the January 12, 1965 issue of *The Daily Jeffersonian*, the newspaper shared the step-by-step process in an article entitled "The Draft: Facts and Figures." Among the items in the article were the local board number and address to register, the importance of keeping one's draft card in their possession at all times, and the requirement that draftees were to let their local board know of any changes with the draftee's marital or college status. Moreover, the six-item article included what happens if the draftee fails his physical exam, how the induction process unfolds, and the length of military service. Finally, the article closes by saying, "*...the rest of the two years will be spent putting that knowledge to use somewhere in the world" (pg. 15)*. Not to be outdone, the clerk of one local board in Florida held a weekly radio program in which she invited listeners to call in and ask her questions about the draft process *(Channeling, September 1967, pg. 4)*.

———————

At some point between his initial registration and induction, the soldier would receive his draft card. Appearing on the wallet-size card would be the soldier's name, date, and place of birth. The card would also include his physical characteristics, including height, weight, color of hair and eyes, and complexion. Additionally, the card would include the signature of the local board clerk. Lastly, the card would also have the individual's Selective Service Number, which consisted of four sets of numbers. The first two numbers correspond to the state where the soldier registered for the draft. The second set of numbers would indicate the number of their local draft board. For Ohio soldiers from Monroe

County, the first two sets of numbers would be 33 and 86. The third set of numbers would indicate the year the soldier was born (1950 would read 50), while the fourth set of numbers would indicate the soldier's line in sequence of others born that year. The higher the last set of numbers, the lesser chance of being called. The draft card of a soldier from Monroe County, Ohio, born in 1950 with a higher number, might read: 33 86 50 365.

———————

In most ways, the job of the local board was complete once the soldier had boarded the bus and headed for the induction center. The local board had met their quota of new soldiers for now and could return to their lives until they were issued a new quota. Nevertheless, the pressure placed on members of local boards was constant. This was especially true of the larger boards that had only minutes to spend on each registrant's paperwork. Consequently, the process sometimes became impersonal and challenging because these larger local boards tended to rely heavily on the advice of local clerks, who were often less qualified to make such critical decisions than the other board members.

Moreover, there was an extreme uneasiness because board members were making life-and-death decisions for young men in their community, many they may have known since birth. In the hands of these board members lay the future fate of young men who may have been raised alongside members' own children, sat beside these same children in school, played sports with them, and even worshipped with them on Sunday mornings. Quite possibly, the balancing act and the choice of who is sent to the military and probably Southeast Asia and who remains stateside *"...is being made by one of the neighbors of the (young) man" (In Pursuit of Equity, pg. 20).* Sadly, there may have been instances where personal relationships, favoritism, wealth, and political power were utilized to decide who would go and who would stay.

However, the responsibility of the local board to fill a certain quota of soldiers for military service was greatly assisted by males who enlisted. Consequently, this reduced the task of the local board in meeting their quotas. For males deciding this route, they were allowed to choose their branch of service and MOS. Following their physical, aptitude test, and interview, they attended basic training, and would eventually become a soldier, airman, marine, or sailor.

Additionally, some boards, especially in the larger cities, would have hundreds, possibly thousands, of individual draft forms to review, organize, and arrange for the next step in the process. Furthermore, it is not generally known how often local board members receive updates on new procedures or policies or how often they are read by local board members. According to one source, the Ohio state Selective Service Board sent/issued nearly one hundred memorandums to local offices during the first nine months of 1966. About two-thirds of the memorandums focused on administrative aspects, while the remainder dealt with procurement quotas *(In Pursuit of Knowledge, pg. 174)*.

While members of smaller boards were commonly known, the same could not be said of larger boards, where *"...the identity of local board members...is one of the best kept secrets in America...the people who do know, tend to come from small towns."* Moreover, *"...the point is clear that board operations are not usually intensely personal" (In Pursuit of Equity, pg. 20)*. The friendliness of the local board existed only in theory. They had a job to do, albeit impersonal at times, and a quota of new soldiers to fill the military ranks.

For example, the Department of Defense communicated to the Ohio Selective Service Board that it needed over 2,700 men from the state to fill its September 1965 quota. The number included four from Monroe County, twenty-six from

Monroe County's neighbor to the north, Belmont County, and three from Noble County *(Daily Jeffersonian, September 2, 1965, pg. 2)*. The January 1966 call asked for two inductees from Monroe County, two from Belmont County, and none from Noble County *(Daily Jeffersonian, January 21, 1966, pg. 1)*. Six months later, the numbers had increased to thirteen inductees needed from Monroe County and eight from Belmont County *(Daily Jeffersonian, July 18, 1966, pg. 1)*. The April 1967 draft called for four hundred and seventy-six new inductees from Ohio, including two from Monroe County, five from Belmont County, and one from Monroe County's neighbor to the west, Noble County *(Daily Jeffersonian, March 11, 1967, pg. 2)*. Finally, in May 1967, the quota of new inductees for local draft board in Monroe County was set at four, while the neighboring board in Belmont County was set at nine and Noble at three *((Daily Jeffersonian, April 17, 1967, pg. 1)*.

Last but not least, the general absence of uniform directives from the Selective Service System commonly made the specific job of the local board difficult. The lack of hard-fast policies and procedures for classifying deferments, hardship cases, economic contribution to the community, and exemptions not only created misunderstanding, misinterpretation, and ambiguity but variability and discretion in the way boards arrived at their decisions. The lack of uniformity may make it seem that one local draft board is more stringent in its decision-making than a board on the other side of the city or county. Moreover, the lack of clarity at the top, combined with a sense of autonomy, the belief that since they were volunteers they could not be held to conformity, and the difficulty in keeping track of changes in policies, led some boards to *"...simply ignore the guidelines provided to them by national and state headquarters..." (Rough Draft: Cold War Military Manpower Policy and the Origins of Vietnam-Era Draft Resistance, Rutenberg, 2019, pg. 167)*.

Clearly, the capricious decisions made by some local draft boards brought attention to an already broken system and a developing belief that *"...If a large number of individual boards are responsible, in the final analysis, for making their own decisions about classification problems, differences are almost sure to occur." (In Pursuit of Equity, pg. 83)*

Despite the differences among local boards in the selection process, it is said that Gen. Hershey refused to include the state or territorial leaders or himself in the deliberations. He believed that local board members knew their population of potential soldiers best.

Throughout, the Selective Service System never wavered in its trust and confidence of local draft board members to keep up with local draftees and their life changes. At one time, a draftee could be single and classified 1-A, and in a matter of days or weeks, the future soldier may get married, enroll in college, change jobs, or welcome a baby. When one or more of these changes occurred, the local board would have to wait for the draftee's information to arrive from Washington, DC, before the board could re-evaluate the soldier's classification.

In some cases, the responsibility of a local board to keep up with a draftee's situation was made easier by the actions of the draftee themselves. Some registrants were even known to include some humor. The Pottawattamie County (Iowa) draft board received a letter from a young man requesting a medical deferment. In the space provided on the form, the draftee was to describe his ailment. He wrote "romantic fever." The board would have granted the young man's request if the draftee meant "rheumatic fever." However, the board declined the request by stating in a return letter to the young man, saying *"...the government does not recognize lovesickness as a debilitating disease." (Channeling, January 1961, pg. 4)*

51

When the initial draft questionnaire asked for the name and address of a person other than family or a member of the household who will always know the registrant's whereabouts, one potential draftee responded, somewhat sarcastically, writing *"...Selective Service local board no. 44, Berkshire County, Lee, Massachusetts." (Channeling, June 1962, pg. 1)*

A newlywed wrote to the local draft board telling them she was seeking an annulment for her 2-day-old marriage. It seems that her husband told her the reason he married her was to avoid the draft *(The Record Herald, Washington Court House, Ohio, August 19, 1965, pg. 2)*. Speaking of marriage, one bride-to-be called the local draft board office to ask if her boyfriend had passed his physical exam. When asked why the young woman needed the information, she answered that her boyfriend promised to marry the young woman if he passed his physical. However, if he failed the physical, the young draftee said all bets were off! The young woman was quite unhappy when she was told by the clerk that the results of the physical were confidential. If the potential bride wants the results of the physical, she must get them from her boyfriend. Hoping for exclusion from serving, another man, unable to read or write, asked his wife to write a letter to the local draft board, explaining how much he was needed at home. Rather than follow her husband's wishes, the wife pleaded with the local board to take him because he was a no-good alcoholic and didn't help around the house.

One draftee from South Dakota wrote to his local board, stating...

> *"Sir. I suppose you wonder where have I move (sp.) to. I planed (sp.) to go to Puerto Rico and give you my new address as soon as I got there, but the police change (sp.) my plans. I stole a motorcycle and my new address is the LA County Jail. I don't know for how long, but I supose (sp.) I should let you know. If you*

want more information let me know. Sincerely yours."
(Channeling, May 1966, pg. 3)

Although they worked long hours with limited guidance and in-service training, received no pay, and were commonly scorned by some in their community, the members of local draft boards performed their job with dedication and devotion and believed in what they were doing. Besides helping the federal government in meeting quotas for military service, local board members were convinced they were assisting certain young, unmarried teenage men who were not long out of high school by helping them choose a career path, giving them discipline, aiding them in building life skills, and find direction and purpose in life through military service.

Furthermore, the commitment of these board members was shown in their dedication. One board member from West Virginia supposedly rushed back into a burning building to remove vital SS records *(Channeling, September 1962, pg. 3)*. One member of a local board from Missouri reported that one of its members, a veteran of service in the Mexican border war and WWI, has attended 194 of the board's 196 meetings since becoming a board member in 1948 *(Channeling, January 1963, pg. 1)*. A local board clerk in Michigan reports that at one point in the previous year (March 1962) she registered five boys without a birthday. They were leap-year babies born on February 29! *(Channeling, January 1963, pg. 3)*. Another board member from Las Vegas has missed only one meeting in nearly 23 years *(Channeling, April 1963, pg. 4)*. Still another board clerk in Kansas reported that a set of triplets recently registered for the draft. The three brothers: Garry, Harry, and Larry, all have the same middle name...Herbert *(Channeling, July 1963, pg. 4)*. A local board member from Wisconsin reports to have traveled nearly 10,000 miles during his 15 years on the board and 196 meetings *(Channeling, September 1963, pg. 2)*. When a 9.2 magnitude earthquake hit Alaska on Good Friday, March 27, 1964, countless buildings were destroyed, and over one hundred and twenty-five lives were lost. Despite the tragedy, one local board opened its doors two days later and registered over two dozen young men for possible military service *(Channeling, May 1964, pg. 4)*. One local board member from Idaho did not miss a single meeting during his twenty-five-year tenure *(Channeling, June 1965, pg. 1)*.

Still, other examples of devotion by local boards were shown when boards took part in Career Day at local high schools to explain the draft process and procedures. Countless other boards served coffee and donuts the morning their registrants departed for physicals and induction. One local board in New Jersey went as far as sending off its inductees with a prayer, patriotic music, and special remarks from a former Congressional Medal of Honor winner. Another board in nearby New York not only hosted a breakfast for the draftees and their families but gave the young men a New Testament Bible, provided by the Gideons, along with a sack lunch supplied by the local girl scouts *(Channeling, June 1968, pg. 3)*.

Some draftees were even known to express their thanks to the local board for their guidance. One registrant on leave from active duty stopped by the local draft board in Rappahannock, Virginia, to say thanks. When asked by the local clerk what he liked about being in the Army, the soldier replied, saying, *"...one of the nicest things about being in the Army is that you don't have to worry about being drafted" (Channeling, March 1962, pg. 4)*. Wishing to express their appreciation to the local clerk for her assistance in helping them navigate the registration process, four young inductees sent the clerk an Easter lily. The note accompanying the flower was signed by Joe, Dave, Rich, and Al *(Channeling, January 1964, pg. 4)*.

———————

Not long into his first term, President Richard Nixon, signed an amendment to the Military Selective Service Act that returned selection by lottery to the draft process for the first time since World War II. At exactly 9:00pm on December 1, 1969, CBS interrupted regular Monday evening programming, beginning with *Mayberry RFD*, to cover the first draft lottery since WWII. Standing in front of a barrel filled with three hundred and sixty-six blue capsules, Representative Alexander Pirnie, from New York, the ranking Republican on the Armed Services Committee, reached into the barrel and drew out the first capsule. Inside was the date September 14. This meant that all men born on that date between 1944 and 1950 would be the first to be called to military service. The last capsule chosen from the barrel was June 8.

Within three years, the Department of Defense announced the suspension of the draft. And with that, the Military Selective Service Act.

Nevertheless, the conflict in Vietnam continued to draw soldiers to Southeast Asia.

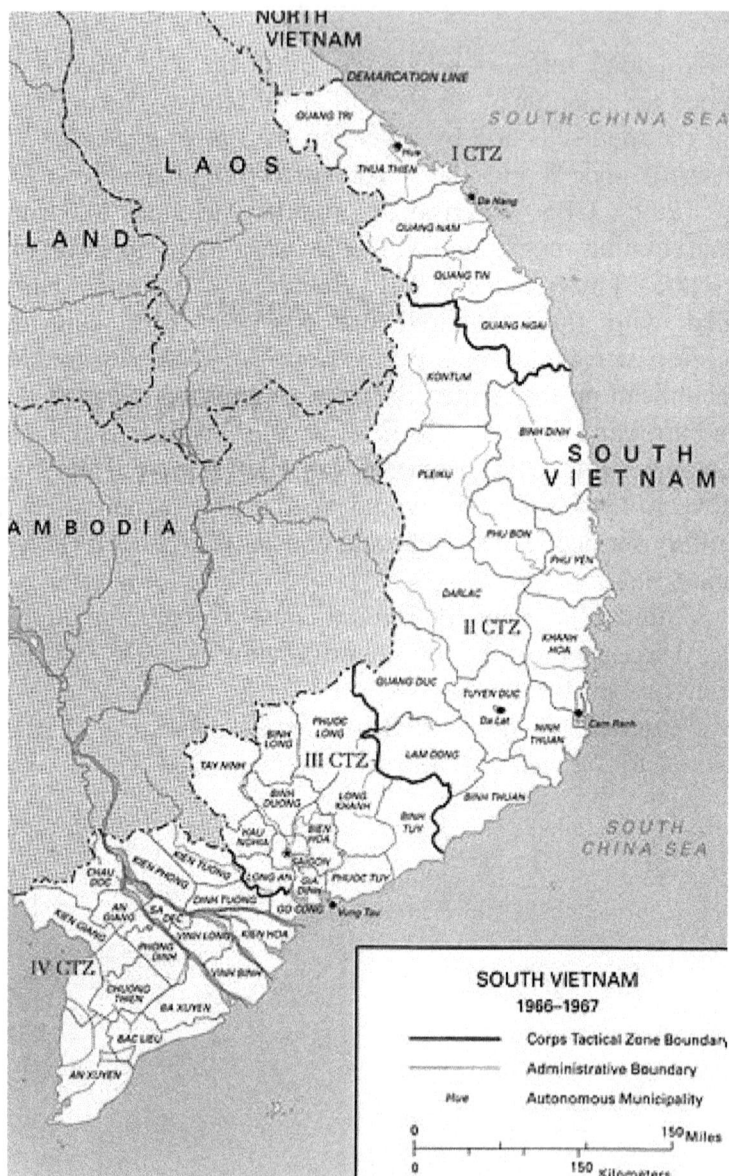

SOUTH VIETNAM
1966–1967

	Corps Tactical Zone Boundary
	Administrative Boundary
Hue	Autonomous Municipality

0   150 Miles

0   150 Kilometers

Chapter III

Vietnam, once spelled as two words...Viet Nam...is located in Southeast Asia and is approximately 120,000 square miles, or the size of New Mexico. From north to south, the country measures just over 1,000 miles long and around thirty miles wide at its narrowest point. It is bordered to the north by China, on the east by the South China Sea, to the southwest by the Gulf of Thailand, and to the west by Laos and Cambodia.

Although Vietnam has nearly two thousand miles of coastline, the inland areas in the north and central parts of the country are hills and dense forests. Mountains and tropical forests comprise the vast majority of the remaining land. The extreme southern part of the country is predominantly delta, and some parts are no more than a few feet above sea level.

Best described as mixed, the temperatures can range from the 60s during the early weeks of the year in the north to the high 70s and low 80s in the south. Many parts of the country experience light and persistent drizzle from early February to late spring. The middle months of the year, May thru October, are considered the monsoon season and can bring heavy rains and typhoons. The last few months of the year are mostly dry.

During the decade of the 1960s, the population was estimated to be between thirty-two and forty-two million. The heaviest population was concentrated in two main areas: Hanoi in the north and Saigon in the south. The major cities between Hanoi and Saigon are Hue and Da Nang. Both are located on the coast in the eastern part of the country.

The country is divided into forty-four provinces or local governments. The provinces are further divided into districts.

By most accounts, the origins of the conflict in Southeast Asia and the U.S. involvement can be traced to the broader regional differences immediately following World War II.

A few weeks before the atomic bomb was dropped on Hiroshima on August 6, 1945, a plan was advanced at the Potsdam Conference to temporarily partition Vietnam at the eighteenth parallel. As part of that plan, Japanese forces in the country's south would surrender to the British, while Japanese troops in the north would surrender to the Chinese. Within a few days, a communist movement began in the north to seize political control of the whole country. A provisional government is formed with Ho Chi Minh as its president. In the south, British General Douglas Gracey is appointed to command all French forces until a French command can be established. Gracey's orders were to oversee the efforts below the 18th parallel, including the liberation of the territory, disarm all Japanese forces, and maintain law and order among the French who wanted to colonize South Vietnam and those loyal to Minh who wished the country to be united under the flag of communism.

Upon the formal surrender of Japanese troops in late summer, American Lt. Col. Peter Dewey, an officer with the U.S. Office of Strategic Services, was sent to Vietnam to search for missing pilots. As a member of a seven-man team, he was also directed to gather information on the growing unrest in the country. Siding with the French, Gracey armed over one thousand French troops to keep the peace. In short time, Minh's followers were ousted from their governmental positions in the south of the divided country. However, Dewey let it be known that he favored Minh's efforts, albeit communist. Gracey immediately ordered Dewey out of the country, to which he complied. On the way to the airport on September 26, 1945, Dewey's car ran a roadblock manned by several of Minh's soldiers. The soldiers, thinking Dewey was French, fired several rounds at his car, killing Dewey and injuring his driver. Dewey is considered by some to be the first American killed in the Vietnam conflict.

As the calendar flips to 1946, Gen. Gracey is ordered to depart South Vietnam, giving the French full authority to oversee order in the country. In March, Ho Chi Minh was formally elected president of the Democratic Republic of Vietnam (DRV). Before long, an agreement is signed between Minh's government and the French, recognizing the DRV as a free state, having its own government and army. Further, the French government agrees to carry out a referendum on the country's unification. However, differences began to develop between the two parties when the French discovered that Minh had been in contact with and was taking advice and direction from the Soviet government. More, Minh's forces begin attacking French civilians in Hanoi. The French responded by attempting to drive Minh's troops out of the city. For the next several years, the political differences between the parties continue to fester.

Fearing the spread of communism beyond the region, Pres. Harry Truman approved $10 million in military aid to the French in May 1950. The following month, war broke out in Korea when the army of the Democratic People's Republic of Korea (North Korea) crossed the 38th parallel into South Korea. In August, the U.S. sent Military Assistance Advisory Group (MAAG) members to Saigon to provide material assistance to the French and indirect military aid to the South Vietnamese government. In December, representatives from the U.S. and France signed an agreement for mutual defense for the region.

———————

For eight years, the French troops fought the Viet Minh to

control the region, especially North Vietnam. Finally, following two months of heavy fighting in the spring of 1954 and a shattering defeat for the French at the Battle of Dien Bien Phu, the French sought a negotiated truth with Minh's forces and began a peaceful withdrawal. A conference is held in Geneva, Switzerland, to negotiate a resolution for dismantling French-dominated Indochina and the growing differences among countries in the region. The attendees at the conference involved representatives from national powers, including China, the Soviet Union, France, and the United States, and regional ones like South Vietnam, Cambodia, Laos, and North Vietnam. Ho Chi Minh, who wanted to end French colonial rule in the country and unify Vietnam under a single communist regime, led the delegation from North Vietnam. From the conference emerged several documents known as the Geneva Accords.

First, the accords established a cease-fire zone in Vietnam at the 17th Parallel, or latitude 17 degrees north, as the line of demarcation between North and South Vietnam. To the north of the line would be the Democratic Republic of Vietnam, or North Vietnam, under the control of Minh and the Vietnamese Communist Party. The authority south of the 17th Parallel would lay in the hands of the non-communist Republic of Vietnam, which wanted a governmental structure more closely aligned with western principles of democracy. The accord further stated that a demilitarized zone, or DMZ, would be established within three hundred days, requiring both military forces to leave the zone. Additionally, any communist troops from North Vietnam currently in Laos or Cambodia were to be removed. Finally, the accord deemed nationwide elections would occur within two years to unify Vietnam. However, none of the ten articles produced at the Geneva Conference would be binding because none of the participating parties signed the document.

In the meantime, Pres. Dwight Eisenhower, the second

U.S. president involved in the conflict in Southeast Asia, announced that additional aircraft would be sent to the region. More, the Department of Defense announced it will send around two hundred Air Force mechanics to assist MAAG operations with the maintenance of U.S. aircraft.

To the American government, the lines were clearly drawn. The Minh government to the north sought to unify the country under communist rule. Conversely, the South Vietnamese government set its sights on preventing a communist takeover.

In November 1955, more members of an advisory group from the U.S. arrived in South Vietnam to offer the government advice and assistance on meeting and overcoming the growing communist effort. Within a year, the U.S. had its first recognized casualty in Southeast Asia: Air Force Technical Sergeant Richard B. Fitzgibbon, Jr., of North Weymouth, Massachusetts.

Fitzgibbon left for Vietnam in early January 1956 as a member of MAAG, the Military Assistance Advisory Group. In addition to training South Vietnamese personnel, he was a crew chief on a Douglas C-47 plane. While on a flight on June 8, 1956, the aircraft came under enemy fire. During the incident, Fitzgibbon reprimanded a member of his flight crew, radio man and Staff Sergeant Edward Clarke, for not doing his job. After landing, a disgruntled Clarke headed to a bar on base for a drink. After several more drinks, Clarke, heavily intoxicated, left the bar and encountered Fitzgibbon, who was handing out candy to children on a nearby street. Still angry over what had happened earlier in the day, Clarke pulled out his firearm and shot Fitzgibbon several times. Chased by local authorities, Clarke quickly fled the scene and took refuge in a nearby building. He died moments later from falling or jumping from a second-story balcony. Fitzgibbon was 35. He is recognized by the Pentagon as the first American to die in Vietnam (*San Diego Tribune, May 29, 1999, pg. B-10*).

At the time of Fitzgibbon's death, the number of MAAG personnel in the region was around three hundred and fifty. Following the withdrawal of French troops later in the year, the number of MAAG in the region would increase two-fold.

Before long, a second soldier, Capt. Harry Cramer would be among a growing list of American casualties to die in the regional conflict.

Harry Cramer was born in Johnstown, Pennsylvania, in 1926 and came from a long line of military pedigree. In addition to his father serving in WWI, Cramer's grandfather, Wilson Cramer, served in the Civil War with the Pennsylvania Volunteers. The younger Cramer graduated from West Point in 1946 at 20…the youngest of his 800-member class. The following year he would be married.

During the next few years, Cramer would attend airborne training at Ft. Benning, Georgia, see military service in the Korean conflict, and serve in Japan as a military advisor. Then, in early summer 1957, he was deployed to Nha Trang in Khanh Hoa Province, located on the east coast of Vietnam between Da Nang and Saigon, as a team member that trained South Vietnamese soldiers. On October 21, 1957, during an ambush drill Cramer was overseeing, a South Vietnamese soldier standing near Cramer was ready to throw an explosive when it detonated prematurely, instantly killing Cramer. He had been in Vietnam less than one hundred twenty days and was awarded the Silver Star and Purple Heart for his military service. Additionally, he was one of six men from the USMA Class of 1946 to die or be missing in action in Vietnam and the first of over 325 from the academy to die during the conflict in Southeast Asia. He was thirty-one at the time of his passing and had been married since June 1947.

The number of soldiers killed in Vietnam now unofficially stood at three. But, as expected, the number of U.S. casualties would more than triple during the next 36 months as America's military presence in Vietnam increased. And just like each of those eleven sons of Monroe County, those soldiers killed in Southeast Asia between 1959 and 1961 had a backstory.

Army Major Stanley Staszak was born on March 5, 1920, in Essex County, New Jersey. When not in school, he worked on a farm with his father, who was in the dairy business. Upon graduation from high school, he enlisted in the Army. Following, he was accepted at West Point, where he was the manager for the West Point soccer team, and graduated in 1943. During his fifteen-year military career, Staszak was stationed in Panama, Germany, and Yugoslavia. In the latter part of his life, he became a member of MAAG and was deployed to Gia Dinh Province, near Saigon, where his wife and two kids joined him. At age thirty-nine, Staszak died of a possible brain hemorrhage in his sleep on April 4, 1959. He was one of two members of the USMA Class of 1943 to die or be missing in action in Vietnam.

Records indicate that on the evening of July 8, 1959, six officers of an eight-man MAAG were in an old sawmill that the U.S. military had converted into a two-story building. Located on the Bien Hoa compound and not far from division headquarters northeast of Saigon, the building contained a mess hall on the first floor and an officers' quarters up a flight of stairs. The advisors had just finished dinner and settled down to watch the movie "*The Tattered Dress.*" The group of six advisors included 37-year-old Army Major Dale Buis, a native of Pender, Nebraska, a West Point graduate, and a seventeen-year veteran of the military. Near Buis was Master Sergeant Chester Ovnand, 44, from Copperas Cove, Texas. Moments earlier, he had written a letter to his wife and dropped it off to be mailed. Before arriving in Vietnam, Sgt. Ovnand had served in WWII and Korea and had less than four months left in his deployment.

Just as the lights came on and Ovnand began making his way to the back of the hall to change the movie reel, five to ten guerillas poked their guns through the windows of the renovated sawmill and began firing. Moments earlier, terrorists had attempted to throw a bomb through a side window, but it bounced back and exploded, killing one of the attackers.

According to the July 12, 1959 issue of the *Stars and Stripes* magazine, "...Major Buis promptly hit the floor, crawled across the room and forced open the door. The opening of the door startled one of the terrorists who was getting ready to toss a bomb into the room. The bomb went off in the doorway, killing Buis and the terrorist." Meanwhile, Ovnand, mortally wounded, crawled across the floor and attempted to climb up the stairs. The raid lasted less than 10 minutes.

Buis, who had arrived in Southeast Asia in November, was less than 2 months away from celebrating his 38th birthday. He left behind a wife and three young sons, ages 5, 6, and 8. It is said that Ovnand's wife learned of his passing while watching the *Today Show* on tv. Ovnand, who planned to retire in three years following a 20-year career in the Army, was the first of five soldiers from Copperas Cove to die in Vietnam. In addition, Buis was the only casualty from Pender, Nebraska, to die in Vietnam. At the time of his passing, the population of Pender was less than 1,200.

Buis and Ovnand are considered to be the first two soldiers killed by enemy fire. Subsequently, their names are the first two engraved on the Vietnam Veterans Memorial Wall...Panel 1E, Line 1.

As the decade of the 1950s ended, the North Vietnamese forces continued their push for a unified and communist country by building a supply route through Laos and Cambodia to support guerilla attacks in the south. To facilitate the movement of men and materials, a specialized North Vietnamese Army unit, Group 559, developed a primitive route along the Vietnamese/Cambodian border, with offshoots into Vietnam along its entire length. The path would become known as the Ho Chi Minh Trail.

Beyond the death of Dewey, Fitzgibbon, Cramer, Staszak, Buis, and Ovnand, U.S. casualties in Vietnam would grow exponentially.

Beyond the election of John F. Kennedy as the thirty-fifth president of the U.S. and an increase in the number of MAAG personnel in Vietnam, the decade of the 60s would begin with the crash of a military DC-9 near the border of Thua Thien and Quang Nam provinces on February 17, 1960. On its way from Saigon to Hue, the plane crashed into a mountain north of Da Nang, killing all onboard. Those killed include Navy Lt. Commander George Alexander, 37, of Los Angeles, California. Also on the plane were Navy Lt. Commander Roger Mullins, 39, of Decatur, Illinois, and Navy Chief Petty Officer and chief aviation electronics tech William Newton, 42, of Newberg, Oregon. All three were with the MAAG. It is believed that Mullins piloted the flight and was assisted by Alexander.

One week later, Air Force Staff Sgt. Maurice Flournoy, 30,

of El Campo, Texas, died from drowning while in Laos. As the son of a barber and a beautician mother, he was class president and played football during his freshman year in high school. In his sophomore year, he was a member of the Future Farmers of America and lettered in both track and football. Flournoy lettered again in both football and track his junior year. Upon his death, it is said that his mother received the following telegram:

> *"It is with deep regret that I officially inform you that your son, Staff Sgt. Maurice W. Flournoy has been missing since 21 Feb. 1960 when he fell from a river vessel into a swift river..." and an "... Extensive search is now being conducted...."*

His body was recovered on March 3. He leaves behind a mother, father, and brother, two years older.

On March 8, 1960, the *El Campo Citizen* notified the public that a military funeral for Maurice would be held on March 11. The newspaper further stated:

> *"Stationed in Laos, near Red China, Maurice lost his life when he fell from a river boat while on a picnic cruise Feb 21. Details from the Government state four Americans dived into the swiftly moving current to rescue him but his body was never sighted. Six days later the remains were recovered and flown to San Francisco by military transport."*

Flournoy's uncle, Rev. Charnel Flournoy, participated in the funeral service. Like so many others who would serve in Vietnam, Staff Sgt. Flournoy's brother served in the military.

Staff Sgt. Flournoy was one of fourteen soldiers from Wharton County, Texas, to die in Vietnam between 1960-1971 and one of seven from the city of fewer than 8,500 residents. Like Alexander, Mullins, and Newton, Flournoy was with the MAAG. Moreover, he may be among the first of over two hundred U.S. military personnel to die in Laos.

Navy Chief Petty Officer and aviation electrician Richard

Stephan, age 28, died on August 31 in Quang Tri Province. He was a member of the local national guard before graduating from high school. Following graduation, Stephan joined the Navy and served tours of duty in Guam and Hawaii. Along the way, he also taught physics at Naval Air Technical Training Center in Oklahoma and sang in the ship's choir while serving aboard the USS Midway. In 1960, he became a member of the MAAG in Vietnam as an instructor for aircraft maintenance. Shortly after arriving in Southeast Asia in July 1960, Stephan began to experience breathing issues. A trip to the hospital required him to travel along a dangerous route filled with enemy mines and ambushes. Subsequently, he chose not to seek medical assistance. When his breathing worsened on August 29, he saw a military doctor. By then, it was too late. Stephan died from malaria and pneumonia two days later.

He left behind a wife of six years and two young children...a girl, age 5, and a boy, who celebrated his 4th birthday four days before Stephan died. CPO Stephan was the second youngest of nine kids.

With his death, the number of military deaths in Southeast Asia stood at eleven.

The twelfth member of the U.S. Armed Forces to die in Vietnam in the early years of the 1960s was Navy Lt. Tom Cress. As a pilot with four years in the military, Cress, 26, from Milwaukee, Wisconsin, died when his plane crashed into the ocean off Japan on January 6, 1961. He was the second pilot killed in action.

To date, the largest single-event loss of American lives in Southeast Asia was on March 23, 1961, when a military plane carrying seven soldiers crashed while on its way from Vientiane, Laos, to South Vietnam.

Flying a specially-designed plane meant for intelligence

gathering, the passengers were bound for some R&R in the "Paris of the Orient" (Saigon). During the flight from Laos, the pilot turned north toward Xieng Khouang(ville), Laos. The crew was directed to use radio-detection-finding equipment to determine frequencies used by Soviet and North Vietnamese pilots and to monitor the construction of enemy airfields in the area. Unfortunately, not long into the flight, the plane began receiving anti-aircraft gunfire from Pathet Lao fighters. The gunfire sheared off one of the plane's wings, causing it to go down.

Onboard the fatal flight that day were Air Force Staff Sgt. Alfons Bankowski, 30, of Stamford, Connecticut, the flight engineer on the C-47 plane. A veteran of the Korean War, he had been in the Air Force for over 12 years. Bankowski is survived by his mother, a single parent, three sisters, and four brothers. His mother received a telegram informing her of her son's death five days after the crash. Bankowski's remains were never recovered.

Also killed in the crash was Air Force Staff Sgt. Frederick Garside, 24, of Plymouth, Massachusetts. His father was a Navy veteran of WWII. Garside had a brother die two months after being born in 1938, and his mother died one year later. Staff Sgt. Garside was the second soldier from Massachusetts to die in the Vietnam conflict. Years later, his remains were found along with two other soldiers on the flight in side-by-side unmarked graves. Garside's body was identified by a picture found in his clothing. He was buried in the family plot in Plymouth on a day of below-freezing temperatures.

Also on the flight was Air Force Capt. Ralph McGee, 29, of Port Sulphur, Louisiana. McGee was the first soldier from Louisiana to die in Southeast Asia. Years later, McGee's open passport was found at the crash site, and this assisted in identifying his remains.

A fourth casualty of the flight was Air Force 2nd Lt. Glenn Matteson, 23, of Dallas, Texas. He entered basic training at

Lackland Air Force Base in San Antonio in November 1959. After 8-weeks of training, Matteson was transferred to Harlingen, Texas, for 8-months of advanced training. He graduated in the early fall of 1960. Following, Matteson volunteered for more training with a C-47 plane at England Air Force in Lake Charles, Louisiana. One classmate said, *"He was intelligent, dedicated, friendly, and a good leader. As such, he stood out among the class and became our class commander." (Faces on the Wall, May 24, 2005)*

Also on board was Air Force Staff Sgt. Leslie Sampson, 24, of Richey, Montana. He would be one of two soldiers from Richey, population of around five hundred, to die in Southeast Asia. He was married.

The last two casualties onboard the deadly flight were Army Warrant Officer Edgar Weitkamp, 31, from York, Pennsylvania, and Air Force Capt. Oscar Weston, Jr., of Norfolk, Virginia. Weston had celebrated his 30th birthday eighteen days earlier. While Matteson had been in the military less than two years, Weitkamp and Weston had a combined fifty-four years of military service. Moreover, Weitkamp worked as an attaché at the embassy in Laos. Unfortunately, like Bankowski, Weitkamp's body was never recovered.

Less than a month after the plane crash in Laos, Army SP4 Theodore Feland died in Gia Dinh Province. Feland, 26, was from Sonoma, California, and was in South Vietnam with the MAAG. He had been in the military for four years, and it is believed that he took his own life on April 20, 1961.

As the tenth U.S. soldier to die in 1961, Army Sgt. Gerald Biber, 25, grew up in Benkelman, Nebraska. Stationed in Laos as a radio operator for MAAG, he was killed by small arms fire on April 22. Despite having served eight years in the military, Biber is believed to be the first radio operator to die in the Vietnam conflict.

Similar to so many others serving in Southeast Asia at the time, Army Sgt. John Bischoff, 31, of Mountain Rest, South

Carolina, was serving with MAAG in Laos. Like Biber, Bischoff was killed on April 22, 1961, by small arms fire, and his body was never recovered. According to a post on *The Wall of Faces*, Biber and Bishoff were part of a 4-man team ambushed while on a mission alongside several Laotian soldiers. Biber, Bishoff, and Army Sgt. Orville Ballinger,…

> *"…jumped aboard an armored car, heading south on Route 13, in a breakout effort. According to Lao survivors, they crouched behind the turret, but the car came under heavy grenade attack. Sgt. Bishoff fired a machine gun from the vehicle until he was shot through the neck and killed. Sgt. Biber had already been wounded and was apparently killed by stick grenades thrown against the armored car. The vehicle was halted and its crew captured. Sgt. Orville R. Ballinger, demolitions sergeant, escaped through the Jungle and linked up with some Lao soldiers. They found a boat and were going downriver when they were surprised and captured by the Pathet Lao seven days later…."*

The third soldier killed in April 1961 was Army Major Walter Moon. As a Rudy, Arkansas resident, population of less than 100, Moon was with the MAAG in Laos. He was believed to have been captured around April 22 and died in captivity at age thirty-eight. His wife received a letter from her husband. It was dated April 19. In it, Moon wrote that *"…everything was fine…and looked forward to getting back home for a long vacation"* (*The Bakersfield Californian, May 4, 1961, pg. 5*). Moon left behind a wife and two children. Unfortunately, like several others killed in the early years of the conflict, Moon's body was never recovered.

The December 24, 1961, edition of the *Wisconsin State Journal* listed Biber, Bishoff, and Moon as missing and being held prisoner by the Communist Pathet Lao forces (*pg. 17*).

As a working member of the MAAG, Army Lt. Colonel

Odis Arnold, 45, of Santa Monica, California, passed away on June 30 from a heart attack while serving in Gia Dinh Province. He had served in the military for sixteen years and was the oldest U.S. soldier to pass away to date in the conflict.

Air Force Sgt. Bruce Jones of Niles, Ohio, was the first soldier to pass away in the second half of 1961. He passed away on August 10 while serving in Thailand. Subsequently, he is not only the youngest to die in the early years of the conflict, but he was the first person to die from the state of Ohio. Jones...

> *"...19...was killed when, apparently by accident, he touched off the automatic ejection seat of a parked jet fighter Thursday and was blown from the cockpit...was hurled from the seat of the F-100 jet onto the concrete ramp at Bangkok's Don Muang Military Airport. He died of a skull fracture...The death was classified as accidental"* (*Circleville Herald, August 12, 1961, pg. 4*).

Jones, off duty at the time of the accident, was stationed in Japan and was in Thailand on temporary training duty.

Five days later, another U.S. soldier died in Thailand. This time it was Air Force Master Sgt. Floyd Studer, 34, of Port Allegany, Pennsylvania. Like countless other casualties in the early years of the conflict, Studer was with the MAAG. Unfortunately, he died when the helicopter he was in crashed northeast of Bangkok.

The last known soldier to pass away during the first thirty-six months of the Vietnam conflict was Army SP4 James "Tom" Davis of Livingston, Tennessee. He played football in high school and married his high school sweetheart following graduation. Davis had three years of college behind him but left his senior year to join the Army. In a letter to his father, a veteran of WWII, SP4 Davis wrote, *"...you did your job in the 1940s; now it's my turn."*

The younger Davis received basic training in South

Carolina, then went to Fort Devens, Massachusetts, for advanced training. Finally, in 1961, he received orders to go to Vietnam with a secretive MAAG intelligence unit. He arrived on a civilian passport. The group's role in Southeast Asia was to pinpoint enemy radio transmissions using highly sophisticated detection equipment. Between his basic and advanced training and leaving for Southeast Asia, his wife gave birth to a baby girl.

Three days before Christmas 1961, Davis, two other U.S. Army radio direction finder operators, and several South Vietnamese Army members left their compound near Tan Son Nhut airbase on the outskirts of Saigon to triangulate the precise position of enemy radio transmissions in nearby Hau Nghia Province. Riding in the front seat of the last of the three trucks, Davis was accompanied by his South Vietnamese driver. As the other two trucks stopped after gathering the needed coordinates, Davis told his driver to pull ahead to get one final reading.

> According to the *Coffelt Database of Vietnam Casualties*, "On 22 December 1961 at approximately 1140 hours, Davis was riding in the front of a ¾ ton truck, which was proceeding west on Viet Nam (sp.) provincial highway Number 10. An electronically controlled mine was exploded near the rear of the truck and immediately after the explosion approximately 10 Viet Cong opened fire with rifles, automatic weapons and hand grenades. Davis managed to open the door and escape from the vehicle; however, approximately 50 feet from the truck, he was hit in the head by a bullet...Death was apparently instantaneous."

SP4 Davis's body was returned stateside on January 3, 1962. He was 25 and had been in the military for less than two years. Three weeks after his passing, the 3rd Radio Research Unit base was renamed Davis Station in his memory.

Consequently, it became the first military compound in Vietnam named for a fallen soldier. Historians will remember Army Specialist 4 James T. Davis as the first U.S. battlefield fatality in Vietnam.

If nothing else, the first several years of America's involvement in the Vietnam conflict could be viewed as a forerunner of things to come.

First, most casualties will be young men between 20 and 30, and many had fathers or siblings who served in the military. Next, the soldier casualties will come from all parts of the U.S., from Connecticut to California and from Nebraska to Texas. Likewise, nearly every county, city, town, or village in America will experience the pain connected with the conflict in Vietnam. This goes for rural, suburban, and urban as well. In addition, all military branches will experience loss, as will all ranks and pay grades. Some of the American losses will occur beyond Vietnam's boundaries. Finally, the variety of casualties from the conflict will run the gamut from accidental to self-inflicted, homicide to disease, and from killed in action to missing in action.

As expected, U.S. military casualties in Southeast Asia would increase dramatically as the American presence in the region expanded. In 1962, the number of American soldiers killed tripled from the previous year from less than twenty to over fifty. Included among the list were nearly three dozen deaths involving helicopter or airplane crashes. Among them was the crash of a C-47 aircraft carrying nine passengers, eight Air Force members, and two Army soldiers.

The plane took off on Sunday, February 11, from Saigon. The crew's mission was to drop off leaflets from South Vietnamese President Ngo Dinh Diem, wishing everyone below a Happy New Year. After dropping off the leaflets over the capital, the plane headed northwest toward Da Nang for the same purpose. Unfortunately, the aircraft and crew did not reach Da Nang...they supposedly hit a mountain in Lam Duong Province.

However, this would not be the only aircraft crash with multiple fatalities. By the end of the year, there would be no less than eleven airplane or helicopter crashes in Southeast Asia in no fewer than fifteen different provinces. One of these crashes involved Air Force Capt. Robert Bennett, 31, of Cincinnati, Ohio, whose plane was believed to have been shot down in An Xugen Province as it was about to drop napalm on Viet Cong troops. According to the November 6, 1962, edition of the *Charleston (WV) Gazette*, Capt. Bennett was...

"...*in a Vietnamese Air Force B26 fighter bomber in a night...mission. It crashed-apparently shot down-180 miles southwest of Saigon. The B26 messaged that it was going in for an attack after sighting a target. Then the radio went dead...Bennett is survived by the widow and their four children...*" (*pg. 2*).

Also among the over fifty deaths during the year were over twenty-five members of the MAAG. Included in the list is Army Staff Sgt. Raymond Parks, 31, of Dennison, Ohio. During the morning hours of July 14, Parks, a member of the Army Special Forces out of Fort Bragg, North Carolina, was riding aboard a civilian-operated airplane when it was shot down over Laos. His remains were never recovered.

Other soldiers to die in 1962 was the first Filipino soldier to die in Southeast Asia, E5 Al Suminguit Padayhag. He died of a heart attack and had been in Vietnam for less than four months. Air Force Capt. Robert Simpson, 35, died in Ba Xugen Province while on a training mission with a South Vietnamese pilot. Simpson, a twelve-year military veteran, had served in WWII and Korea. He was from Panama City, Panama, and his body was never recovered.

The deaths of over seventy U.S. service members in less

than seven years and in no less than twenty different provinces indicate an expanded American presence in the region. However, the increasing death rate and the expanded presence of American troops in the region were only a precursor of things to come.

One year later, the number of casualties would almost double to nearly one hundred twenty-five. Of that number, over one-half were members of the Army, and nearly one in three were members of the Air Force. Helicopter or plane crashes killed most of the Air Force soldiers. Those killed in action in Southeast Asia in 1963 came from thirty-six different states, with California losing fourteen soldiers and Texas with twelve lives lost. Among the list of those killed was Staff Sgt. Robert Hain, 30, of Dorchester, Massachusetts, who died from friendly fire on May 6, and Air Force E3 Richard Hill from Houston, Texas, who died three days before his twenty-second birthday. Sadly, Air Force Capt. Thomas Gorton from Toledo, Ohio, would lose his life in a helicopter crash on December 6…his thirty-fourth birthday.

In 1964, the number of U.S. military casualties in the region would double and surpass two hundred. Army SP4 Billy Duane Good, of Dunbar, West Virginia, was among those losing their life. He was a member of the 362nd Signal Battalion and died when the vehicle he was driving overturned while negotiating a curve in the road. SP4 Good was the first of over seven hundred soldiers from West Virginia, population of approximately 1.8 million, to die in Southeast Asia, bestowing upon the state the unwelcomed honor of having the most soldiers killed per capita. SP4 Good was born on Christmas Day, 1938, and had been in the military for over four years. He was 25 and married.

For several reasons, the fifteen months between August 1964 and November 1965 marked a turning point in U.S. military involvement in Southeast Asia.

In August 1964, the U.S. Navy destroyer USS Maddox was operating in waters off North Vietnam when the ship's crew was fired upon by several boats from the North Vietnamese Navy. Although there were no U.S. casualties, the incident prompted the passage of the Gulf of Tonkin Resolution, which gave Pres. Johnson the power to assist any country in Southeast Asia that was threatened by communist aggression. The resolution allowed the president a pretext for entrance into the Vietnam conflict. However, Pres. Johnson did not immediately act on his powers because of the U.S. elections set for November 3.

On February 6, 1965, around three hundred Viet Cong soldiers attacked the U.S. airfield at Camp Holloway, near Pleiku, in the central highlands of Gia Lai Province. Although the attack was over in minutes, it destroyed nearly a dozen U.S. aircraft and cost seven U.S. soldiers their lives. Six of the seven deceased soldiers were less than twenty-six years old, and the oldest was thirty-five. While one of the soldiers killed had served in the military nearly two decades and two had served over eight years, the remaining soldiers had been in the military an average of eighteen months.

Less than 24 hours later and in retaliation for the attack on Camp Holloway, Pres. Johnson issued the command to begin bombing selective North Vietnam targets in the north of the country. Deemed Operation Flaming Dart, the goal was to destroy enemy barracks just north of the DMZ. Undeterred by the bombings, however, the enemy launched a second attack on another U.S. facility less than a week later. The second attack in Binh Dinh Province caused the death of nearly two dozen American military personnel. Among those casualties was an 18-year-old Army Pfc. Larry McClanahan, of Yakima, Washington, 19-year-old Army Pfc. Walter Rickard, of Lahaina, Hawaii, 20-year-old Army Pfc. Lavon Stephen of Roswell, New Mexico, and 21-year-old Army Pfc. Paul Bays of Rosemont, West Virginia, who was fourteen days away from celebrating his twenty-second birthday. Many of those killed in the attack were involved in the maintenance and repair of helicopters.

Pressured by several members of Congress to step up the bombings, Pres. Johnson approved plans for the sustained bombing of several fixed targets in North Vietnam, including major roads. On March 2, Operation Rolling Thunder commenced with nearly one hundred fifty U.S. fighter bombers and about twenty South Vietnamese Air Force aircraft taking part in the bombing.

One week later, nearly 1,500 U.S. Marines were ordered to South Vietnam to guard the airbase at Da Nang against a possible enemy attack. By the end of the month, almost 25,000 military personnel were in the country, and about 1 in 4 were Marines. The latter act was seen as the first direct U.S. involvement in the Vietnam conflict.

On April 25, Marine Lance Cpl. Randall Campbell, 20, was killed by a booby trap while on patrol in Thua Thien Province. Born in Montreal, Quebec, he was among the countless Canadians who crossed the border and enlisted in the U.S. military. At the time, it was illegal for Canadian citizens to fight in a war Canada was not formally involved in. Campbell is believed to be one of the first Canadians to die in the Vietnam conflict.

Less than two months later, a second Canadian serviceman died. On June 18, Marine Pvt. Melvin Suthons, 21, from Welland, Ontario, was killed from small arms fire. Three more Canadian-born soldiers would die in Vietnam during the following six months. Marine Pvt. Stefan Stalinski, 20, the youngest of the five soldiers, was from Montreal, Quebec, and died on July 8. Lance Cpl. Francis J.D. Delmark, 22, died on August 18, and Pvt. Robert Kunkel, 23, the oldest of the group, died on November 16 from wounds received on August 18. While all five soldiers were Marines, Delmark and Kunkel were killed in Quang Ngai Province, Campbell in Thua Thien Province, Stalinski in Quang Tri Province, and Suthons in Quang Nam Province.

In late summer, Pres. Johnson announced the call-up of 50,000 U.S. troops to be deployed to South Vietnam. This brought the number of troops committed to the region to over 125,000. Additionally, Pres. Johnson said that the monthly "draft" call would increase the number of soldiers for military duty from around 17,000 to nearly 35,000 monthly. Less than one month later, Pres. Johnson signed an executive order that removed the marriage exemption from the draft. However, married fathers between nineteen and twenty-six were still exempt. In addition, soldiers who were married before midnight on August 26 would be exempt from military service. It is said that countless men drove to Nevada because the state did not have a waiting period for two people to get married.

Four days later, however, General Lewis Hershey, the Director of the Selective Service System, clarified Pres. Johnson's order by announcing that all married, childless men between the ages of nineteen and twenty-six would be eligible for military service beginning in January 1966. Consequently, a soldier's prompt decision to marry did not exempt them from military service. It only deferred their possible entrance into the military.

On October 22, Army Pfc. Milton Lee Olive, III, and four other soldiers were pursuing several enemies in the jungle near Phu Coung, in Binh Duong Province, when one of the enemy threw a grenade toward Olive and the others. Immediately, Olive threw himself on the grenade, saving the lives of his fellow soldiers. In addition, he was around sixteen days from celebrating his nineteenth birthday. As a result of his actions, he was awarded the Medal of Honor, the first African-American in the Vietnam conflict to receive the honor. Before entering the military, Olive had moved to Mississippi to live with his grandparents so that he could work alongside others to register black voters.

Additionally, the number of deaths among young soldiers in Southeast Asia was increasing dramatically. Included among those who lost their lives in Vietnam in 1965 is Army Pfc. Terry Wright of Ft. Wayne, Indiana, and Army Pfc. James Ward of Milwaukee, Wisconsin. Pfc. Wright, who had been in Vietnam less than two months, passed away on October 10 from a sniper's bullet. Ward was in Vietnam for less than two months and died the next day from small arms fire while on a search and clear operation. Both soldiers were seventeen and would be two of several seventeen-year-olds killed that year. The others include Pfc. Alan Barnett of Astoria, Oregon, and Pfc. Carl Daniels of New Orleans, Louisiana. Both Army soldiers arrived in Vietnam on August 20, were in A Company, 2nd Battalion, 8th Calvary, 1st Calvary Division, and died in Pleiku Province on November 4, 1965. Army Pfc. Anthony Pendola of Peoria, Illinois, who began his tour of duty on August 18, died on November 6 from small arms fire. Like Barnett and Daniels, Pendola died while serving in Pleiku Province. He left behind a wife and a two-month-old baby girl.

The sixth 17-year-old to lose his life in Vietnam in 1965 and the second to pass away on November 6 was Philadelphia, Pennsylvania, Marine Cpl. Charles Antonelly. He enlisted in the Marines after attending Edison High School in Philadelphia. He received basic training at Parris Island, South Carolina, between March and June 1962. Cpl. Antonelly received additional training as a helicopter mechanic.

Ironically, he died when his helicopter went down in Thua Thien Province. He was the first from his high school, Thomas Alva Edison, to die in Southeast Asia. By the time of the end of the Vietnam conflict, there would be over fifty others from the high school to die in combat fighting. Subsequently, the school is known to have the highest casualty rate during the Vietnam conflict of any high school in the U.S. As one of the most poverty-ridden areas of Philadelphia, many soldiers were known to have gotten into trouble before entering the military. Most were given a choice by the court: jail or military service.

Within days of the death of Pfc. Wright in mid-October, Pres. Lyndon Johnson ordered every soldier under 18 years old out of combat. Unfortunately, the orders arrived too late for Ward, Pendola, and several other seventeen-year-old soldiers. Pfc. Daniels was around forty-five days from celebrating his eighteen birthday, while Barnett died eleven days before his eighteenth birthday.

———

Far above, however, the singular event that most fully marked the turning point of America's involvement in the Vietnam conflict happened in the latter half of November in the dense jungles of the central highlands. The nearly week-long engagement would mark the first time that many of the 25,000 U.S. troops currently on the ground in Vietnam would face North Vietnamese troops. Furthermore, the battle would account for almost fifteen percent of all U. S. military casualties in 1965. The engagement marked the deadliest week for American casualties in the conflict. It would come a matter of days after two anti-war protesters set themselves on fire to demonstrate their rage against the conflict in Southeast Asia.

On November 2, Norman Morrison, a thirty-two-year-old Quaker from Baltimore, Maryland, immolated himself in front of the Pentagon. One week later, Roger LaPorte, a member of the Catholic Worker Movement, immolated himself in front of the United Nations Building in New York City. LaPorte was twenty-two and a former seminarian.

In the early days of October, U. S. military intelligence noted a growing presence of North Vietnamese and Viet Cong troops in the rural Ia Drang Valley in Gia Lai Province. The build-up would later cause Pres. Johnson to double the size of draftees. Additionally, American military intelligence uncovered an enemy plan to attack a special forces camp southwest of Pleiku. The enemy's plan was to first attack the camp and then lie in-wait in the jungles surrounding the camp and ambush any troops coming as reinforcements. With the help of U. S. air support, the initial attack on the camp was turned away. Still, the ambush of the reinforcements caused the South Vietnamese troops to suffer several casualties.

In a short time, American commanders decided to take the initiative and send troops into the Ia Drang Valley to suppress any further increase or advancement of enemy troops. The plan was to first bomb the area using B-52 airplanes, followed by a large-scale assault of U. S. and South Vietnamese Army (ARVN) regulars. In addition, troop leaders saw this as an opportunity to introduce a new facet to the conflict: the use of helicopters to deliver, supply, and remove dead and wounded from the battlefield. The encounter between the Allied forces and the PAVN troops lasted four days and caused heavy losses on both sides.

Of the two hundred and thirty-four lives lost in the Ia Drang Valley during the last two weeks of November 1965,

81

nearly each of the fifty states and the District of Columbia had at least one soldier die in the battle. The only states not to lose a native son in the deadliest battle to date in the conflict were Colorado, Connecticut, Maine, Nebraska, New Hampshire, Rhode Island, and Vermont. Of the soldiers from Pennsylvania that were killed, two of them, Army Pfc. Samuel McDonald and Army 2nd Lt. Larry Leroy Hess, were buried in Gettysburg National Cemetery. McDonald died on November 15, and Hess two days later.

In addition, there were no less than seven soldiers from Puerto Rico killed in the first major battle of the Vietnam conflict. This includes Army Sgt. Elias Alvarez-Buzo, Sgt. Ramon Bernard, and Sgt. Antonio Ramon Bernard-Robles, who died on November 15 at LZ X-Ray. Also losing their lives were Army Staff Sgt. Megdelio Caraballo-Garcia, SP4 Ramon Kuilan-Oliveras, Pfc. Julio Ernesto Morales Gonzalez, and Pfc. Miguel de Jesus Vera Duran. The last four soldiers died on November 17 at LZ Albany.

Also killed on November 17 in the Ia Drang Valley was Army Staff Sgt. Clarence Vereno Beverhoudt from the Virgin Islands, and Filipino Army SP5 Ishmael Juson Paredes. Beverhoudt, 36, would be the first of fifteen soldiers from the Virgin Islands to die in Southeast Asia. Paredes, also 36, had been in the Army for over a decade and left behind a wife and three children in Jersey City, New Jersey. Paredes would be one of nine Filipinos to die in the conflict.

Included in the list of Ohio soldiers who lost their lives on November 17 was *Staff Sgt. Glenn McCammon* of Woodsfield. He was 32. McCammon would be one of nearly two thousand soldiers to lose their lives in Southeast Asia in 1965.

_____

The large numbers of casualties on both sides of the

battlefield would also usher in several new phrases to the conflict, such as body count and kill ratio. Moreover, the battle of Ia Drang would signal an increase in American troops in Southeast Asia. By the time Pres. Johnson called a halt to the bombing of select targets in North Vietnam on Christmas Eve 1965; the U.S. military presence in South Vietnam had increased from under 24,000 troops the year before to almost 185,000…a nearly 700% increase. Moreover, the number would increase to approximately 400,000 within twelve months.

Similarly, U.S. casualties increased nearly 800% by the close of 1965…from over two hundred and fifteen in 1964 to over thirteen hundred the following year. Pres. Johnson hoped the halt in the bombing would bring the North Vietnamese to negotiations. It did not.

1966

With no movement from the North Vietnamese toward an accepted peace settlement, Pres. Johnson lifted the bombing moratorium on January 31, 1966, and Operation Rolling Thunder resumed with U.S. bombers hitting sites north of the DMZ. Ironically, the move came on the heels of *Time* magazine naming Army General William Westmoreland as their 1965 Man of the Year. With American troop strength in Southeast Asia nearing 200,000, new military operations by U.S. and ARVN troops to fight the communist advance in South Vietnam increased dramatically, over twenty in January alone. By the end of June, the number will have increased almost tenfold. The list of operations would include Operation Marauder in the Mekong Delta, Operation Crimp in Binh Duong Province, involving joint U.S. and Australian troops, and Operation Van Buren, which comprised American and South Korean military units. As expected, the number of U. S.

military lives lost would increase proportionally.

A military spokesperson for the Department of Defense announced in early spring that nearly fourteen hundred U. S. servicemen had been killed in the conflict since the beginning of the year, adding that the average number of lives lost among the four military branches, Army, Navy, Air Force, and Marines, was around one hundred every week.

One of the over four hundred U. S. soldiers to die in January was Army Pfc. Joseph Quiroz. He was born in Chicago, Illinois, on March 9, 1944, and enlisted in the Army at age 20. Pfc. Quiroz began his duty tour in Vietnam on December 14, 1965, and died forty-six days later on January 29, 1966, in Binh Dinh Province, when the helicopter he was traveling in was hit with mortar and automatic weapons fire. He was 21 and was one of sixty-one soldiers that died that day. Quiroz was a member of Our Lady of Guadalupe Catholic Church...the first Mexican American Catholic Church in Chicago. Reportedly, the church suffered more than any Catholic Church in the U.S., losing twelve of its parishioners during the Vietnam conflict; five were killed within five months of each other in 1968. At his death, he was receiving $117.90 per month. In addition, Pfc. Quiroz lost an older brother, John, in the Korean War.

Among the list of no less than twenty soldiers killed during January from Ohio from the Army included Cpl. Raynald Amador, Staff Sgt. Wallace Baker, Sgt. Francis Beagle, Sgt. James Coats, Pfc. Billy Deweese, Pfc. Charles Frederick, 2nd Lt. Thomas Grant, Staff Sgt. William Gutter, SP5 David Jackson, 2nd Lt. Matthew Pechaitis, Sgt. Grant Rhodes, Pfc. Robert Smith, Pfc. Charles Swartz, Pfc. Michael Timmons, SP4 Richard Webster, and Pvt. Wilbur Wise. Also losing their lives during January 1965 were Marines Capt. Lawrence Helber and Cpl. Nathan Cole, Navy CPO Thomas Bruck, and Air Force Staff Sgt. James Lute.

Baker and Smith died the day after New Year's Day, while

Rhodes died two days later. Beagle, from New Matamoras in Washington County, died one day after. Lute was killed on January 7, and Cole and Timmons the day after.

Bruck, Pechaitis, and Swartz died on the same day, January 10, and Amador died the following day. As for Jackson, who began his tour of duty in Vietnam on Christmas Eve, 1965, he died on January 17. Like Timmins, he was from Columbus.

Coats and Deweese died on the same day two weeks later, on January 25, and Gutter and Webster four days after that. Helber, whose body has never been recovered, Wise, Grant, and Frederick died during the last week of the month.

Between January and June 1966, no less than one hundred and fifty-five Ohio soldiers died in Southeast Asia. This would eclipse the one hundred and ten deaths for the previous five years! The latter six months of the year would be no different. One hundred sixty-six additional Ohio soldiers would lose their lives by year's end.

———————

On February 18, a helicopter struck a power line over the Saigon River in Bien Hoa Province, killing all seven soldiers onboard. Included in the casualties were Army 2nd Lt. Carol Drazba of Dunmore, Pennsylvania, and 2nd Lt. Elizabeth Jones of Allendale, South Carolina. Both were twenty-two years old, nurses attached to the 51st Field Hospital, and the first females killed in the Vietnam conflict.

Drazba, a 1964 graduate of the State Hospital School of Nursing in Scranton, joined the Army on September 23, 1965, during her second year of the nursing program. Following basic training, she was assigned to Fort Huachuca, Arizona, and then Fort Sam Houston, Texas, where she was commissioned as a 2nd lieutenant. She volunteered for duty in Vietnam and began her tour there on October 13, 1965. At the time of her death, she had been in the military for less than two years.

Second Lt. Jones was a nurse graduate of the Medical School of South Carolina. She was assigned to the U.S. Army hospital at Fort Jackson before going to Vietnam on October 13, 1965. At the time of her passing, Lt. Jones was engaged to be married to Army Lt. Colonel Charles Honour, and her mother had recently mailed Lt. Jones a wedding dress. Sadly, Lt. Col. Honour was one of the passengers aboard the helicopter when it went down on February 18. Also onboard were SP4 Christopher Lantz, 18, of Cleveland, Ohio, SP4 Gary Artman, 19, of Oklahoma City, Oklahoma, and Capt. Thomas Stasko, 30, of Aurora, Colorado. The seventh soldier to lose his life that day was the helicopter pilot, Capt. Albert "Bert" Smith, 27, of Washington, DC. He was the son of UPI White House correspondent Merriman Smith. All aboard the helicopter were members of the U.S. Army.

Not long after Army Staff Sgt. Barry Sadler's musical tribute to SP5 James Gabriel, a member of America's Special Forces and the first Hawaiian to be killed in Vietnam, became a major hit, *"The Ballad of the Green Berets"* was tempered by the words of a *U.S. News and World Report* article proclaiming that the conflict in Vietnam had become a stalemate. Despite the magazine's bold declaration that neither the U.S. nor its enemy was likely to emerge the winner, the first American magazine to make such a statement, American troop strength had exceeded a quarter of a million in the region. The U.S. efforts to fulfill its military obligation to the South Vietnamese government were further promoted when the Philippine government voted to send some 2,000 troops to Vietnam. The Philippines became the fourth nation to send troops to the region, joining the U.S., Australia, and South Korea.

However, the growing flames of unrest in the U.S. surrounding America's presence in Southeast Asia was aided a few weeks later when a Japanese tv station aired an interview with a downed American pilot. Commander Jeremiah Denton, a Navy pilot, was shot down and captured in July 1965 while on a bombing mission over Thanh Hoa Province. During the May 2, 1966 interview, Denton, with his eyes blinking rapidly with each word spoken, affirmed his support for the American presence in the region, despite his captor's commands to do the opposite and criticize American involvement in Vietnam. However, on closer look, U.S. military intelligence officers discovered that Denton was using Morse Code to spell out the word "torture" with his blinking to convey that American prisoners were being brutalized by their North Vietnamese captors.

With few exceptions, the last six months of the year were a carbon copy of the events of the previous six months.

For starters, around another forty military operations began in the region, including six in July, seven in August, and no less than ten in September. During the last three months of the year, an additional nine military operations would start in October and thirteen during November and December. As expected, military casualties increased during the six months.

Among the fifty-one Ohio soldiers to die in July and August were Monroe County cousins, Army *Pfc. Jack Pittman* and Marine *Pvt. Duane Greenlee.*

Pittman was injured on July 18 when his vehicle hit a claymore mine as it traveled on Vietnam Highway QL-13, also known as Thunder Road. One week later, he died from his wounds in a San Francisco, California, hospital. Also killed in the same vehicle that carried Pittman was Army Pfc. Patrick Dwyer of Philadelphia, Pennsylvania, and Army Pfc. Donald

Priest, from Monroe County, New York. Both soldiers were 23 years old and had fathers that served in WWII. Combined, Dwyer, Pittman, and Priest had been in Vietnam for less than fifteen months.

Exactly one month later, on August 25, Pittman's cousin and fellow Beallsville, Ohio, resident Pvt. Duane Greenlee was killed in Quang Nam Province by small arms fire. Unlike Pittman, who was an only child, Greenlee was the oldest of nine children, and his father had served in WWII.

Similarly, several more Canadian-born U.S. soldiers died in Vietnam. Among the list was Marine Pvt. Frank Crabbe, 19, from Montreal, who died on February 2 when the vehicle he was in ran over a mine in Quang Nam Province. Next, it was Marine Pvt. David Hann, 19, who died in Quang Ngai Province on March 4 from small arms fire. His death was followed by the passing of two more Canadian soldiers in April. Marine Pvt. Daniel Sauve, at 18, was the youngest soldier from Canada to die in the Vietnam conflict. He died on April 21 from accidental homicide. Five days later, Marine Pvt. Hans Lorenz, a radio operator, died from burn wounds he received on April 11 while on duty in Quang Nam Province. He was the seventh U.S. Marine from Canada to die in Vietnam in the last twelve months.

On May 9, Marine Lance Corporal Austin Corbiere, 23, of Little Current, Ontario, died while serving in Quang Nam Province. He was the fourth Canadian soldier to die in Quang Nam Province within a year. Additionally, Army Sgt. Thomas Williams of St. Catherines, Ontario, was the first Canadian soldier to die while serving with the U.S. Army. He had been in the military for over fourteen years, most recently as a cannon specialist, and died on July 18 from a heart attack. Sgt. Williams was 38 years old. Three weeks later, Marine Corporal Dennis Schmidt died from small arms fire while serving in Quang Tri Province. He had been in the military less than one year, had celebrated his 21st birthday two months earlier, and was buried in Nova Scotia.

Less than one month later, the United States Coast Guard reported the loss of two members, the first of seven members of the USCG to die in Southeast Asia. According to the *Pacific Stars and Stripes* magazine, the USCG Cutter Point Welcome was patrolling waters in the Gulf of Tonkin on August 11 when it was mistaken for a North Vietnamese vessel by three American warplanes. The initial strike hit the U.S. vessel's bridge, killing the commander at the time, Lt. JG David Brostrom, 25, of Los Altos, California. Immediately, the Chief Petty Officer began to steer the ship away from further attack. However, believing the vessel was attempting to elude, the American pilots opened fire on the boat a second time, killing Petty Officer 2nd Class Jerry Phillips, 27, of Corpus Christi, Texas. The remaining eleven crewmembers were unhurt. Brostrom, who had turned twenty-five two days earlier, was a graduate of the Coast Guard Academy in New London, Connecticut, and the son of a retired commander. He was cremated, and his remains were committed to the Pacific Ocean. Phillips was married and had 3 sons.

Within a few weeks of the U.S. Department of Defense announcing the largest draft call during the conflict, around 50,000 men, two more Canadian soldiers would die while serving in Southeast Asia. The first, Army Pfc. Robert Steel of Windsor, Ontario, lost his life when an explosive was accidentally detonated nearby. He died on October 4 at the age of 19. Nearly three weeks later, Navy pilot Lt. John Francis, 33, from Weston, Ontario, died in a fire aboard the aircraft carrier USS Oriskany while stationed in the Gulf of Tonkin off the North Vietnamese coast. The fire on the Oriskany began when a flare was accidentally ignited and then thrown near a magazine locker. Francis was one of the thirty-four officers, twenty-four of them pilots, and ten crewmen to lose their lives that day.

Also among those losing their lives aboard the ship was yet another seventeen-year-old. This time, it was Navy Airman Apprentice Greg Hart of Seattle, Washington. He was the youngest member of the vessel to lose his life that day. In addition, the fire also claimed the life of Navy Lt. Commander William Garrity, a Catholic priest and chaplain aboard the Oriskany. While giving last rites and seeking to comfort those injured and dying from the fire, Garrity was overcome with heat and smoke, becoming a victim himself. Father Garrity was forty and one of six soldiers from Havre, Montana, population of around ten thousand, to die in the Vietnam conflict.

The last of the Canadian soldiers to die in Vietnam while serving with U.S. troops was Marine Lance Corporal John Reeves, 23, of Winnipeg, Manitoba. He drowned on December 23 while serving in Quang Nam Province. The conflict in Southeast Asia would claim the lives of one hundred and thirty-four Canadian soldiers.

The year ended with several significant actions being undertaken regarding the regional conflict.

Less than one week after Thanksgiving, the U.S. and its allies in Vietnam agreed to a North Vietnamese and Viet Cong proposal, which called for three ceasefires to coincide with the upcoming holidays. The first ceasefire would begin at 7:00am on Christmas Eve and conclude at 7:00am on December 26. A second moratorium on fighting would begin on the morning of New Year's Day, 1967, and last twenty-four hours. The final ceasefire would start on February 8 and last four days. It would mark Tet, the Vietnamese new year, celebrated in North and South Vietnam.

Around the same time that Bob Hope was making his third Christmas trip and humorously telling troops near Cu Chi, northwest of Saigon, that "they have a lot of tv competition back in the states and should get on the ball...if they don't, the war may be canceled..." the U.S. Army was deploying its newest element to step up water patrols in the Mekong Delta. Known as the Mobile Riverine Force, it comprised Army and Navy personnel deployed on several watercraft, complete with machine guns and other weapons. Beyond patrolling the hundreds of miles of delta waterway, the MRF could rapidly move troops from one location to another when needed.

1967

With each passing year, it seemed that America was being drawn deeper and deeper into the conflict in Southeast Asia and civil unrest at home, and 1967 was no different.

First, there was an increase in troop size in Southeast Asia. In addition to U.S. troops, numbering over 375,000, ARVN strength was quickly approaching 750,000, and over 50,000 from other allies. Subsequently, increased troop strength in the region was followed by increased military operations. During the first six months of the year, there were no less than one hundred and seventy new operations in Vietnam, including Operation Cedar Falls in Binh Duong Province, involving nearly 16,000 American troops and just as many ARVN troops, Operation Sam Houston near the Vietnam-Cambodia border, and one of the most extensive operations in the war, Operation Junction City, in Tay Ninh Province, that involved over 30,000 U.S. troops and over 5,000 ARVN soldiers. The region would have nearly as many new operations during the last six months.

In like manner, the increase in military troops and operations also increased U.S. casualties, combat and otherwise.

Not long after the U.S. Supreme Court overturned the conviction of world heavyweight boxing champion

Muhammad Ali for draft evasion, U.S. Air Force Major General William Crumm was piloting a B-52 bomber when it collided in mid-air with another bomber, twenty miles offshore of Vihn Bihn Province. The collision happened on July 7, as the two planes changed positions because one had navigational issues. While seven crewmembers survived the incident, the crash took the life of Major General Crumm, 48, and a dozen other crew members. Among the others losing their lives was Air Force Capt. David Bittenbender, 26, Air Force Major Paul Avolese, 35, and Air Force Master Sergeant Olen McLaughlin, 39. Crumm, Bittenbender, and Avolese were all from New York, while McLaughlin was from Tampa, Florida. Of the four officers lost in the collision, only the body of Avolese was recovered. The others are classified as missing in action. Major General Crumm was the highest-ranking officer killed in the Vietnam conflict.

Three weeks later, an explosion and fire aboard the USS Forrestal cost the lives of one hundred and thirty-four sailors. The Navy class aircraft carrier left Norfolk, Virginia, on June 6, headed for Vietnam and the Gulf of Tonkin. It is believed the carrier arrived around July 24 and anchored just off the coast of Quang Nam and Quang Tin provinces. For several days, the planes aboard the Forrestal flew bombing missions over North Vietnam. On the morning of July 29, just before 11:00am…

> *"…a Skyhawk bomber, taking off on a mission against North Vietnam, had 'spewed' flame in a hot start, probably caused by excess fuel. The flame struck a missile aboard an F-4 Phantom. The missile tore loose and struck the fuel tank of another plane. The fuel ignited and spilled over the deck, becoming a river of fire that vaporized steel and entered the bowel of the ship through holes ripped in the decks by explosions. With the carrier's fate at stake…sailors rushed to other rockets--which might explode at any moment--to*

heave them over the side...." *(Life magazine, August 11, 1967, pg. 21)*

Despite the best efforts of the Forrestal's crew and seaman from other ships in the area, including the USS Bon Homme Richard and the USS Oriskany, which had experienced an onboard fire nine months earlier, the fire aboard the Forrestal burned for several hours. Of the lives lost that day, nearly one-third of the sailors came from Texas, Pennsylvania, New York, and Florida.

Among the thirteen crew members from Texas to lose their lives was Navy Seaman Ray Chatelain, 21, of Tenaha, Texas, a population of less than one thousand. He had volunteered for a second tour of duty in Vietnam and was placed on the Forrestal. Chatelain was the fourth soldier from Shelby County, Texas, to die in Southeast Asia in 1967.

Among the dozen Pennsylvania crew members to die from the fire aboard the Forrestal was Petty Officer Third Class Richard Sietz from Gettysburg. As a third-generation sailor, Sietz's father was a ship captain, and his grandfather served in the German Navy following WWI. As he was assisting in fighting the onboard fire, a bomb exploded nearby, killing PO Sietz. He had been married for less than a year when his wife gave birth to a baby girl one month after his passing. Seaman Kenneth Dyke of Huntington Station, New York, was one of the nine 19-year-olds to die upon the Forrestal. During the fire, he fell overboard and was initially rescued by a nearby helicopter. However, as Dyke was being pulled up, he lost his grip and fell back into the ocean. His body was never recovered.

Among the ten soldiers from Florida to die in the worst accident aboard a Navy vessel since WWII was Airman Charles Kieser, 20, of Orlando. As the second sailor from Orlando to die in the fire, Kieser had been in the Navy for less than a year. In addition, he was one of two dozen 20-year-olds to die aboard the Forrestal.

Over eighty percent of the one hundred and thirty-four

sailors who perished on July 29, 1967, were between eighteen and twenty-five. The two eighteen-year-olds were Airman Apprentice William Brindle of Wabash, Indiana, and Airman Apprentice James Newkirk of Pensacola, Florida. Petty Officer First Class George McDonald, 47, of Los Angeles, California, was the oldest sailor to die in the fire. He had been in the Navy for twenty-four years.

Also killed in the fire were seven sailors from Ohio, including Seaman James Blaskis, 21, from Euclid; Petty Officer Second Class James Earick, 29, of Bellefontaine; and Petty Officer Second Class John Edwards, 29, from Dayton. The others were Airman Ralph Jacobs, 22, of Columbus; Navy Fireman Ronald Ogrinc, 21, from Columbus; Airman Harold Watkins, 22, from Cleveland; and Seaman Nelson Spitler, from Upper Sandusky, who turned twenty-one on July 2.

There were also seamen from neighboring West Virginia among the fire casualties. This includes Petty Officer Second Class Marvin Adkins from Mallory and Seaman John Stanley Duplaga from Wheeling. Adkins, a 14-year veteran of the Navy, turned thirty-two the day before he died. Duplaga, 22, had been in the Navy for less than a year.

Among the survivors of the fire aboard the USS Forrestal was a thirty-year-old pilot, Lt. Commander John McCain. At the time, his father was the commander of U.S. naval forces in Europe. The younger McCain had requested a combat assignment and was assigned to the Forrestal. When the fire upon the Forrestal placed the vessel out of commission, McCain was transferred to the USS Oriskany, anchored nearby. Three months later, while participating in Operation Rolling Thunder, he was shot down, captured by North Vietnamese forces, and held prisoner for the next several years.

———————

Also among the over eleven thousand U.S. casualties in Southeast Asia in 1967 are three of the nine soldiers known collectively as the "Morenci 9." The group comprised eight members of the Class of 1966 at Morenci High School in Morenci, Arizona, and one friend who dropped out of college to join the others. Of the nine, five were white, three were Hispanic, and one was Navajo. Two of the nine had already received their draft cards...1-A. At least by enlisting in the Marines, the friends believed they would have some say if-and-when they would begin their military service. On July 4, 1967, all nine met and boarded a bus for San Diego, California, and basic training. After completing boot camp, four of the group were placed on a ship headed for Vietnam. One group remained in California for extended radio training while the remaining soldiers waited for their deployment orders. By year's end, three of the nine had been killed in combat.

The first to die was Cpl. Robert Draper on August 2. He was 19 and died during an enemy ambush. Three months later, on November 6, it was Lance Cpl. Bradford King, age 21. As a star linebacker on the football team before his deployment, he had been in Vietnam for less than a month. Both Draper and King were killed in Quang Nam Province.

Three more of the Morenci 9 would die the following year, including Lance Cpl. Alfred Whitmer on April 13 in Thua Thien Province, Lance Cpl. Larry West on May 17 in Quang Nam Province, and Sgt. Jose Moncayo, the oldest of the group. He died less than three weeks later in an ambush while on patrol in Quang Tri Province. Marine Sgt. Clive Garcia died two days after Thanksgiving 1969 from a booby trap while on patrol in Quang Nam Province.

Additionally, the Vietnam conflict would claim three boyhood friends from Midvale, Utah, and all of them would pass away in the span of sixteen days. The three young men lived on consecutive streets in Midvale. The first to pass away was Army SP4 Frank LeRoy Tafoya, who lived on Fifth Avenue. He died on the fourth anniversary of the assassination of Pres. John F. Kennedy, November 22, at age 19, in Binh Thuan Province. Marine Lance Cpl. John "Jimmy" Martinez, 20, lived on Sixth Avenue and died on Thanksgiving Day in Quang Tri Province. Army Sgt. Tom Gonzales, 20, grew up on Seventh Avenue in Midvale and died on December 7 in Binh Dinh Province. He arrived in Vietnam two days before his 20th birthday. Within fifteen months, the last of four soldiers from Midvale, Marine Sgt. James Tueller, would pass away. He died of wounds in Quang Ngai Province on December 23, 1968. Sgt. Tueller was 19.

On the last day of November, a C-7 military plane carrying twenty-six passengers crashed into a mountain in Binh Dinh Province during bad weather. The aircraft was returning from Pleiku to Qui Nhon when it was diverted to Nha Trang. Among those that perished was Capt. Eleanor Alexander, 27, of Riverdale, New Jersey, and 1st Lt. Hedwig Orlowski, known to family and friends as Heddy, 23, of Detroit, Michigan.

After graduating high school in 1957, Capt. Alexander went on to graduate from D'Youville College School of Nursing in Buffalo in 1961. She trained at Madison Hospital in NYC for 6 years and enlisted in the Army on April 5, 1967. Capt. Alexander completed her basic training at Brooke Medical Center in Houston, Texas, and began her tour in Vietnam on June 6, 1967, with the 67th Evacuation Hospital in Qui Nhon as an operating room nurse. She had been in Vietnam less than a year when she died. Surviving were her mother and brother.

1st Lt. Orlowski was born in Tel Aviv, Israel, and attended high school in Wiesbaden, Germany, before moving to Michigan with her family. She trained at Mercy Hospital in Detroit and Hurley Hospital in Flint before entering military service in September 1965. In June 1967, she deployed to

Vietnam with the 85th Evacuation Hospital as an operating nurse.

Also onboard the flight was 1st Lt. Jerome Olmsted, 24, a nurse anesthetist from Clintonville, Wisconsin, who had just observed his sixth month of duty in Vietnam. He was survived by his mother and father and five siblings. Olmsted also leaves behind a wife and a young daughter. A fourth member of the medical team to lose his life on November 30, 1967, was 1st Lt. Kenneth Shoemaker, 26, of Owensboro, Kentucky. A fifth member of the medical team to die in the crash was Army E5 Phillip Ogas of Lindsay, California. He celebrated his 22nd birthday twenty-four days before his passing. Alexander and Shoemaker were nurse anesthetists, while Ogas was an operating room specialist. Like Orlowski, Ogas and Olmsted were from the 85th Evacuation Hospital, while Shoemaker was a medical member from the 67th Evacuation Hospital.

Among the others that perished on the flight were two soldiers from Ohio, two from Washington state, and two each from South Carolina and West Virginia. Alexander, Orlowski, and Olmsted were awarded the Bronze Star and Purple Heart.

Although the plane and its crew and passengers went down on November 30 and were listed as missing, it took rescue crews five days to locate the wreckage because the aircraft went down in dense mountain jungle.

The day before those twenty-six bodies were recovered from the wreckage, a Marine Riverine Force (MRF) flotilla set off on a mission up the Mekong River toward the Rach Ruong Canal. Their mission, part of Operation Coronado IX, was to find and destroy elements of the North Vietnamese Army and Viet Cong gathering along western Dinh Tuong and eastern Kien Phong provinces. Before long, the flotilla began receiving rocket and small arms fire from the western banks of the canal. The fighting was intense. When the two-day battle ended on December 5, it had cost the North Vietnamese and Viet Cong nearly three hundred soldiers. The battle, one of the biggest during the Operation Coronado series, cost the lives of eleven American troops, with around two hundred wounded. As expected, each of the American casualties had a backstory.

Army Pfc. Donald Cote, 20, of Mountlake Terrace, Washington, had been in Vietnam for less than six months. Beyond being one of four twenty-year-olds to die in the battle, Cote was the third soldier from Mountlake Terrace to be killed in 1967. Upon his passing, he received the Purple Heart and was posthumously promoted to Corporal.

At eighteen, Pfc. William Moseley, from Moorestown, New Jersey, was the youngest of the Army soldiers to lose his life along the banks of the Rach Ruong Canal during Operation Coronado IX. Pfc. Moseley, whose father had been in the military for two decades and retired as a major, had been in Vietnam less than two months.

Army Pfc. Richard Russ, 20, of Wilmington, North Carolina, began his tour of duty in Vietnam two weeks before he died and was nineteen days away from celebrating his twenty-first birthday. Before entering the military, he worked at WECT TV in Wilmington. Russ, a Purple Heart recipient, was killed by a sniper while exiting a helicopter during the early hours of the battle.

Described by a fellow soldier as "mucho machismo" in a post on *The Wall of Faces*, Army Sgt. John Juarez, 22, was from Colton, California. He died five days before his twenty-third birthday and was less than forty days from completing his twelve-month tour of duty. Juarez was awarded the Bronze Star, the Silver Star, and the Purple Heart. During the four years following his death, Cote would lose his mother, sister, and two brothers.

Like Sgt. Juarez, Army Sgt. Donald Miller was less than

forty days from completing his deployment to Vietnam. He was married and died one month shy of his twenty-fifth birthday. As a Purple Heart recipient, Miller is the only soldier from Alexandria, Kentucky, to die in Vietnam.

The first of the two nineteen-year-olds to lose his life along the banks of the Rach Ruong Canal on December 4, 1967, was Army Cpl. Bryant Young from Salt Lake City, Utah. He was awarded the Bronze Star, the Silver Star, and the Purple Heart.

As the second nineteen-year-old to die in the battle, Sgt. Alvester Winston was from Baltimore, Maryland. As a NCO (non-commissioned) medical officer, he had celebrated his birthday two days earlier. According to the *Coffelt Database of Vietnam Casualties*, Winston's…

> *"…unit was patrolling a small river aboard armored troop carriers when it was suddenly subjected to intense fire from a Viet Cong force on the river banks. As Specialist Winston's platoon made a beach landing and began penetrating dense foliage, it was hit by another withering enemy barrage. The insurgents were firing rockets, automatic weapons and rifle grenades from well fortified (sp.) bunkers and immediately pinned the friendly troops down. Hearing calls for medical aid from two comrades who fell fifty meters to his front, Specialist Winston raced through a savage curtain of fire to the injured soldiers. As he began treating their wounds, he was struck by an enemy sniper's bullet. Heedless of his own serious wound, he continued his lifesaving efforts even though he realized the Viet Cong had pinpointed his position. He was mortally wounded while valiantly shielding his patients from a raking fusillade…."*

The body of Sgt. Winston was recovered on December 8.

As the oldest of the Army casualties in the battle, Master Sgt. William Pollard was forty-two. Like Pfc. Moseley, Pollard was from New Jersey, specifically Swedesboro, with a population of around 2,300. He had been in the military for twenty-two years, first in the Navy in WWII and then in the Air Force, before his deployment to Vietnam.

The third of the twenty-year-old soldiers to lose their lives in the Mekong Delta on December 4 was *Pfc. Charles Schnegg* from Beallsville, Ohio. Besides being the sixth of the nine Army soldiers to lose his life in Kien Phong Province during the battle, Schnegg was the fourth soldier from Monroe County, Ohio, to die in Vietnam. Moreover, Schnegg was the third to lose his life from the village of Beallsville, with a population of less than five hundred.

The two Navy crewman to lose their lives during the two-day battle were E3 Adrian Howell from Lucedale, Mississippi, and E3 Robert Moras from Escanaba, Michigan. Like Miller, Moseley, and Russ, both sailors were recorded as being killed on the west side of the canal in Dinh Tuong Province.

Howell, the fourth twenty-year-old soldier to lose his life that December day, would have turned twenty-one on January 28th. He was wounded during the ambush and died later that day. According to the December 11 edition of the *Hattiesburg American*, Howell was *"...George County's first Vietnam combat casualty."* At the time of his passing, his monthly pay was $170.10, and was one of six children in his family.

Fellow Navy man Moras, 21, had been in Vietnam less than two months. According to the *Coffelt Database of Vietnam Casualties*, his MRF unit's mission

> *"...was to escort armored troop carriers transporting Vietnamese Marine personnel to the operations area, to provide them with close fire support, and to perform blocking operations to prevent the enemy's escape. While proceeding up the Rach Ruong Canal, Monitor 111-2, came under heavy rocket, recoilless rifle, machine gun and small arms fire from prepared enemy positions along both sides of the canal. Fireman Moras commenced firing immediately and maintained*

a deadly suppressive fire into the enemy positions. Although seriously wounded when his boat sustained two B-40 rocket hits, he courageously refused to leave his mount and continued to lay devastating fire on the enemy positions until he was fatally wounded by a third rocket which hit directly on his machine gun mount...."

For his heroism, Moras received the Silver Star, America's second-highest military honor, along with four other medals. He was the first soldier from Escanaba to lose his life in Vietnam.

By year's end, there were nearly 500,000 American troops in Southeast Asia and about twelve thousand loss of U.S. lives. The number is roughly double the loss of lives from 1966. Five hundred and seventy-three soldiers from Ohio lost their lives in Southeast Asia in 1967.

The first casualty of the year was Army Pfc. Allan Schulz, 19, of Marion. He died in Bien Hoa Province on January 1, 1967, and had been in Vietnam for 34 days. Oddly, Schulz's death occurred during the 48-hour New Year's truce, and he was the first of two dozen soldiers from Marion to die in the conflict. West Point graduate and Navy Commander John Peace, 38, is recorded as the last Ohio soldier to die during the year. He was a pilot aboard the USS Kitty Hawk, and his aircraft disappeared from radar while on a bombing mission on December 31. It is believed that the Hudson, Ohio, native was shot down near the North Vietnamese city of Vinh in Nghe An Province. Peace's body was never recovered, and he remains missing in action.

Sadly, the U.S. number of troops dying in the region would grow even more prominent in the coming year.

1968

With nearly 17,000 reported casualties, 1968 would be the deadliest year for American soldiers during the Vietnam conflict. More American lives would be lost in 1968 in Southeast Asia than in the Revolutionary War, the War of 1812, and the Spanish-American War combined...nearly two times more! On average, almost three hundred twenty-five soldier lives were lost each week of the year, or around fifty each day. Subsequently, once again, the old adage rang true: the more things changed, the more they stayed the same.

The year's events began on January 21 when PAVN forces attacked a Marine base at Khe Sanh. Located less than twenty miles south of the DMZ in Quang Tri Province, the base lay along Route 9 and ran west through South Vietnam, ending in eastern Laos. The base was first hit with artillery, which destroyed a large portion of the base's ammunition and mortar rounds. Lasting nearly two months, the 6,000 Marines battled no less than 20,000 North Vietnamese to keep the base's critical location. The first battle of Khe Sanh would cost the lives of over one hundred and fifty Marines.

Less than two days later, on January 23, North Korea captured the USS Pueblo and its crew of eighty-three. North Korean officials claimed the ship was gathering intelligence about the communist country and the vessel was within its territorial boundaries. Naval officials say the ship was in international waters and was between thirteen and twenty nautical miles offshore. During the eleven months of imprisonment, the North Koreans took countless pictures of the crew for propaganda purposes. In many of these pictures, the crew was shown flipping the "middle finger" as a sign of protest. The imprisoned sailors told their captors that the middle finger was a sign of "good luck" in Hawaiian culture. The crew was released after nearly a year of repeated torture, abysmal living conditions, and meager food.

Within a week, the Viet Cong and North Vietnamese Army launched a major offensive during the Vietnamese lunar new year holiday period called "TET." Both parties hoped the offensive would force the U.S. and its allies out of the divided country, negotiate a settlement, and simultaneously end America's bombing of cities in North Vietnam. Unfortunately, the truce did none of these. Consequently, the enemy unleashed its coordinated attack plan throughout the country. For several reasons, this caught the U.S. and its allies off-guard.

First, the timing of the enemy offensive came as a complete surprise to America and its allies because the attacks took place during a temporary truce. Similarly, the timing of the offensive allowed countless communist troops to travel south under the guise of visiting relatives south of the DMZ. Finally, the offensive coincided when many South Vietnamese soldiers were on holiday leave.

During the first phase of the offensive on January 30 and 31, the enemy forces attacked populated centers like Hue and Saigon and countless military locations with mortars and rocket attacks, followed by a rush of enemy troops. By early February, battles were taking place in over one hundred South Vietnamese cities and in all but a handful of provinces. The last of the initial fighting occurred in places like Bac Lieu Province in the Mekong Delta during early February and ended shortly after that. Conversely, the action in and around Hue lasted until late winter and cost the lives of nearly 225 American soldiers. In contrast, the ongoing battle at the U.S. base at Khe Sanh lasted until spring. The main focus of enemy troops in Saigon included Tan Son Nhut air base, the palace, and the U.S. Embassy.

Surprised by the well-organized attacks, Gen. William Westmoreland, commander of American forces, asked that an additional 200,000 U.S. troops be deployed to the region. This would be in addition to the nearly one million combined

American, ARVN, Australian, and South Korean troops already there.

With communist troops surrounding Saigon, the panic was widespread and enemy troops, some dressed in civilian clothing, blended in with citizens. On February 1, one of these supposed infiltrators was brought before the Saigon police chief and was shot in the head. The execution, captured by an American photographer, would be shown in newspapers worldwide. Additionally, the picture would become another rallying point for anti-war protestors.

During the first phase of the wave of attacks between late January and mid-February, U.S. casualties exceeded five hundred and fifty in Saigon, nearly two hundred and twenty-five in Hue, and countless ones at Khe Sanh. The highest casualty rate during the offensive happened on February 18, when over five hundred and forty American soldiers were killed. As a result, a new draft call was issued for nearly fifty thousand new U.S. troops within a week.

Among those American soldiers that lost their lives during the first TET offensive was a second member of Our Lady of Guadalupe Catholic Church in Chicago. On the next to the last day of January, Army Cpl. Edward Cervantez lost his life in Phu Yen Province while on combat patrol. He had turned twenty-one on December 19, 1967. As the oldest of seventeen children, Cpl. Cervantez was a batboy for the Chicago White Sox. It is said that after night games, it was not uncommon for White Sox manager, Eddie Lopez, to give Cervantez a ride home in Lopez's limousine. A third member from the church, Pfc. Alfred Urdiales, 18, died on February 7 while on duty in Quang Tri Province.

The North Vietnamese and Viet Cong began a second TET offensive not long before Mother's Day, 1968. Known as mini-TET, the secondary offensives concentrated on two main areas: a second assault in Quang Tri Province, just below the DMZ, and the city of Saigon. When the fighting had subsided in these two areas, American losses numbered over eleven hundred and fifty.

Included in the U.S. losses was yet another parishioner from Our Lady of Guadalupe Catholic Church. The soldier, Pfc. Charles Urdiales, 24, died on May 13 in Binh Duong Province. He had been in Vietnam less than forty days and was a cousin to Pfc. Alfred Urdiales. Also losing his life that year was eighteen-year-old Marine Pvt. Pedro "Peter" Rodriguez. Although he lived in Gary, Indiana, he was a member of Our Lady parish. Pvt. Rodriguez died on Memorial Day, May 30, from small arms fire while serving in Quang Nam Province.

Less than a month later, a sixth member of the church, Army Sgt. Raymond Ordonez, 20, would die in Hau Nghia Province. By year's end, an additional four soldiers from the church would lose their lives in Southeast Asia.

———

Included among the Allied forces to lose soldiers during the enemy offensives was the country of New Zealand. While the New Zealand presence in the conflict in Vietnam dates to April 1963, when a team of surgeons entered the country as humanitarian aid, military troops did not begin arriving until a year later. In 1965, the same year a detachment from the Royal New Zealand Artillery set foot in Southeast Asia, the South Pacific country recorded its first death in the region. Sgt. Alastair Don, 37, and BDR (Corporal) Robert White, 28, were killed when their vehicle hit a land mine on September 14, near Ben Cat, in Bien Duong Province. A third soldier, Staff Sgt. Graham Grigg, 32, would die on December 4 in Saigon when a bomb exploded near him.

The following year, New Zealand soldiers came under the

operational control of Australian forces. Before long, New Zealand was being pressured by American military leaders to send additional troops to Vietnam. No soldiers from New Zealand died in 1966, but there were two the following year, including Capt. Peter Williams, who died one month before his 30th birthday from a booby trap, and Cpl. Maurice Manton, 29, who died on September 2 in Phuoc Tuy Province. As expected, when New Zealand troop numbers increased in 1968 to nearly five hundred and fifty, the rate of casualties also saw a rise to double digits.

The first soldier to die that year was Private Haere Hirini, 31, who passed away from his wounds during the first TET offensive. The last was Lt. Corporal Donald Bensemann. He was killed in action on November 16, seventeen days after his 20th birthday. In between, there would be six more soldiers from New Zealand to die during the year. The following year, it would be no different when twelve would die. Nearly two-thirds of the thirty-seven soldiers from New Zealand that died in Vietnam did so between 1965 and 1969.

Similarly, no less than seventeen more U.S. soldiers would die in Southeast Asia that had attended Edison High School in Philadelphia. The list would include three soldiers killed during May and June and two each in February, March, July, September, and December. By year's end, the total of lives lost from Edison would stand at thirty-eight. Five of the seventeen that died in 1968 were killed in Quang Nam Province, three in Quang Tri Province, and three in Thua Thien. In like manner, the list of deceased includes three that were eighteen, four that were nineteen, six that were twenty, one that was twenty-one, and two that were twenty-two years old. The oldest of the group was twenty-five. Finally, one soldier from Edison had served six years in the military, and another had served two years. The remaining fifteen that died in 1968 had one year or less in the military.

Among the list of Edison deaths is Army Sgt. Robert Torres, 20, who was killed in Long An Province. In the February 12, 1968, edition of the *Philadelphia Inquirer*, his obituary stated that he had completed one year of college at Philadelphia Community College when he enlisted in the Army in March 1966. He planned on becoming a pharmacist. Sgt. Torres had been in Vietnam for thirty days. Also losing his life in Southeast Asia was Army E4 Laurel "Earl" Blevins III, 22, who died on August 18. The radioman was supposed to complete his tour of duty three days before his death.

Also killed during the first six months of 1968 was Monroe County, Ohio, soldier Army *SP4 Richard Rucker*, who died on May 30 from friendly fire while battling enemy troops in Saigon. Rucker died the day before the U.S. recorded the most-deadly day of the conflict: May 31. That day alone, no less than two hundred forty-five American military lives were lost.

A sixth soldier from Monroe County, Ohio, would be killed less than three weeks later. Army *Staff Sgt. James Ravencraft*, 33, was from Clarington and is believed to have died on June 18 in Phong Dinh Province, having arrived in Vietnam on May 7. His remains were not identified until March 1975.

Quite possibly, however, the most shocking event during the first six months of 1968, militarily and politically, came in the mid-evening on Sunday, March 31. In a televised speech before the American people, Pres. Lyndon Johnson began his words by telling viewers about the situation in Southeast Asia, including the TET offensive, the continued infiltration of communist troops into South Vietnam, and the increasing loss of American lives. Then, after nearly forty minutes, he seemingly took a long breath and continued his speech...

> *"...in these times as in times before, it is true that a house divided against itself by the spirit of fraction...is a house that cannot stand...I have concluded that I should not permit the Presidency to become involved in partisan divisions that are developing this political year. With American sons in the fields far away, with the American future under challenge right here at home, and our hopes and the world's hopes for peace in the balance, I do not believe that I should devote an hour or a day of my time to any personal partisan causes or to any duties other than the awesome duties of this office, the Presidency of your country. Accordingly, I shall not seek, and I will not accept, the nomination of my party for another term as your President..."*

Clearly, it seems Pres. Johnson saw the proverbial writings on the wall and the political and racial divisions developing in the U.S.

For starters, Johnson, whose approval rating among Americans was just above 35% at the time, had narrowly survived the primary election in New Hampshire. The results had Johnson defeating his fellow Democratic candidate, Sen. Eugene McCarthy, by a mere six percent. Within a week, a third candidate entered the presidential race: New York Senator Robert Kennedy.

Secondly, it was the racial unrest of the previous year. The first signs of unrest occurred not long after Easter 1967 when students at two local colleges in Nashville protested upon hearing that civil rights advocate Stokely Carmichael had been denied the right to speak on campus. The riots lasted three days between April 8-10, and around one hundred were arrested.

On June 11, a race riot erupted in Tampa, Florida,

following the shooting death of a nineteen-year-old African-American man by a white police officer. The teenager was believed to have been among three men who robbed a store in the city. During the four-day riot, around five hundred members of the Florida National Guard were called in to assist the local police. When peace was restored on June 15, there had been over one hundred arrests and nearly $2,000,000 in property damage.

Subsequent riots followed in Cincinnati, Ohio, on June 12, in Atlanta, Georgia, on June 17, and in Buffalo, New York, on June 26. The following month there were no less than ten riots in major cities across America. In the east, riots occurred in New York City and Rochester, New York. In like manner, there were riots in the Midwest in states like Ohio, Michigan, and Minnesota and in southern ones like Alabama. Rioting began in Los Angeles, California, within a week of the Tampa unrest. The most destructive riots occurred during the last few weeks of July in Detroit and Newark, New Jersey.

The three months of rioting resulted in nearly ninety deaths and almost 15,000 arrests. Five cities alone...New Haven, Connecticut; Louisville, Kentucky; Newark, Milwaukee, and Detroit...accounted for over two-thirds of all arrests. In Detroit alone, there were over seven thousand arrests during six days of riots.

Similarly, countless anti-war protests were happening in cities across the U.S. While some protesting occurred before 1965, the movement seemed to "take off" when Pres. Johnson issued Operation Rolling Thunder in March of that year. In mid-April, protests were held in New York and San Francisco. One of the most prominent protests occurred in October 1967 when over 100,000 protesters to America's growing involvement in Vietnam gathered at the Lincoln Memorial in Washington, DC. During that mass protest, not only were countless demonstrators arrested, but draft cards were *"...fluttering like fallen leaves in the wind" (The Daily*

Jeffersonian, October 17, 1967, pg. 13). Among the songs that may have been played at the protest were *"We've Gotta Get Out of this Place"* by The Animals (1965), *"Bring 'em Home"* by Pete Seeger (1966), and *"I Feel Like I'm Fixin' to Die Rag"* by Country Joe McDonald (1967). Within the last song are found the immortal lyrics...

> *"...it's one, two, three, what are we fightin' for?" Don't ask me, I don't give a damn, Next stop is Vietnam."*

In addition, there were ongoing domestic challenges to Pres. Johnson's efforts to combat poverty, the Civil Rights and Voting Rights Act, and his Age Discrimination in Employment Act. This is to say nothing about the unexpected domestic events, like the assassination of Rev. Dr. Martin Luther King in Memphis, Tennessee, in April, continued rankling surrounding peace talks with North Vietnam in May, the assassination of Sen. Robert Kennedy in Los Angeles in June, the heavy-handed police crackdown that accompanied the Democratic convention in Chicago that August, the election of Richard Nixon to the office of president in November and the collapse of the Silver Bridge connecting Point Pleasant, West Virginia, and Gallipolis, Ohio, on December 15, 1967, which cost the lives of forty-six individuals.

––––––––––

The months of July and August 1968 saw the death of two more nurses, bringing the total to four that had been lost so far in the Vietnam conflict.

Second Lt. Pamela Donovan, 26, of Brighton, Massachusetts, was the only member of her Irish immigrant family to gain U.S. citizenship. She wanted to become an American citizen so she could serve in the Army Nurse Corps. Trained at Fort Sam Houston, Texas, 2nd Lt. Donovan served with the 85th Evacuation Hospital in Qui Nhon, in Binh Duong Province. Before her deployment to Vietnam in March of 1968, she underwent intensive jungle training to better understand the conditions in Southeast Asia. Unfortunately, 2nd Lt. Donovan died from pneumonia on July 8.

Lt. Col. Annie Ruth Graham, the highest-ranking officer among the eight nurses to lose their lives in Vietnam, had served in WWII and Korea before deploying to Southeast Asia. As a member of the 91st Evacuation Hospital, it was not uncommon for her to send money back home to help with family expenses. Lt. Col. Graham suffered a stroke on August 8 and was immediately evacuated to a hospital in Japan. She died six days later at the age of 51.

Also, there continued to be instances of friends who would sign up together for military service...the Buddy System. Such was the case with longtime friends Steven Amescua and Anthony Blevins of Turlock, California. They joined together in September 1967.

Sadly, Marine Pvt. Amescua was killed by enemy mortar fire on May 15 in Quang Tri Province. He was part of Operation Scotland III, had been in Vietnam for sixty-three days, and was three months away from celebrating his nineteenth birthday. Pvt. Amescua would be awarded the Purple Heart.

His "buddy" and friend, Marine Pvt. Anthony Blevins, was born in Austria. On the night he died, he was not scheduled for duty but was asked to help guard a bridge in Quang Nam Province from enemy attack. Unfortunately, the Viet Cong attacked, and Blevins was killed that night. It was just over three months after Amescua had died. Pvt. Blevins was killed on August 23, along with nearly one hundred and ten other soldiers in Vietnam. While in the country, his pay totaled less than $200 a month, including a military base pay of $113.40, hostile fire pay of $65, and $8 foreign duty pay. Pvt. Blevins died nine days before his twentieth birthday. On the day Blevins' mother received the news of her son's death, she discovered she was pregnant with her third child.

———————————

Going into the year, there had been nine chaplains to die in Southeast Asia since the first U.S. ones arrived in 1962. In like manner, there had not been two members from the same family to be killed in the conflict to date. However, both instances were about to change.

The first chaplain to die in Vietnam prior to January 1, 1968, was Rabbi Meir Engel. He died of a heart attack at age fifty in 1964. Three chaplains died two years later in 1966, including Father William J. Barragy in May 1966. He was the first chaplain to die in combat. In September, a Congregational minister, Rev. William Feaster, was wounded by enemy artillery fire and later died from infection. Father William Garrity, 40, was one of six Havre, Montana, soldiers to die in Southeast Asia. Stationed aboard the USS Oriskany when it was engulfed in flames in October 1966, he died while attempting to offer last rites to those injured and dying aboard the burning vessel. Also killed in Vietnam in 1966 was Father Michael Quealy. He passed away from enemy machine gun fire while comforting wounded soldiers and giving last rites during a battle on November 8 near Saigon.

The following year, four more chaplains died in the Vietnam conflict. Baptist chaplain Rev. James Johnson, the only black chaplain to die in the conflict, would die in a plane crash in Ninh Thuan Province on March 10 along with a dozen other soldiers. Nine days later, Father Charles "Charlie" Watters lost his life from enemy gunfire while assisting medics and providing pastoral care to injured soldiers in Kontum Province. Army Major Ambrosio Grandea was born in the Philippines as the second of seven children and was an ordained minister in the Methodist church. He was *"...hit by fragments from a hostile mortar round while conducting religious service on May 25..."* in Quang Tin Province (*Coffelt Database of Vietnam Casualties*). Major Grandea was taken to a hospital in the Philippines and died three weeks later. Awarded the Silver Star and the Purple Heart, he was thirty-four and married at the time of his death. Father Vincent Capodanno was the last of four chaplains killed in Vietnam in 1967. A Navy chaplain, he was killed on Labor Day in Quang Tri Province by enemy machinegun fire while administering last rites to a fallen Marine. The following year, three additional chaplains were to die in Vietnam.

The first was Father Aloysius McGonigal on February 17, 1968. He was killed from small arms fire while administering last rites to Marines along the banks of the Perfume River in the city of Hue, Thua Thien Province. Father McGonigal, a major in the Army, had an office in the MAAG compound in Hue. He was forty-six. Five days later, Father Robert Brett, 46, an Army major, was killed during the siege of Khe Sanh in Quang Tri Province while pastoring to wounded soldiers. Major Brett, who had arrived in Vietnam less than four months before his death, was known to have officiated as many as ten masses a day! The twelfth chaplain to die in Vietnam since the beginning of the conflict, and the last to die in 1968, was Army captain and Rabbi Morton Singer, who died on December 17 in a plane crash while on his way to officiate at a Hannukah service in Quang Tin Province. At thirty-two, he was known to run each Sunday morning with soldiers who had received punishment demerits. Capt. Singer had been in-country for forty-two days before dying.

On March 21, 1968, Army Staff Sgt. Samuel Nixon, 25, of Mulberry, Arkansas, died from wounds he received while serving in Thua Thien Province. As the fifth of ten children, Sgt. Nixon followed his older brother, Dale, into the Army. The younger Nixon was married, had two children, and had been in Vietnam less than ninety days. His brother, Army

Capt. William Dale Nixon, 28, was killed six weeks later, on May 8, in Chau Doc Province. As the oldest child, he had joined the Army at age eighteen and had been in Vietnam for less than one hundred days. Capt. Nixon had escorted his brother's body home to Arkansas in March. The Nixons are one of thirty-one sets of brothers to die in the Vietnam conflict.

During the same year that U.S. troop strength would exceed one-half million in the region, American ally Australia would register over five hundred combat troops in Southeast Asia. As one of America's staunchest partners, the Australian presence in the conflict goes back to the summer of 1962, when, like their Pacific neighbors, New Zealand, Washington pressured them to send troops to fight the expansion of communism. By the end of 1964, there would be around two hundred troops in Vietnam. When the first wave of soldiers arrived in 1965, they were placed alongside American troops fighting in Bien Hoa Province. Additional Australian troops, aircraft, and ships would arrive in 1966 and 1967. By 1968, the number of Australian soldiers would hover around eight thousand.

Most likely, the country's first combat death was Warrant Officer Class Two and advisor Kevin Conway, who died on July 6, 1964. He would be the only Australian to die that year in Vietnam. One year later, there would be no less than sixteen deaths of Australian soldiers. Included among the over fifty casualties in 1966 was twenty-one-year-old Errol Noack.

As the only child of a single parent, Noack was raised by his father, a commercial fisherman, along with aunts and uncles. In 1965, while working with his father, the younger Noack received notice that he had been called for military service. On May 24, 1966, after only ten days of service, he died of gunshot wounds in Phuoc Tuy Province.

By 1967, Australian military casualties would increase to around seventy. The number of deaths would jump to over one hundred the following year. The deadliest day of casualties for the Pacific country was May 13, 1968, when between twenty and twenty-five military lives were lost in the Battle of Moral-Balmoral in Binh Duong Province.

At year's end, the unofficial number of U.S. military casualties in Southeast Asia stood at 16,899. This would be the high-water mark for American casualties during the conflict, as military deaths would decrease dramatically in the following years. Of this number, three Ohio soldiers would die on the first day of the year.

Army Sgt. Norman Anderson, 25, of Delaware, Ohio, died when his helicopter went down in bad weather in Binh Dinh Province. The remains of Sgt. Anderson were recovered two weeks later, on his birthday, January 15.

Also on the deadly flight that killed all ten soldiers onboard was a second Ohioan, NCO (non-commissioned) medical officer SP4 David French, 20, from Canton. According to a post on *The Wall of Faces* by French's roommate in Vietnam, *"...He took my place on a Huey to deliver paychecks."* As only one of eleven members of the United Church of Christ to die in Southeast Asia, the remains of SP4 French were recovered on January 18.

A third Ohio casualty on January 1, 1968, was Army Pfc. Robert Murphy, 21, of Euclid. He passed away due to wounds received on December 31 in Phuoc Tuy Province when his escort convoy was ambushed by Viet Cong troops along highway QL-2. *"The engagement was sharp and short, lasting only eight to ten minutes" (Coffelt Database of Vietnam Casualties).* Pfc. Murphy, who had begun his tour of duty in Vietnam twenty days earlier, was awarded the Purple Heart.

On the last day of the year, the conflict would claim the lives of two Ohio soldiers, Marine Pvt. Ricardo Galvan, 19, of Lorain, and Army Cpl. Kenneth Tuttle, 19, of Martins Ferry, in Belmont County.

Pvt. Galvan, 19, died in Quang Nam Province from a gunshot wound to the head. He would be one of over one hundred and thirty soldiers from the Akron area to die in the conflict. Cpl. Tuttle, who began his tour of duty thirty-three days before his death, was killed in Kontum Province from small arms fire.

In between the death of Sgt. Anderson on January 1, and the passing of Cpl. Tuttle, on December 31, no less than nine hundred Ohio soldiers died in Southeast Asia...or about three a day. A majority would die during the TET offensive in the first six months of the year.

———————

Just as 1968 would mark the year with the highest number of American troops and casualties, about 17,000, in Southeast Asia, the year would bring several other "firsts."

For starters, the cost of the war to American taxpayers would exceed $75 billion. This total was just under the amount spent on the War of 1812, the Mexican-American War, the American Revolution, the Spanish-American War, and the U.S. Civil War combined...$85 billion.

Most importantly, the year would mark the first time in nearly a decade that a Republican was elected to the U.S. presidency. Prior to Pres. Richard Nixon's victory in November over Democratic candidate and former vice-president Hubert Humphrey, in which Nixon won the popular vote by less than one percentage point but the electoral vote by over one hundred, there had been two Democrats in the White House between 1961 and 1969...Pres. Kennedy and Pres. Johnson. Before that, there had been only one

Republican in the presidency between Pres. Roosevelt in 1932 and Kennedy in 1961…Pres. Eisenhower.

1969

When Pres. Nixon was inaugurated on January 20, 1969, he not only became this country's 37th president but the fifth U.S. president to be involved in the nearly two-decade-long conflict in Southeast Asia. The first president to deal with the military issue was Pres. Truman, not long after he took office in 1945. Despite the turnover in the White House and the hope for a negotiated "peace with honor," the loss of life among U.S. service personnel in Southeast Asia continued unabated.

On January 1, no less than twenty American servicemen lost their lives in Vietnam in eleven different provinces and Laos, including seventeen members of the Army and one each from the Air Force, Marines, and Navy. Among the three lost lives in Quang Nam Province was Marine Pvt. Thomas Jourdanais, 20, from Waterford, New York. He was killed when he stepped on a land mine while exiting a helicopter and had been in Vietnam for a mere eleven days. Also declared dead in Quang Nam Province was Navy Chief Petty Officer Joseph Nemeth, 35, of Cleveland, Ohio. He died from head injuries while in a recreational area on China Beach on Christmas Day, 1968. Nemeth, a fourteen-year veteran, left behind a wife and three children.

The list of deceased also includes Army SP4 Wayne Lindsay, 34, who was one of three soldiers killed in Laos. He would be one of around sixty Canadians to lose their lives in Southeast Asia and the first soldier from Burnaby, British Columbia. A second soldier from Burnaby, Marine Pvt. Harry Kellar, 19, would lose his life less than two months later. Also killed in Laos on the first day of 1969 was Army Staff Sgt. Michael McKibban, 22, from Klamath Falls, Oregon. He had been in the region for one month, arriving on December 1, 1968.

117

Army Staff Sgt. Rodney Yano, 25, of Kealakekua, Hawaii, was crew chief aboard a helicopter hovering above the jungles in Bien Hoa Province, marking the location of enemy bunkers with white phosphorus, when one of the grenades detonated prematurely. This caused ammunition in the helicopter to explode, sending the aircraft and its two passengers crashing to the ground. Yano had been in the Army for six years.

Undeterred by the current conditions around them, around seventy-five riders took off on their bicycles on January 18 in what *The New York Times* called *"...the world's most hazardous sports event: a six-day bicycle race through half the length of Vietnam." (January 19, 1970, pg. 3)*

The race, a modified version of the former Tour de Vietnam, suspended in 1954 when the Geneva Accord took effect dividing the country, began in the coastal city of Whatrang, around two hundred miles north of Saigon. However, this year's event was considerably shorter than the last one held in 1956. The previous race began just south of the DMZ and ended over 1,300 miles to the south in Camau, the capital of the country's southernmost province, Ca Mau. The race, this time, was sponsored by the South Vietnamese government to show that it controls the countryside and its roads. Riders will pedal about one-third of the distance of the former race.

The initial leg of the current race took the riders south from Whatrang to Phanrang, a distance of about sixty-five miles. Along the way, riders passed the large Army base at Cam Ranh Bay. The second day of the race took the riders northwest toward the mountainous Lam Dong Province and the city of Dalat, nearly one mile above sea level. From there, the tour headed south, passing through populated areas controlled mainly by the Viet Cong. The in-between legs would take the riders through the outskirts of Saigon and then into the flatlands of the Mekong Delta. The race would finish in the provincial capital of Long Xuyen.

Most of the riders were from South Vietnam, including one sergeant from the South Vietnamese Army, an eighteen-year-old, and his forty-six-year-old father. No American riders took part in the race. Along nearly every mile of the race, the participants were escorted by military helicopters hovering overhead and teams of security personnel on the sides of the road. The NYT article noted that *"...About $424 goes to the winner."*

On the same day President Nixon was sworn in on the steps of the U.S. Capitol by Chief Justice of the Supreme Court Earl Warren, thirty soldiers, including three Ohioans, lost their lives in Vietnam. Army Major Richard Zimmerman was from St. Clairsville, Belmont County. He was an observer aboard a two-person reconnaissance helicopter doing low-level scouting in Binh Duong Province for any signs of enemy bunkers, campsites, or trails. Moments after receiving enemy ground fire, the aircraft crashed, killing Zimmerman and the pilot. Zimmerman, 31, an eight-year veteran, was one of two soldiers from St. Clairsville to die in Vietnam, and both were killed in the same year. Zimmerman left behind a wife, daughter, and two sons.

The other Ohio soldiers to die on January 20 include Navy HM1 (hospital corpsman) Norman Pierre of Chillicothe and Army Sgt. Paul Ballard, 21, of Columbus. A sixteen-year veteran, Pierre, 34, was killed in a vehicle crash in Da Nang, in Quang Nam Province. Ballard, 21, known as "Stinky" by family members, died from small arms fire while in Tay Ninh Province. He was fifty-five days away from completing his tour of duty in Southeast Asia.

Between January 1 and Nixon's inauguration, over thirty-two additional soldiers from the Buckeye State lost their lives in Vietnam. This includes four soldiers on January 4 and five on January 12. Despite the optimism brought on by the start of peace talks on January 25 in Paris involving the U.S., South Vietnam, North Vietnam, and the Viet Cong, there were another two dozen soldier casualties during the last eleven days of the month. This brought the month's total to around fifty-six. Except for four days, at least one Ohio soldier was killed each day during the month. Moreover, the casualty rate would jump in the next two months to seventy-three in February and seventy-six in March.

The rise in February casualty rates was primarily attributed to the communist offensive known as TET 1969. Initially, the attacks were centered on U.S. military installations in or near Saigon. They began when enemy troops began mortar fire in the early morning of February 23. Within a short time, the attack was repulsed. Except for an Army photographer, there were no other American casualties.

Around the same time, enemy troops began attacking over one hundred other sites across South Vietnam, including the port and airbase at Da Nang, damaging several aircraft. In the north, fighting took place near the DMZ on February 25. The attacks cost the lives of countless American soldiers.

Among those from Ohio killed on February 23 were Army SP4 Robert Buck, 22, from Reynoldsburg, who was killed in Binh Duong Province; Marine Chief Warrant Officer 2 Clyde Callahan, 46, from Caldwell, who died in Quang Tin Province; and Marine Pvt. Richard Heifner, 22, from Ashland. Heifner would be the second soldier from Ashland to be killed within two weeks.

Other Ohio soldiers losing their lives in fighting on February 23 were Army Sgt. Douglas Hinkle, 24, from Toledo; Marine Cpl. Jerry Howerton, 21, from Portsmouth, who began his tour of duty thirty-two days before being killed by small arms fire in Quang Nam; and Army SP5 Thomas Preston, 21, from Parma.

One of the last three Ohio soldiers to die on February 23 was Navy Seaman Nicholas Pyle, 21, from Columbus. Pyle, whose father served in WWII, died in Hua Nghia Province from rocket/mortar fire while part of the riverine forces. He was on his second tour of duty in Vietnam. Also among the list of Ohio casualties on that day were Army Cpl. Richard Ritzler, 20, from Tiffin; Army SP4 Jerry Spradlin, 20, from McGuffey, who was killed in Long Khanh Province; and Marine Lance Corporal Woots Wadkins, 19, from Sciotoville. He was killed while on patrol in Quang Nam Province. Meanwhile, neighboring West Virginia lost six soldiers in the attacks of February 23, five Marines and one Army soldier, while Army Sgt. David Sundquist of Minneapolis, Minnesota, died on his 22nd birthday from a mortar attack.

The following day recorded the loss of two Ohio soldiers. Army Sgt. Charles Carpenter, 27, from Lebanon, was killed in Kontum Province *"...from wounds received while on perimeter guard when mistaken for hostile forces and area came under friendly gunship fire"* (*Coffelt Database of Vietnam Casualties*). He was an eight-year veteran and a recipient of two Bronze Stars and a Purple Heart. Marine Pvt. Duane Davis was from Huntsville and died from wounds while serving in Quang Nam Province. As a wireman, his position required him to install and maintain cable networks that linked outposts and headquarters. He was 19.

On February 25, nine native sons of Ohio lost their lives, including four each from the Army and the Marines and one member of the Navy. Among the Marines losing their lives at FSB (Fire Support Base) Neville, in Quang Tri Province, was Cpl. Gerald Zawadzki, 21. While growing up in Brooklyn, Ohio, he was an assistant troop leader in his boy scout troop. Like countless other Marines, Cpl. Zawadzki did his basic training at Parris Island, South Carolina. Marine Pvt. Robert

Brogan, 18, and Marine Pvt. Randolph Ramsey, 19, were among the over two dozen Marines killed at FSB Russell, also in Quang Tri Province. A third Marine killed that day was Pvt. Samuel Wall, also 19. He died in Quang Nam Province. Brogan and Wall were from Cincinnati, while Ramsey was from unincorporated Williamsfield, Ohio, in Ashtabula County. Additionally, Ramsey had been in Vietnam only twenty days and Wall seventeen.

The four members of the Army killed on February 25 were Major Thomas Fox, SP4 Larry Woolum, Pfc. Frederick Ratliff and Sgt. James Titus.

Woolum, 20, from Marion, was engaged and planned to marry upon his return from Vietnam in September. Instead, he died in Thua Thien Province after stepping on a booby trap. Woolum was twenty years old, while Ratliff, who was killed in Bien Duong Province when his base camp came under enemy attack, and Titus, who died in Kien Hoa Province in an enemy firefight, were twenty-one. Fox, 31, a graduate of the Ohio State University and a trained surgeon, died ten days after contracting hepatitis while in Pleiku Province. A plaque at the University of Cincinnati, Department of Surgery, bears the following...

> *"In dedication of 'The Gloved Hands'...and "as a fitting testimony to Dr. Fox's character and purpose in life: 'Make every effort to supplement your faith with virtue, and virtue with knowledge, and knowledge with self-control, and self-control with steadfastness, and steadfastness with godliness. II Peter 1:5-6." (post, The Wall of Faces)*

While Ratliff and Titus were both from Columbus and Woolum from Marion, Fox was the third soldier to die that day from Cincinnati.

The lone Navy seaman from Ohio killed on February 25 was Second Class Petty Officer Kenneth Davis, age twenty-two, from Zanesville. As one of two medical corpsmen serving with the Marines at FSB Russell in Quang Tri Province, he died when regiments of the North Vietnamese Army attacked in the early morning hours. He was married, had a 22-month-old daughter, and received a monthly pay of around $290.

During the first quarter of the year, nearly two hundred soldiers from Ohio would die in Southeast Asia. This includes over fifty in January, over seventy in February, and over seventy-five in March. On the second Sunday of March alone, the 9th, there would be over seventy-five U.S. casualties, and nearly one in four were soldiers from California, New York, and Pennsylvania.

Among the soldiers killed was Army Cpl. Gregorio Pangelinan, 26, from Mongmong, Guam. Just before 6:00pm, the armored personnel carrier he was driving hit a landmine while traveling on highway QL-19 in Binh Dinh Province. He had been in Vietnam for thirty-seven days and was one of around seventy Guam soldiers to die in Southeast Asia. Pangelinan's son, age 5 at the time of his father's passing, followed his dad into the Army and obtained the rank of Major.

The lone soldier from Ohio to be killed on March 9 was *Navy HM3 William "Bobby" Lucas*. Not only was he the seventh soldier to die with a "Monroe County connection," but the fifth graduate of Beallsville High School that did not make it home from Vietnam. The other graduates include Jack Pittman, Duane Greenlee, Charles Schnegg, and Richard Rucker. Lucas, 20, had been in-country for four months and was killed in Quang Nam Province with the Marines.

Nearly two weeks later, the United States Coast Guard would lose its fifth member in less than nine months. Chief Petty Officer Morris Beeson, an eighteen-year veteran, died from small arms fire on March 22 while his vessel, the Point Orient, was patrolling waters off Binh Dinh and Quang Tri Provinces. As the only military member from Pitkins, Louisiana, to die in the conflict, he began his second tour on September 20, 1968. He was 37 and married. His death follows the passing of Lt. Jack Rittichier, 34, of Barberton, Ohio. His helicopter was shot down over Laos on June 9, 1968. However, his body was not recovered until thirty-five years later. Seven months later, on December 5, E3 Heriberto Segovia Hernandez, 20, a member of the USCG Cutter Point Cypress, died from small arms fire while aboard a launch boat conducting surveillance on a canal in the waters of An Xugen Province. He was from San Antonio, Texas. Not only was he the youngest member of the USCG to die in Southeast Asia, but he was also the only unmarried member of the branch.

By August, two additional members of the USCG would lose their lives in the region. First, it was Petty Officer Michael Painter, who died on August 8, 1969, aboard the USCG Cutter Point Arden when a mortar misfired. He was 26, from Moscow, Idaho, and his son followed him into military service. During the same incident, LTJG Michael Kirkpatrick, 25, was injured and died the next day. He was 25 and from Gainesville, Florida.

Beyond the loss of nearly two hundred more Ohio soldiers in the following three months, April thru June, there were several more "firsts" in the conflict.

On Maundy Thursday, April 3, the day Christians around the world gathered in observance of the Last Supper, the U.S. Department of Defense announced that the death toll for Americans killed in Southeast Asia had surpassed 33,500. The number was nearing the number of Americans killed in the Korean conflict. The announcement came around the same time that the number of American troops peaked in Southeast Asia at over 540,000.

True to one of his campaign promises made during the

1968 elections, Pres. Nixon announced that 150,000 U.S. troops would withdraw from South Vietnam over the next twelve months. The troop withdrawals were part of an administrative policy known as Vietnamization, which placed more of the military responsibility for fighting the enemy upon South Vietnamese troops.

While "fragging," the deliberate attempt by a soldier to inflict harm on another soldier by using a grenade or other explosive device, had been known to have taken place in Vietnam as early as the mid-1960s, the practice increased dramatically in 1969. One of the most publicized incidents during the conflict occurred on April 21 in Quang Tri Province.

According to military records, the deadly set of events may have been set in place earlier in the day when Marine 1st Lt. Robert Rohweller, 25, of Jacksonville, Florida, a four-year veteran on his second tour of duty in Southeast Asia, reprimanded several soldiers in his company for refusing to go on patrol. The lieutenant's actions so angered one of the soldiers that he vowed revenge. Around 2:00am, those in a nearby…

> "…hooch were awakened by an explosion. An M26 fragmentation grenade had detonated in the neighboring company office directly under the cot upon which Lieutenant Rohweller slept and inflicted shrapnel wounds of the head, chest, and abdomen." (Coffelt Database of Vietnam Casualties)

When confronted, three soldiers confessed to participating and singled out a private who left the detonated grenade. At the trial, the fourth soldier, the guilty ringleader of the group, confessed, saying, "…I did that m…………," adding, "He won't f… with nobody else no more." (Coffelt Database of Vietnam Casualties)

Military personnel was aided in their investigation when the guilty private was discovered wearing the pin to the deadly grenade on one of his fingers. The private pleaded guilty to premeditated murder and conspiracy to murder and was sentenced to forty years imprisonment. While serving his sentence, he was killed by another inmate.

Less than three weeks later, the *New York Times* ran a front-page article that exposed the Nixon administration of secretly bombing portions of the Ho Chi Minh Trail in Cambodia. The story would eventually lead the Republican president to begin an all-out search to find the source of the leak, beginning with wiretaps of several *Times* reporters. The efforts would conclude with the Pentagon Papers and the Watergate scandal.

Around the time John Lennon, and his wife, Yoko Ono, were holding their second "bed-in" and recording the anti-war song entitled *"Give Peace a Chance,"* the youngest American soldier in the Vietnam conflict was killed. Marine Pvt. Dan Bullock was fourteen when he entered a recruiting station in Brooklyn, New York, and enlisted for military service. Bullock, born in 1953, altered his birth certificate to read 1949. He was sent to Vietnam in May 1968 after basic training at Parris Island.

On the night of June 7, Bullock was transferred from cleaning detail to night watch because another Marine had dislocated his thumb the day before during a pick-up boxing session. Just after midnight, while under enemy attack, Bullock, and three other Marines stationed at An Hoa Combat Base in Quang Nam Province, jumped into a nearby foxhole. Within minutes, one of the attackers threw a bag filled with explosives into the foxhole. The explosive killed Bullock and three other U.S. Marines from F Company, 2nd Battalion, 5th Marine: Lance Corporal Larry Eglinsdoerfer, 21, from Milan, Michigan; Pvt. Donald Bunn, 21, from Ft. Wayne, Indiana; and Pvt. Jason Hunnicutt, from Petaluma, California. Hunnicutt was the second youngest to die in the foxhole that night. He was nineteen. Not only did Bunn and Hunnicutt die on the same day, but they began their tour of duty in Vietnam on the same day...March 19. A fifth Marine from the same outfit, F Company, 2nd Battalion, 5th Marines, Pvt. Steven Montgomery, 19, from Hayward, California, was on the base perimeter, and also died in the attack. At fifteen, Bullock was the youngest U.S. serviceman killed in Southeast Asia. He had been in Vietnam for less than three weeks.

In all, there were nearly two dozen Marines that lost their lives in Quang Nam Province on June 7. Among the losses were three soldiers from Wisconsin, including Cpl. Frederick Benishek, 19, from Antigo; Pvt. John Krzmarcik, 19, from Wausau; and Pvt. William Zahn, 20, from Milwaukee. In like manner, there were two soldiers from New Jersey, including Lance Corporal Donald Arribi, 20, from Cliffside Park, who died four days before his twenty-first birthday, and Pvt. Larry Hansen, from Penns Grove, had arrived in Vietnam eight days before he died.

The lone Ohio soldier killed on June 7 was Pvt. Bruce Pankuch, 23, from Middleburg Heights, Ohio. Following graduation from Massanutten Military Academy, Virginia, in 1965, Pankuch became crew chief aboard a helicopter. Around 2:00pm on June 7, he was aboard a helicopter that suffered hydraulic (fluid) failure and crashed shortly after take-off. He was an only child.

The average age of the Marines that lost their lives in Quang Nam Province on June 7 was nineteen. Among the nineteen, three were eighteen, ten were nineteen, and seven were twenty years old. Of the remaining soldiers, four were twenty-two, and one, Pvt. Pankuch, was twenty-three.

True to one of his election promises, Pres. Nixon announced the reduction of nearly 25,000 troops from Southeast Asia the following day. However, it was too late for the about six dozen soldiers who died on June 7, including the twenty-five members of the Army who were killed, six from the Air Force, and two from the Navy.

Among the Army soldiers to be killed was Sgt. Richard DeLaney. While he was one of the ninety or more soldiers from Vermont to die in the conflict, DeLaney was the only soldier from Essex. He was nineteen. Navy Seaman Curtis Hendrickson, 23, from Winger, Minnesota, died on his way to a meal, falling between two moored pontoon boats. Air Force Sgt. Clifford Lefler, 23, was one of four airmen from the 366th Supply Squadron, 366th Tactical Fighter Wing, stationed at the base. He was from Milford, Ohio.

On the same day, June 8, 1st Lt. Sharon Ann Lane died when enemy rocket fire hit the 312th Evacuation Hospital. Most of her patients were North Vietnamese soldiers. Lt. Lane, 25, a nurse from Canton, Ohio, was the eighth female nurse to die in the conflict. She is considered the only U.S. servicewoman killed by hostile fire in the Vietnam conflict.

Similarly, another chaplain would be killed on the same day that 1st Lt. Lane would die. United Presbyterian Church minister Lt. Colonel Don Bartley was killed when the truck he was riding in hit a landmine southwest of Da Nang in Quang Nam Province. At the time of his passing, he was assisting in producing a tv program on Vietnam chaplains. Rev. Bartley, 36, left behind a wife and two children. He was less than two weeks away from completing his twelve-month tour of duty.

However, the U.S. loss of life was brought to the public's full attention on June 27, 1969.

On that day, *Life* magazine identified 242 soldiers that had lost their lives in Southeast Asia. The number represents the average number of U.S. soldier casualties for seven days during the conflict. The front of the magazine bore the picture of Army SP5 William Gearing of Rochester, New York. He was killed on May 19 in Quang Tri Province and would have turned twenty-one in seventy-two days. To the left of Gearing's face on the magazine cover was written: "The Faces of the American Dead in Vietnam: One Week's Toll."

Following the release of names of those killed in Southeast Asia by the Pentagon, the magazine asked many of the families of the deceased soldiers to submit photographs of their fallen loved ones. Of the nearly 220 photos received, over one hundred and seventy showed the soldier in his dress uniform or military fatigues. The remaining photos showed the soldier in his high school cap and gown, senior class picture, or street clothes.

Nearly one in four Americans saw the article and the accompanying photos. Unlike anything Americans had seen before, the eleven randomly-ordered pages of photos put a name and a face to many of the soldiers who had fought…and died…in Southeast Asia. More, the article demonstrated that the conflict in Southeast Asia was both collective and, at the same time, highly personal.

Those two hundred and forty-two lost lives came from forty-six of the fifty states. As expected, California lost twenty-four soldiers, Michigan seventeen, Texas eleven, and Florida ten. Additionally, the article mentioned four soldiers from Puerto Rico that died. These include Army Sgt. Pedro Rios, 40, who died in Quang Tri Province. He was a sixteen-year veteran of the military and died on May 21. Two days later, a pair of Puerto Rican soldiers were killed on the same day and in the same province. First, it was Army Staff Sgt. Heriberto Marrero-Estrada, 20, from Bayamon, Puerto Rico. Then, several hours later, it was a twenty-one-year-old Army corporal named Jose M. Galarza-Quinones from Rio Piedras. Both men were casualties on May 23 while serving in Thua Thien Province. As the fourth soldier from Puerto Rico to pass away in seven days, Army Pfc. Ramon Vazquez Nieves, 21, was from Puerto Nuevo. He was among the three dozen soldiers killed that day in Quang Ngai Province. These four soldiers from Puerto Rico would be among the nearly 350 from the island to die in the Vietnam conflict.

Also mentioned was Army 1st Lt. Donald Ide. Educated mainly in India, where his dad was serving with the U.S. diplomatic corp., the family was later transferred and resided in Beirut, Lebanon. 1st Lt. Ide stepped on a land mine in Hua Nghia Province and was killed instantly. He died on May 25 at age 25 and had been in the military for just over eighteen months. His cousin, Dan Evans, was the governor of Washington at the time of Ide's passing.

Among the two hundred and forty-four deaths were nine soldiers from Ohio. Army Sgt. James Duffy, 20, had begun crossing off the days until he flew home to Brunswick, Ohio. The last day he marked off a day from his calendar was May 24. He had fifty-five days remaining in Vietnam. It was likewise for Army SP4 Floyd Barber, 23, of Franklin. He was killed in Kontum Province and was twenty-one days from completing his tour of duty. And the same could be said for Youngstown native and Army Pfc. Patrick Hagerty, who passed away in Pleiku Province on May 31. At 19, he was less than two weeks from completing his year-long tour of duty.

Like many that tragically lost their lives in Southeast Asia, Army 1st Lt. James Luckett, 27, died in an ambush on May 23. He was known as "Pappy" because he was much older than most of the men he commanded. Born in Balboa in the Panama Canal Zone, he was not only a graduate of the Ohio State University with a degree in Philosophy but was one of sixteen known Eagle Scouts to lose their life during the Vietnam conflict. He left behind a wife and a two-year-old daughter, and he would be one of two soldiers from the canal zone to die in Vietnam. Similarly, three other Ohio soldiers died on May 25 or were injured that day and later passed away.

First, it may have been Army SP4 Ophrey Irvin, 25, from

Chillicothe, who died from small arms fire while in Quang Ngai Province. He was married and had 2 children. Marine Cpl. Daniel Pucci, 22, of Berea, was hit with shrapnel from an enemy mortar attack while in Quang Tri Province and died in a hospital in Japan on June 2. He had been in the military for around fifteen months. Both Army Cpl. Wayne Garven, 21, from Mt. Vernon, and another soldier were scheduled to go out on night patrol on May 25, but only one was needed. The two soldiers flipped a coin to see who would go. Garven lost! That night, he stepped on a booby trap in Hua Nghia Province and died.

Army Pfc. Henry Hausman was a casualty when the enemy ambushed the military vehicle he was riding in on May 27. He was nineteen and lost his life in Phuoc Long Province. On May 29, Army Pfc. Charles McMillion, 20, was killed in Hau Nghia Province. He had been in Vietnam for twenty-four days. Like Lt. Luckett and Sgt. Duffy, Pfc. Charles McMillion is among the 20+ soldiers whose photo does not appear in the magazine article.

In like manner, eight soldiers from neighboring West Virginia were mentioned in the June 27 *Life* issue. The list includes six members of the Army, including Army Cpl. Roy Clark, Army Pfc. Freddie Coffman, Army Sgt. Mark Haverland, Army Pfc. Wesley Ice, Army Cpl. David Kinney, and Army Pfc. James Workman. The two Marines losing their lives were Cpl. Larry E. Boyer and Pvt. Gordon Perry.

Of the list, four died in Quang Ngai Province (Clark, Haverland, Ice, and Kinney), and one each in the provinces of Kien Hoa (Workman), Quang Nam (Perry), Quang Tin (Coffman), and Quang Tri (Boyer). Similarly, seven soldiers were between twenty and twenty-three years old, and one was nineteen. Most unsettling, two soldiers had been in Vietnam less than thirty-two days, and one soldier had less than forty-five days before he was to leave for home.

With these West Virginia soldiers' passing, the number of

soldiers killed in Southeast Asia from the state now stands at nearly five hundred and thirty. There will be another one hundred and seventy-five military lives lost from the Mountain State before the conflict in Vietnam ends.

Another soldier mentioned in the article is Army Sgt. William Anthony Evans, 20, of Milwaukee, Wisconsin, who was the oldest of eight children. On March 2, he was the patrol leader of an 11-soldier squad on a secret mission inside Cambodia when the group was ambushed. While waiting for air support, a rocket-propelled grenade hit nearby, fatally wounding him and another platoon member, Army E5 Michael May, 21, of Vassar, Michigan, an Infantry Operations and Intelligence Specialist. According to a post on the website *Findagrave*, Evans began his tour in Southeast Asia on the same day he died: March 2. If the post is accurate, Evans joins the nearly one thousand soldiers who died on their first day of military service in the Vietnam conflict.

Moreover, because neither the remains of Sgt. Evans nor E5 May was ever recovered; they remain on the list of nearly two thousand soldiers missing in action or not accounted for from the Vietnam conflict. Both may be the first of almost five hundred American soldiers to be killed in Cambodia.

Also mentioned in the article is Marine Pvt. Ralford Jackson, 20, of Tuba City, Arizona. Pvt. Jackson, a radio telegraph operator, was killed in Quang Tri Province on May 22, when rocket/mortar fire had a direct hit in a foxhole he was in. He was less than two months away from celebrating his twenty-first birthday. As the oldest of twelve children, he was one of over forty-two thousand Native Americans to serve in Southeast Asia and is believed to be the first Hopi Indian to be killed in Vietnam. Pvt. Jackson was married and had two young daughters.

Not surprisingly, the article also confirmed a growing trend with the conflict; the largest group of soldiers killed in Southeast Asia were between 18 and 21 years old. Specifically, the article showed that sixteen lost their lives at age 18, thirty-seven were 19, seventy-four were 20, and forty-three reached the age they could legally vote and drink…21. Among those losing their lives was Army SP5 William "Billy" Gearing, whose face appeared on the magazine's cover and served with the 3rd Detachment, 7th Psychological Operations Battalion.

SP5 Gearing grew up in Greece, New York, just outside of Rochester, and attended Olympia High School. He was drafted in 1968 and enlisted for a third year in the Army, hoping to be sent to military school instead of Vietnam. In early December, he was sent to Vietnam, and later that month was able to travel to Chu Lai, Quang Nam Province, to see the Bob Hope Christmas Show. Unfortunately, Gearing was killed by enemy mortar fire in Quang Tri Province on May 19, sixty-six days from celebrating his twenty-first birthday. With his passing, he became the seventh soldier from Olympia High School to lose his life in the conflict and the fifth to die in Quang Tri Province. Among the list of five was Army Sgt. Jeffrey Bruce who died on February 10 of that same year when the boat he was in capsized, and he drowned. While in high school, both Gearing and Bruce played on the football team. Gearing was the center, and Bruce was the quarterback. An eighth soldier that attended the school would die four weeks later in Quang Ngai Province.

Army Cpl. William Seigle was from Sapulpa, Oklahoma, located on the old historic Route 66 and around fifteen miles southwest of Tulsa. He was a machine gunner with Company D, 2nd Division, and died from enemy mortar fire in Thua Thien Province on May 27, 1969…his 21st birthday. Cpl. Seigle had been married around seventeen months and had a four-month-old daughter. Also killed on the same day in Thua Thien Province was Sgt. William Anderson of Templeton, Pennsylvania. He died in Dihn Tuong Province from small arms fire, and his funeral was held on his 19th birthday. Staff Sgt. James Francis, 22, from Napa, California, was also killed on May 27, along with seven others from C Company, 1ˢᵗ Battalion. The seven-hour battle in which Staff Sgt. Francis and the others lost their lives occurred in Kontum Province. He was scheduled to leave Vietnam in less than two months. Army E4 Duane Curtis Bowen was from Ramona, California, and died in Chau Doc Province on May 28. He was in a forward firebase when it was attacked by enemy rocket fire. Before his death, Bowen had visited the military PX and purchased an engagement ring for his fiancé. E4 Bowen died two days before his 21st birthday.

Among the oldest soldiers mentioned in the *Life* article were four soldiers. They ranged in age from thirty-five to forty. This includes Army Lt. Col. Robert H. Carter, 35, of Morganton, North Carolina. As an infantry commander, he died on May 27 in the same battle that killed Staff Sgt. James Francis. The helicopter carrying Lt. Col. Carter had just landed when he was hit by sniper fire. Marine Staff Sgt. Ernest C. Munoz, 36, from San Antonio, was killed on May 26 when he stepped on a booby trap during the second day of Operation Pipestone Canyon in Quang Nam Province. He was married and had seven children. Army cannon crew member Sgt. Orville Hampton died on May 24 in Binh Long Province when an explosion occurred while he was loading one of the cannons. He had been in Vietnam for less than fifty days and was thirty-seven years old. Finally, the most senior soldier mentioned in the article was Army Sgt. Pedro A. Rios. He was killed in Quang Tri Province on May 21 and is buried in Ponce, Puerto Rico. Sgt. Rios was 40. Combined, these four soldiers had over a half-century of military service.

———————

Lastly, Army members comprised over one hundred and ninety of the two hundred and forty-two soldier deaths mentioned in the article. Marine losses number just shy of fifty, with most occurring in the provinces immediately south of the DMZ. The provinces, Quang Tri, Thua Thien, Quang Nam, Quang Tin, Quang Ngai, Hue, and Da Nang, were collectively called I Corps by the military.

Navy losses include Navy GMG3 (Gunner's Mate Petty Officer 3rd Class) Andrew Rice, 20, of Fort Richardson, Alaska, on May 23. It is believed that he fell off the boat while on an inland waterway in Dinh Tuong Province and drowned. He had been in the country sixty-six days. Navy HM2 (hospital medical corpsman 2nd class) Chris M. Pyle, 21, grew up in Kansas but moved to Oklahoma in 1963. His initial deployment to Vietnam was delayed because shortly before he was to leave, he broke his arm. While serving as a medic with a Marine unit fighting in Quang Nam as part of Operation Pipestone Canyon, the unit came under heavy attack, with several soldiers needing medical attention. According to a post on *The Wall of Faces*...

> *"...The call went out for 'Corpsman Up!' and Doc Pyle started running toward the wounded. Several other Marines began hitting booby-traps. According to many eye witnesses (sp.), someone tripped a booby-trap (sp.) that released a grenade from a tree, and dropped it down toward the wounded. Doc Pyle never missed a beat, he caught the falling grenade, stuffed it into his flak jacket, and dove into a ditch. His action prevented the explosion from harming anyone of the many wounded, or the Marines assisting them..."*

Navy HM2 Pyle died on May 28, and his body was escorted to the U.S. by his brother, John, who was also serving in Southeast Asia at the time. Pyle's family found it ironic that he became a medic, especially since he liked hunting but would always have someone clean the animal because he didn't want to do it.

The third Navy soldier mentioned in the article was Navy HM3 Richard L. Cox, 21, of Shakopee, Minnesota. Trained at the Great Lakes Naval Station, it was not uncommon for HM3 Cox to bring classmates home to Shakopee during the weekends or holidays. Like Navy HM2 Pyle, Cox was serving with a Marine group in Quang Nam Province during Operation Pipestone Canyon when he stepped on a booby trap on the afternoon of May 27 and died from his injuries. Before leaving for Vietnam, HM3 Cox had gotten married. He had been in Southeast Asia for seventeen days and is one of the twenty-five soldiers in the *Life* article without a photo.

Likewise, the last six months of the year brought just as many revelations at home and abroad.

In early July, the first combat troops to withdraw from the war zone began exiting Vietnam. The initial group, around 800, comprised members of the Army's 9th Infantry Division and landed at McChord Air Force Base near Tacoma, Washington, on July 8. They would be followed by soldiers from the 3rd Marine Division.

For only the second time since the U.S. intervened in the Vietnam conflict in 1956, the number of American soldiers killed in the region declined. This was especially true for Ohio soldiers. During July, less than fifty Ohio servicemen were killed, compared to an average of nearly sixty monthly casualties for the first six months. Except for August, which saw a slight increase in Ohio soldiers killed in Southeast Asia, the monthly casualty rate would continue to shrink during the next six months. By December, the number of Ohio soldiers to die would be less than two dozen.

Among the forty-eight soldiers from Ohio to die in July was Army Pfc. Thomas Johnson, 19, from London, southwest of Columbus. He was born on Veterans Day, 1949, and died on July 4, in Dinh Tuong Province, from small arms fire. Marine Lance Cpl. Leon Parker died the following day while serving in Quang Tri Province, and Army SP4 Francis Rigdon, from Manchester, the day after that. He came from a family of seven. While Pfc. Johnson and Lance Cpl. Parker were nineteen, SP4 Rigdon was 21.

Included among the sixty August casualties was Marine Pvt. James Blake from Sandusky. He died on August 3 in Quang Nam Province from small arms fire. Pvt. Blake would have celebrated his 20th birthday in thirteen days. Also killed during September was Navy Petty Officer First Class Robert Arnold, 24, of North Madison. As a six-year veteran stationed aboard the USS Harnett County in the Gulf of Thailand, he was on board a helicopter that went down in a rainstorm following take off from the aircraft carrier. He was a door gunner on board the helicopter and was survived by his mother and one sister.

Among the September list of forty-six deaths was Army SP4 John Futo from Cleveland and Army Warrant Officer Terry Denney from Sandusky. Futo died one day after his 21st birthday, on September 1, while serving in Quang Ngai Province. Denney was killed when the helicopter he was piloting was hit with ground fire, clipped several tree limbs, and crashed to the ground in Binh Dinh Province. WO Denney died on September 9…six days away from celebrating his 20th birthday on September 15.

Among the thirty deaths in October was Army Capt. Stanley Adams, 26, from Dayton. A graduate of the Air Force Academy, Class of 1965, he died on November 4 when his plane went down while on a mission in Phong Dinh Province, in the Mekong Delta. Adams was one of nearly three dozen members of the Christian Church (Disciples of Christ) to die in Southeast Asia. Air Force Lt. Colonel Bernard Knapic, 39, from Youngstown, died moments after one of the engines on the aircraft he was piloting caught fire while departing Tan Son Nhut Air Base near Saigon. He was a fourteen-year veteran and was buried in Arlington National Cemetery.

November claimed the lives of forty Ohio soldiers, including three on the same day, November 12. The first was Marine Pvt. Jerome Higgins, 19, from Springfield. After destroying an enemy bunker, he rescued two fellow Marines from the battlefield. He then assisted in loading them onto a medivac helicopter. However, a sniper mortally wounded him upon returning to the firefight in Quang Nam Province. For his courage, Higgins was awarded the Silver Star. Also killed that day was 1st Lt. Joseph Lofton from Akron. As a helicopter co-pilot, he was providing air support for fellow Marines near An Hoa Air Field in Quang Nam when his aircraft was hit with enemy fire and crashed. Lofton, a former Boy Scout, was 24 and had been in South Vietnam for six weeks. The third soldier from Ohio to die on November 12 was Army SP4 Thomas Landrum from Fairborn. He would become one of over five hundred soldiers from the 1st Brigade, 5th Division, to die in the Vietnam conflict. Landrum, 24, was killed while serving in Quang Tri Province.

Twenty-one Ohio soldiers lost their lives in Southeast Asia in December. Included among the list was Air Force Airman 1st Class Patrick Martin, 20, from Batavia. Killed less than 24 hours before the Christmas truce took effect, he was one of two airmen killed when their aircraft crashed less than fifteen minutes after taking off from an airfield in Phuoc Tuy Province. Army SP4 Dennis Boland died in Binh Long Province on December 26, three days before his 21st birthday. According to the *Coffelt Database of Vietnam Casualties*, Boland *"...was killed while on a military mission retrieving mines when a mine exploded for unknown reason."* It is said that Boland had a red Chevelle 396 waiting for him in the family driveway at his Cincinnati home.

As summer turned into fall, the anti-war movement in

America continued to surge. The growing crusade was aided when two songwriters with the Motown label, Norman Whitfield and Barrett Strong, co-wrote what many believe to be one of the most famous songs of the Vietnam conflict. The song *"War"* opens with a phrase being repeated several times…

> *"War…what is it good for?*
> *Absolutely nothing."*

The lyrics that follow further define and answer the chorus. Among them…

> *"War, I despise*
> *'Cause it means destruction of innocent lives*
> *War means tears to thousands of mother's eyes*
> *When their sons go out to fight and lose their lives*
>
> *(War) It ain't nothing but a heartbreaker*
> *(War) Friend only to the undertaker*
> *War is the enemy of all mankind*
> *The thought of war blows my mind*
> *War has caused unrest, within the younger generation*
>
> *(War) It ain't nothing but a heartbreaker*
> *(War) It's got one friend that's the undertaker*
> *War has shattered many young men's dreams*
> *Made them disabled, bitter and mean*
> *Life is much too short and precious to be fighting wars*
> *these days*

At about the same time, the North Vietnamese released three American prisoners of war. The first was Navy pilot Lt. Robert Frishman, who had been held as a POW since his plane was shot down in October 1967. Also released was Air Force Capt. Wesley Rumble. His plane was shot down in April 1968. The third prisoner, Navy Seaman Petty Officer Second Class Doug Hegdahl, had been in a North Vietnamese prison camp since the spring of 1967. After falling overboard from his vessel, the USS Canberra, stationed in the Gulf of Tonkin, he stayed afloat for several hours before being rescued by local fishermen. Hegdahl was promptly handed over to North Vietnamese military officials when he reached the shore. While all three were released as part of a propaganda effort by the North Vietnamese on August 5, 1969, Hegdahl's release proved the most beneficial for U.S. military intelligence.

During his time in captivity, Hegdahl memorized the names, personal information, and capture dates of over two hundred and fifty fellow POWs to the tune of *"Old McDonald Had a Farm."* Hegdahl's first-hand knowledge was crucial in helping the U.S. government determine the names and conditions of those soldiers being held as prisoners by the North Vietnamese.

The following month brought a mix of good and not-so-good news. On September 2, the world learned of the passing of communist leader Ho Chi Minh at his residence in Hanoi. It was reported that Minh, 79, died of heart failure. The U.S. and its allies hoped that with Minh's passing, the issue of peace in the divided country would take on added importance. Three days later, Americans learned of the horrific events that had taken place in March of the previous year in Quang Ngai Province, when between 300 and 500 unarmed villagers were killed by American troops. The My Lai Massacre would lead to the arrest of over two dozen U.S. soldiers; however, in the end, only one, an Army lieutenant, would be convicted. One week later, Pres. Nixon announced plans to withdraw an additional 35,000 troops from the region. Within the same week, and to further his plan to reduce American troop strength in Southeast Asia, the president canceled draft calls for the last two months of the year.

On the next to last day of the month, the American people began hearing a song on radio stations that sought to remind listeners of the simple life. While it was not his intent, country singer Merle Haggard's *"Okie From Muskogee"* went a long way to instill pride in America. The pro-war faction who supported the conflict in Vietnam soon adopted the song as their "rallying" song. With simple and heartfelt lyrics, it's no wonder the song became an instant hit.

"We don't smoke marijuana in Muskogee
We don't take our trips on LSD
We don't burn our draft cards down on Main Street
'Cause we like livin' right, and bein' free

We don't make a party out of lovin'
But we like holdin' hands and pitchin' woo
We don't let our hair grow long and shaggy
Like the hippies out in San Francisco do

And I'm proud to be an Okie from Muskogee
A place where even squares can have a ball
We still wave Old Glory down at the courthouse
And white lightnin' still the biggest thrill of all..."

The last three months of 1969 also saw countless other events surrounding the conflict in Southeast Asia.

On October 2, Hannah Elizabeth Crews, 23, from Lenoir, North Carolina, died from head injuries she received when her jeep was involved in an accident in Bien Hoa. Although she was the third member of the American Red Cross to die in Vietnam, Crews was the first female casualty of the organization's *Donut Dollies* to die in the regional conflict. The first Red Cross workers to lose their lives were Vernon Lyons from Wichita Falls, Texas, and Paul Samuels. Lyons died on August 29, 1967, when his jeep ran over a landmine near Da Nang. Samuels was killed in Khe Sanh during the early stages of the 1968 TET offensive. He was forty-four while Lyons was forty-eight.

Hannah Crews joined the Red Cross after graduating first from Peace College, a private women's prep school in Raleigh, North Carolina, affiliated with the Presbyterian Church, and later with a degree in History from Appalachian State University, Class of 1968. Shortly after that, she began teaching in nearby Winston-Salem, North Carolina. Then, wanting to offer more of her life to others, she joined the Red Cross on June 15, 1969, as a recreational aide. While attending training classes in Washington, DC, she learned of the organization's history, qualifications, and what was expected of her as one of the Donut Dollies.

Originally called the American Red Cross Supplemental Recreation Activities Overseas program, or SRAO, the Dollies can trace their roots as far back as WWII and the Korean War. Others believe the group goes back even further, possibly to WWI when they were called "Donut Lassies." They were given that name because they served soldiers refreshments. Many had fathers that served in the military. However, as time went on, volunteer qualifications and duties were expanded beyond simply serving refreshments to soldiers. By the 1960s, the organization had put strict entrance policies in place.

First, the volunteer must be a young woman between twenty-one and twenty-four with a college degree. She must also present several letters of recommendation, pass a physical exam, and give no less than one year of service. Moreover, Dollies must be friendly and have the girl-next-door appearance and personality. Above all, volunteers in the program must know Red Cross and military procedures, policies, and protocols. With such strict requirements, it is little wonder that only one in six applicants was accepted into the program.

Beyond simply seeking to boost morale through their presence, volunteers were asked to play card games with soldiers, help soldiers write letters to loved ones back home, or listen when those away from home wanted to talk. They may also be asked to write and perform skits on stage during an appearance at a base or a remote camp. Because most Dollies served in a combat zone, they were issued dog tags since their travel required them to drive on dangerous roads or fly in a helicopter to a firebase in the jungle. It was not uncommon for Dollies to bring along books, cigarettes, candy, soda, and even mirrors to hand out to troops. Radios were said to be a big hit among soldiers because they could dance with the Dollies while listening to music.

The volunteer position also had a bad side. While most soldiers were appreciative, courteous, and respectful of the Dollies during their presence with the troops, there were those instances when sexism came into play. On more than one occasion, some soldiers told the volunteers that women have no place among male troops and should be home in the kitchen and making babies. Besides the possibility of an attempted assault and daily propositions, the Dollies had to occasionally address the issue of a Peeping Tom.

Most likely dressed in the organization's light blue clothing with a skirt just above the knees, bearing the Red Cross patch on the left shoulder of her shirt; a small, red cross on one lapel and the initials ARC on the other; and a name tag that stated her first name only, Hannah Crews, barely five feet tall with a southern drawl, arrived in Vietnam on July 4, 1969. At the time, she was one of over one hundred Dollies in the region. Her living conditions were unlike any she had experienced before. Crews, who wore her hair short, most likely lived in a Quonset hut with several other females and only one bathroom. Hot water was sporadic, as was electricity and air conditioning. At the time, her brother was stationed with the Marines at Camp Lejeune, North Carolina.

On the night of September 26, Crews had just finished a shift at the recreation center and was riding back to her quarters when she fell out of a jeep and suffered a head injury. After being treated, she was admitted for observation. During the night, her condition worsened, and she was transported to the hospital in Long Binh, approximately seven miles away. She died five days later.

Of her passing, three friends wrote...

> *"We remember a day in June when we watched her board a plane for Washington, and the ironical double rainbow in the sky as she departed. We never expected to lose her so quickly but during the three months she was gone, she always remembered her family and friends. Through letters and tapes she repeated frequently, 'I've never been so happy.'...We believe Hannah found her pot of gold at the end of the rainbow." (High Point Enterprise, October 10, 1969)*

Two other Donut Dollies, including Virginia Kirsch and Lucinda Richter, would die in Vietnam. Kirsch, 21, from Brookfield, Ohio, was murdered by an American soldier on August 16, 1970, while she slept in her quarters in Cu Chi, near Saigon. She had been in Vietnam for approximately one week. Richter, also twenty-one, was from St. Paul, Minnesota. She died on February 9, 1971, from complications associated with Guillain-Barre Syndrome while in a military hospital in Cam Ranh Bay.

On Columbus Day, an estimated crowd of 5,000 – 10,000 anti-war protestors breached the perimeters of Fort Dix in New Jersey. The group was protesting the arrest and imprisonment of over three dozen antiwar soldiers from the ASU (American Servicemen Union), comprised of ex-GIs, active GIs, and soldiers that had gone AWOL. Also among the crowd that day lending emotional and physical support were countless women and members of the SDS (Students for a Democratic Society). However, not long after the protestors broke through the outer boundaries of the military complex, they were met with tear gas and members of the Military Police. Eventually, the protestors backed down.

However, three days later, on October 15, antiwar demonstrations took place in New York, Washington, DC, and San Francisco. On that day, it is said that more than one million people nationwide, most wearing black armbands, left their workplaces to demonstrate their opposition to the Vietnam conflict. One month later, no less than 500,000 protestors gathered in the nation's capital in what was the largest antiwar protest in American history.

On November 2, Army Warrant Officer Leo Hester, Jr., from Jacksonville, Florida, was piloting an observation helicopter over Phuoc Long Province when his aircraft was hit by enemy ground fire and crashed. Two others aboard the aircraft also died. He died nineteen days before his 20th birthday, had been in military service less than one year, and was an only child. Hester's father, Navy Lt. Commander Leo Hester, from Heber, California, died March 10, 1967, when his aircraft experienced a catastrophic event and crashed into a mountain in Ninh Thua Province. All fourteen aboard the aircraft were killed. Hester, 42, a twenty-two-year veteran of military service, first volunteered for the Navy in 1941. The Hesters, one of three pairs of father and son to die in the Vietnam conflict, are buried beside each other in Barrancas National Cemetery in Pensacola, Florida.

Of the fifteen recorded casualties on November 7, all of which were members of the U.S. Army, there were only three soldiers from states west of the Mississippi River…Arizona,

Iowa, and Oklahoma. States that lost more than one soldier include Illinois and Pennsylvania. The lone soldier from Florida killed that day was Army Warrant Officer David Greeson, 21, from Melbourne. Before entering the Army in 1968, he was a Melbourne Civil Air Patrol member and attended the Florida Institute of Technology. A helicopter co-pilot, Greeson was shot down conducting reconnaissance near a rubber plantation in Phuoc Long Province. He had been in-country for less than fifty-five days. Greeson's younger brother, Army E5 John Greeson, 18, was a medical NCO and was killed sixteen months earlier in Hau Nghia Province on July 22, 1968. The Greesons are one of a group of thirty sets of brothers that died in the Vietnam conflict. Beyond each being awarded a Purple Heart for their military service, the two brothers are buried beside each other in the Florida Memorial Gardens in Rockledge, Florida.

As November turned into December, the U.S. held the first draft lottery since the early years of WWII and the first in peacetime. Before a nationally televised audience, New York Congressman Alexander Prime, standing in the headquarters of the Selective Service in Washington, DC, reached his hand into a large glass container full of blue plastic capsules, each containing a specific day of the year...January 1 through December 31. The first number drawn out was September 14. Consequently, all eligible men between eighteen and twenty-six and born between 1944 and 1950 were now being called for military service. The last date drawn was July 20.

On December 9, another chaplain, the fourteenth, died in Vietnam. This time it would be Lutheran Church (Missouri Synod) minister and Army Major Roger Heinz. An eight-year veteran of the military, Rev. Heinz, 33, died when his helicopter crashed into a hillside in Quang Ngai Province on

December 9, 1969. The Coventry, Connecticut native left behind a wife and two children.

Less than one week later, Pres. Nixon announced a third phase of U.S. troop withdrawals. The withdrawal would involve approximately 50,000 American soldiers by April of the following year.

Around the middle of December, the Viet Cong announced that it would observe a three-day Christmas truce, beginning December 24 and lasting through December 26. The Allied forces, cautious of such a truce because of past enemy violations, said they would only observe a 24-hour ceasefire. The one-day truce would begin at 12:00am on December 25 and end at 12:00am on December 26.

It can be said that the year ended with mixed results.

On one hand, there were 11,780 American soldiers that lost their lives in Southeast Asia during the year, raising the total number of U.S. lives lost to over 48,000. This includes nearly five hundred and ninety from Ohio. Among the list of other casualties are two more soldiers from Our Lady of Guadalupe Catholic Church, including Marine Pvt. Michael Miranda, 21, who was injured while on night duty patrol and died from his wounds on April 2, and Marine Pvt. Dennis Rodriquez, 19, who died while on patrol. Both soldiers were serving in Quang Nam Province. Also killed during the year was Army Pfc. Kenney Lassiter, 19, from Philadelphia. He and seven other soldiers lost their lives when the enemy attacked the landing zone they were protecting. Lassiter's death brings the number of former students from Edison High School in Philadelphia, known collectively as the Edison 64, to seven for the year and the total number of death from the south Philly school to over forty-five. Nearly one-half of the soldiers died in one of three provinces: Quang Nam, Quang Tri, or Thua Thien.

At the end of 1968, troop strength was 536,100, and deaths to around 30,000. A decrease in troop strength at the end of 1969 brought the number to 475,200 and deaths to 40,024. Both numbers would continue to decline in the coming years.

1970

By most accounts, 1970 would continue to be a year of change at home and abroad.

For starters, the year would be one in which the number of casualties for Ohio service members would decline. During the first three months, there would be less than seventy deaths. The number pales in comparison when placed side-by-side with the number of Ohio military deaths in previous years. In January 1969 alone, over sixty soldiers from the state lost their lives.

Among the first deaths of the new year was Army Pfc. Gary Eicheler and Marine Cpl. John Fatica who died on January 3. Pfc. Eicheler was a 1966 graduate of Cloverleaf High School in Seville, Ohio, and the Wooster Business College in 1969, where he studied accounting. He did his basic training at Fort Campbell, Kentucky, followed by advanced training at Fort Polk in Louisiana. In the course of forty-seven days, he arrived in Vietnam (November 17), celebrated his twenty-first birthday (December 6), won a drawing for a ticket to Bob Hope's Christmas Show (December 9), saw the show from a center seat (December 22), then died on January 3 from injuries while on a combat mission in Binh Duong Province. In a letter his mother received before his death, he wrote, *"...there isn't anything to worry about...because it's pretty safe around here" (Medina County Gazette, January 8, 1970).* His mother, a postal worker, had just returned home when she saw an Army jeep drive up with two officers inside. Pfc. Eicheler's father was a veteran of WWII and died while the younger Eicheler was a sophomore in high school. The younger Eicheler leaves behind a mother and a sister in junior high school.

Marine Cpl. John Fatica, 21, was a construction draftsman from Cleveland. He died in Quang Nam Province and is buried at Fort Logan National Cemetery in Denver, Colorado.

The remaining days of the month would see an additional twenty-four soldiers, including twenty-two from the Army, lose their lives. The two Marines to lose their lives between January 6 and the end of the month were Pvt. John Hargreaves from Brook Park and Lance Cpl. Edward Justice from Cincinnati. Both soldiers were twenty-years-old and died in Quang Nam Province.

Of the remaining casualties from the state, there was one soldier from Akron, Cleveland, Columbus, Dayton, and Hamilton. Similarly, there was one soldier to pass away from Harrison, Huron, Newark, Springfield, Warren, Waverly, Willshire, Winchester, and two from Cincinnati. Army Cpl. Robert Kramer, 20, from Cincinnati, was injured on January 11 in Quang Tin Province and died four days later.

During the next eleven days, eight additional soldiers from Ohio would die in Vietnam. Army SP4 Gary Morris from Lancaster and Army E4 Henry Taylor from Dayton were killed on January 14. Morris, 21, died while on patrol in Quang Ngai Province, while Taylor, 20, died in Binh Dinh Province when his unit came under enemy attack.

On January 18, three Army soldiers from Ohio were killed in Vietnam, including Pfc. David Fowler, 18, from Elyria, who died in Thua Thien Province; 2nd Lt. David Stoppelwerth, 26, from West Chester, who died in Hau Nghia; and SP4 Mark Tonti, 22, from Columbus. He died in Binh Duong Province when a mine was detonated near him. One week later, on January 25, three more Ohio soldiers were killed in Vietnam. This includes Army SP4 Roy Beasley, 21, from Bellevue; Army Sgt. Duane Marhefka, 23, from Kensington; and Army SP4 James Vinciguerra, 20, from Akron. Beasley and

Marhefka were killed in Quang Tin Province, while Vinciguerra in Quang Tri Province. Marhefka had been in-country less than three weeks. The last Ohio soldier to die in January was Army SP4 Richard Mader from Cleveland. He died on January 31 in Binh Thuy Province while on patrol.

While the number of Ohio soldier casualties would briefly decline in February to around twenty, the following four months, March thru June, would increase dramatically. In March, thirty-two sons of Ohio lost their lives, while April, May, and June would show over one hundred and twenty combined deaths. May alone would record no less than forty-five deaths and June nearly forty.

Generally speaking, the increase in casualties may be connected to the region's dry season, which runs from December through May. The rainy season begins in June and runs thru November. Additionally, this may help to explain why nearly 6 in 10 deaths of Ohio soldiers, 182 of 309, in 1970 happened during the dry season.

The list of soldiers killed in February includes Army Pfc. James Carman, 20, from Canton. He died in a helicopter crash in Binh Duong Province on February 1. Prior to entering the military, Carman, a door gunner on a helicopter, was employed by the Royal China Company in Sebring. Carman had a brother who was in the Air Force and was serving in Cambodia at the time of his brother's death.

Four days later, on February 5, two Ohio soldiers lost their lives, including Army Cpl. Paul Lees, 21, from Cuyahoga Falls, and Navy Lt. Richard Stephenson, 25, from Hamilton. Lees died from wounds he received while in combat. Stephenson died not long after his plane was catapulted off the USS Ranger, which was stationed in the Gulf of Tonkin. Crew members aboard the aircraft carrier report that Stephenson's plane went down in the night sky following an explosion.

Stephenson remains missing in action.

On February 14, two more Ohio soldiers were killed in Vietnam. Marine Pvt. James Burke, 18, died in Quang Nam Province when he stepped on a land mine while on night patrol. He had been in Vietnam for less than thirty-five days and was the tenth soldier from Middletown to die in the conflict. Army SP4 Charles Thomas, from Fairborn, was injured on January 1 in Quang Tri Province when his tank hit a land mine. He died from 3rd degree burns over nearly seventy-five percent of his body on Valentine's Day in a military hospital in Yokohama, Japan. Thomas, a 1967 graduate of Fairborn high school, was attending nearby Sinclair College when he was called for military service. His parents were at his bedside when he passed. By month's end, thirteen additional soldiers from Ohio would die in Vietnam, including two soldiers on February 18 and three on February 20.

Army Pfc. David Skala, 23, from Canton, was killed in Pleiku Province. He was drafted on June 26, 1969, did his basic training at Fort Campbell, Kentucky, and was killed on the same day as Army Pfc. James Clark, 20, from Wadsworth. He and seven other soldiers died when their helicopter was shot down over Quang Duc Province while attempting to resupply ground troops.

According to the *Pacific Stars and Stripes*, Clark's *"...copter was the 1,487th destroyed in the Vietnam War since January 1, 1961. Thirteen copters have been downed and destroyed in the past nine days" (February 20, 1970).* He was the eighty-eighth soldier from Stark County to die in-country. A post on Skala's *Wall of Faces* said, *"No wife's (sp.), kids, or grand-kids (sp.)."* Skala and Clark were among the thirty soldiers, twenty-three Army, four Marines, and three members of the U.S. Air Force killed that day.

Multiple deaths of Ohio soldiers also occurred two days later when the conflict claimed the lives of Army Pfc. Clyde

Root from Canton, Army Sgt. William Wood from Alliance and Army Cpl. James Waulk from Washington Court House. Wood was twenty-two, Root was twenty, and Waulk was nineteen. While Wood and Waulk died in Phuoc Long Province from land mines, Root passed away in Quang Tin Province during Operation Frederick Hill. He would be the eighty-ninth soldier from Stark County to die in Southeast Asia.

The last Ohio soldier to die in February was Army SP5 Daniel Proctor, 19, from Cleveland. He was a door gunner on a helicopter that was hit and crashed in Ba Xugen Province on February 27.

March would see an increase in Ohio military casualties of nearly fifty percent. And like February, a number of the losses would occur on the same day.

On the first Friday of the month, the conflict would claim the lives of two soldiers, both members of the Army: Pfc. Thomas Brockmeier, 20, from Marietta, and Sgt. Glenn Lovett, 22, from West Liberty. Sgt. Lovett was the vice president of his 1965 graduating class of Zanesfield High School and attended Ohio State University before entering the military. While both soldiers died on March 7 from enemy fire, Brockmeier in Hau Nghia Province and Lovett in Quang Tri Province, Sgt. Lovett was five days away from celebrating his 23rd birthday.

Exactly one week later, on Friday, March 14, the conflict claimed twenty lives, including sixteen members of the Army, two Marines, and two members of the Air Force. The Army casualties that day was Pfc. Robert Banks from Antwerp, who was six days away from celebrating his 21st birthday, and Pfc. Timothy Echols, 18, from Dayton. Echols died in Pleiku Province when his gun suddenly discharged. Pfc. Banks, who attended Antwerp High School and worked at Mickelson Upholstery Shop before entering the service in February 1969, was killed in combat in Quang Nam Province. Air Force Capt. Dana Dilley, 29, from Duncan Falls, was one of two members of the Air Force killed that day. Capt. Dilley, the lone soldier from Duncan Falls to be killed in Vietnam, was piloting a helicopter for ground troop reconnaissance when it was shot down over Quang Duc Province. Capt. Dilley, who trained at Laughlin AF Base in Del Rio, Texas, left behind a wife and two sons living nearby in Coshocton, Ohio.

Far and away, the deadliest days came in the second half of the month. On March 16, three Ohio soldiers, two members of the Navy and one from the Army, lost their lives.

Army Cpl. Gerald Corlett, 21, from Oregon, Ohio, lost his life in Tay Ninh Province from small arms fire, possibly a sniper, just before midnight. During his brief tenure in the military, less than one year, he was awarded eight medals, including a Bronze Star and Purple Heart. The two Navy personnel, Petty Officer Third Class Gregory Asbeck, 22, from Grove City, and LTJG Charles Pressler, 24, from Bay Village, were killed when their plane, filled with over thirty members of the Navy, crashed upon approach to an airfield near Da Nang in Quang Nam Province. During the flight that originated in Taiwan, the pilots were forced to shut down one of the plane's engines because of overheating. In addition, a large section of the runway had been closed for repairs because of rocket and mortar attacks. Pressler, a graduate of Ohio University and Officer Candidate School in Rhode Island, was an only child. His father was a retired Navy lieutenant,

On March 28, three members of the U.S. military lost their lives in Vietnam. Army SP4 Richard Broyles was from Fairfield and died in a vehicle accident in Bien Hoa Province. Army Cpl. Sidney Rohler, from Wadsworth, was killed while on patrol in Thua Thien Province. Also among the twenty-one service members killed that day was Airman First Class Joseph Soule' from East Canton. He died in Khanh Hoa Province and had been in Vietnam for fifty days. According to a post on *Wall of Faces*, Soule also had three brothers to serve in the military, and one may have been in Vietnam when Airman Soule passed away. While all three soldiers, Broyles, Rohler, and Soule' were twenty at the time of their deaths, Soule' was the only one of the three married.

Two more Ohio soldiers would die during the following forty-eight hours. Army Sgt. William Hainley, 19, died on Easter Sunday, March 29, in Tay Ninh Province. He was from Sandusky and was one of fourteen killed that day at FSB (Fire Support Base) Jay when they came under heavy attack less than five miles from the Cambodian border. Included among the thirteen wounded that day was Marine Lance Cpl. Jackie Lundell from Norwalk. Injured from a grenade's fragmentation, he was taken from Quang Nam Province to a hospital in Da Nang and died the next day from his wounds. Lundell left high school early to join the Marines. He would have turned twenty in less than three weeks. At the time of his passing, Lundell received less than $230 a month and had a sister serving in the WACS (Women's Army Corps) in Fort Belvoir, Virginia. Additionally, he was the only male of four kids. A post on the *Wall of Faces* left the following comment...

> *"...I couldn't understand why you left school to go, but I had more room in the locker when you did, you left alot (sp.) of space for me to use, your passing left a place in our towns (sp.) heart and the heart of a nation..."*

While Lundell would be the first soldier from Norwalk to die in Southeast Asia in 1970, two more soldiers would die the same year. Air Force Tech Sgt. Jack Hawley, 37, died on April 10 in Thailand. He was one of ten soldiers killed when an aircraft crashed into a building housing the Armed Forces

Radio Network in Udon, Thailand. Prior to being deployed to Southeast Asia, Hawley was stationed in Germany. Army SP4 Timothy Thompson, a medic NCO, died on December 13 after stepping on a land mine in Quang Ngai Province while carrying a wounded soldier to safety. Prior to enlisting, he was a Boy Scout, an amateur cb radio operator, and worked in a bakery. He had been in Vietnam for forty-nine days and would have turned twenty-one in forty-nine days.

The following two months, April and May, would record the highest number of casualties of Ohio soldiers during the year…a total of ninety-seven.

On April 1, the U.S. population was 203,392,031. Undoubtedly, the numbers may not include the seventy-plus soldiers who lost their lives on that day or the additional one hundred and thirty-two that died in the same week. For instance, Army Sgt. Gerald Purdon, 21, from Cincinnati, lost his life in Tay Ninh Province. He was stationed on the perimeter of FSB Illingworth when it came under heavy enemy attack. At one point during the attack, his rifle jammed, and he fought the enemy in hand-to-hand combat. Purdon, who was married and was less than two months away from completing his twelve-month tour of duty in Vietnam, had four brothers and two sisters. Also among the two dozen casualties at FSB Illingworth was Army Sgt. Robert Hill, 21, from Lowell, Ohio. The firebase closed three days after the April 1 enemy assault. In addition, three West Virginia soldiers died on April 1, including Army SP4 Everett Ankrom, 20, from Pennsboro; Army Sgt. Jay King, 38, a twenty-year veteran from Newhall; and Army SP4 James Miller, 20, from Martinsburg. Ankrom and King lost their lives in Binh Thuy Province, while Miller, born on July 4th, was killed in Thua Thien Province. Miller was the tenth soldier from Martinsburg to be killed in Southeast Asia, King the third to die from Newhall, and Ankrom the second from Pennsboro.

The following day, the conflict would claim the lives of six Ohio soldiers, or nearly twenty percent of the thirty-nine casualties that day. Army Cpl. Donald Chambers, 21, from Kimbolton, was killed when a booby trap was detonated near him while serving in Quang Ngai Province. Most likely, there may have been more individuals in Chambers' company, D Company, than in his unincorporated town of Kimbolton. Also killed in the same explosion was 1st Lt. Robert Kettering, 24, from Canton. He had attended the Ohio State University. Army SP4 Dale Gronsky, 21, from Wakeman, population around 825, died from a booby trap while on patrol in Quang Tin Province. The fourth Ohio soldier to die on April 2 was 2nd Lt. Orville Kitchen, 23, from Dayton. He was a Wilbur Wright High School graduate and a cadet leader in the ROTC program at the University of Dayton before being deployed to Vietnam. 2nd Lt. Kitchen was killed by sniper fire while in Renegade Woods, Quang Tin Province, and was among thirteen soldiers to die in the battle that lasted several days. Sgt. William Vaspory, 20, died when his helicopter was brought down while on a mission in Ba Xugen Province. Sgt. Vaspory, from Dayton, was a crew member aboard the aircraft. Army Pfc. David Kesterson, 20, was from Port Clinton, located on the banks of Lake Erie. He died from injuries he received sixteen days earlier while stationed in Quang Tin Province. Similar to Cpl. Chambers and SP4 Gronsky, it was a booby trap that ended Pfc. Kesterson's life.

One day later, the conflict took the lives of two more Ohio soldiers: Army SP4 Ron Parsons, 21, from Wapakoneta, and Army *Pfc. Dwight Ball, 20, from Sardis*. Both died in Tay Ninh Province, Parsons, during a rocket attack at the base camp and Ball when an artillery round meant for the enemy landed near him while serving in Renegade Woods. Parsons, nine days away from completing his one-year tour in Vietnam, had 4 brothers and 2 sisters. Ball, who had recently returned from getting married in Ohio, had four sisters and one brother. He was the eighth soldier from Monroe County to die in the conflict.

Over the next four days, five more Ohio soldiers would lose their lives. Army Lt. Colonel Andrew Simko, 39, from Bellaire, died on April 5 when his helicopter was shot down over Binh Dinh Province. He was a West Point graduate and a sixteen-year veteran of the military.

Army member Staff Sgt. Andrew Brassfield, 33, from Sylvania, was killed on April 6 from small arms fire while serving in a reconnaissance mission five miles inside the Laotian border. He joins the company of over nineteen hundred other soldiers whose bodies have never been recovered. Lexington, Ohio, native Pfc. Ralph Reed, 21, was injured on April 6 while on a helicopter mission over Kontum Province. He died ten days later in a hospital. Immediately before taking off, it is said that Pfc. Reed and another soldier, both helicopter crew chiefs, flipped a coin to see which aircraft would deliver supplies and which would fly cover.

Between April 7 and 9, two Ohio soldiers were killed in Vietnam, including Marine Pvt. William Turner, 18, from Cedarville, and Army Sgt. Clayton Whitcher, 22, from Cuyahoga Falls. Both died from small arms fire on April 7, Pvt. Turner in Quang Nam Province and Sgt. Whitcher in Quang Ngai Province. An explosive claimed the life of Army Sgt. Gary Brown, 21, from Warren, on April 9. Pfc. Thomas Gates, 37, from Cincinnati, was injured on April 9 and died in November 1986 from wounds received in Thua Thien Province.

From April 13 thru the end of the month, the conflict would take the lives of no less than eleven more sons of Ohio. On the same day the oxygen tanks aboard Apollo 13 exploded as the crew made their way to the moon, two Ohio soldiers were killed in Vietnam: Army Sgt. William Caldwell, 19, from

However, he did not tell Americans that he had done so until two days later, on the last day of April. Nevertheless, the move brought an immediate response from Americans opposed to the conflict.

One of the first protests began on the Kent State University (Ohio) campus on Saturday, May 2, when the state's national guard was called in over student unrest. The following day, student leaders called for a campus-wide protest on Monday, May 4, beginning at 11:00am. When nearly one thousand students gathered, they were told to disperse by the commanding officer of the guard. At the same time, the guard began moving the protestors toward the school's football field, which was protected by fencing. Upon arriving at the area, the students, with no place to go, turned on the troops. Thinking they were being attacked, the troops sent tear gas and fired several shots into the air to scatter the crowd. The next thing they knew, the student protestors were being fired at by the troops. In the next twenty seconds or so, guard troops fired nearly seventy rounds into the crowd of student protestors, killing four and wounding as many as seventy-five. Among the casualties were honor student Allison Krause, 19, from Churchill, Pennsylvania; Jeffrey Miller, 20, who had transferred from Michigan State University in January; and Sandra Scheuer, 20, who was caught in the gunfire while walking between classes. Like Scheuer, a fourth student, William Schroder, was walking between classes when he was fatally shot. As an honor student and an Eagle Scout, he recently received an award from the Association of the U.S. Army for his studies.

Shortly after midnight on May 14, students near Jackson State University in Jackson, Mississippi, were protesting the Cambodian invasion. Suddenly, law enforcement shot into a crowd. The gunfire lasted less than thirty seconds while over four hundred and fifty shots were fired, resulting in two deaths and injuring around a dozen. The two casualties were identified as a university law student, Phillip Gibbs, 21, and a 17-year-old high school senior named James Green.

During the same two weeks, no less than thirty-three Ohio soldiers lost their lives in Southeast Asia. Among the fourteen that lost their lives in the first seven days was Army Sgt. Joseph Tatum, 20, from Hilliard, who died in Phuoc Tuy Province. His father was an Army corporal during WWII. Army Warrant Officer Donald Parker, 19, from Toledo, died on May 2 when his attack helicopter collided with another aircraft over Cambodia.

The conflict claimed the lives of three soldiers the following day. Army Sgt. John Kotora, 21, from Vermilion, was wounded in Binh Dinh Province but had the strength to make it to a nearby landing zone on his own. After several months in a hospital in Japan, he died from his wounds. Air Force Lt. Col. Lawrence Conaway, 39, from Columbus, died in Ha Giang Province, North Vietnam, when his plane was hit by ground fire and crashed. A veteran of the Korean conflict, his body was never recovered. Army Staff Sgt. Fred Denkins, the third soldier from Ohio killed on May 3, was killed at LZ Betty in Binh Thuan Province during an early morning attack. He was thirty-three and from Cincinnati.

On May 5, two more soldiers from the Buckeye State lost their lives in Southeast Asia. Army Sgt. William Malcolm, 28, from Toledo, was killed near FSB (Fire Support Base) Veghel in Thua Thien Province. According to his obituary that appeared in the *Toledo Blade* on May 18, he was

> *"...A veteran of 12 years of service in the army, Sgt. Malcolm was for four years a commander of the army honor guard at Washington, DC, where he commanded the firing at the funerals of both President John F. Kennedy and Gen. Douglas MacArthur..."*

Army Warrant Officer Thomas E. McDonald, 21, from Brewster, died when his helicopter was shot down over a rubber plantation in Binh Duong Province. The son of a WWII

Navy veteran, the younger McDonald wrote a letter to his parents on May 4…the day before his passing…proclaiming his support of Pres. Nixon sending troops into Cambodia. The letter, which appeared in countless newspapers under the headline *"Dead soldier 'hated to hell' the protestors,"* was also included in the *Congressional Record* of May 19. The letter reads, in part…

> *"The move that President Nixon has taken and is standing pat on is the most significant and outstanding move anyone has taken since this war begun…For 6 years the NVA has been coming across the border killing and destroying US and Vietnamese people, homes, etc., then returning to safety back across the border…Now they can't. We've hit them and very hard…Every day all of us read about the protesting, bombings, and opposition toward the war and the decision of our president toward Cambodia…To be frank, I'm very ashamed of the actions of my own people in the United States. I don't even want to return to all of that. We are here for a purpose and we are, accomplishing our goal…President Nixon is our man. We that are here believe in him, pledge him our votes and support. I truly loathe the man or woman who denounces him and hate to hell every protestor that lives…As for my personal well-being, I'm healthy, suntanned, and safe. My only problem is that I am homesick and miss and love all of you…I'll be going to Australia for R and R and believe me I'm ready. Signed, Mick"* (Dover Times Reporter, May 13, 1970, pg. 1)

McDonald, a Norfolk and Western Railway fireman and a student at Grand Rapids Junior College in Michigan before his military service, had been in Vietnam for eight months.

May 6 proved to be the deadliest day of the month for Ohio soldiers when six lost their lives, nearly fifteen percent of all deaths recorded that day. Of the almost 60 killed that day, all were U.S. Army, except for three Marines. Among the Marines killed was Ohio native and Lance Cpl. Thomas Cravens, 19, from Cincinnati. A machine gunner, he was killed during an enemy night attack in Quang Nam Province.

Included among the Army soldiers killed were Staff Sgt. Kenneth Foutz from Dennison, who died seven days shy of his twenty-fifth birthday; SP4 Paul Kriegel, from Cleveland, who died one day after celebrating his twenty-first birthday; and Sgt. Gary McKiddy from Miamisburg. Foutz was killed in combat in Thua Thien Province. Kriegel and McKiddy died when their helicopters were shot down over Cambodia. McKiddy had flown over 650 missions during his six months in Southeast Asia. The barracks at Fort Hood, Texas, were later named in his honor. Also killed that day was Sgt. Gary Snyder from Toledo and Sgt. Frederick Ziegenfelder from St, Marys, Ohio. Both were serving at Firebase Henderson in Quang Tri Province when they were killed. In addition, Foutz died one week before his twenty-fifth birthday, and Ziegenfelder died nine days before his twenty-first birthday. Both were initially classified as missing in action but later changed to killed in action. The average age of the six soldiers that died on May 6 was twenty-two.

There was one Ohio soldier that died on May 7. Marine Sgt. Robert Phleger, 31, from London, died in Quang Nam Province. He was a ground radio repairer and had recently extended his tour. Phleger, the leader of a seven-man unit, was the last man in a line of soldiers on a reconnaissance patrol when he was attacked by a tiger.

The following seven days were no different when sixteen Ohio soldiers died in the region. On May 8, Army SP4 David Butcher, 19, from Marion, died from wounds he received while serving in Cambodia. The following day, Army Sgt. Michael Ussery, 19, from Brook Park, died in a helicopter crash in Thua Thien Province. He was buried in Flatwoods,

Kentucky.

Army Sgt. Thomas Merriman, 21, from Pauling, and E4 John Merschman, 20, from Delphos, died in Cambodia on May 12. Merriman was less than two months away from completing his tour when he was killed in a mortar attack. According to a post on *Faces on the Wall*, he wrote to a fellow soldier to, *"...pray for me tonight, will you? I asked the lord to forgive my sins tonight. I really want to live for him. Pray that he will hear my prayers."* Merschman, a star on his high school football team, died in a helicopter crash in Pleiku Province at twenty-three. The 1971 yearbook from his high school was dedicated to him. An only child, he was buried in the same cemetery plot as his parents.

Marine Cpl. Roy Wilson was from Lyons, Ohio. He was injured on Mother's Day, May 10, 1970, in Quang Nam Province and died from his wounds in a Da Nang hospital the following day. Wilson, 20, was fifty days away from completing his one-year tour of duty. Pfc. James Charlesworth, 20, from Girard, died in Cambodia from wounds he received on May 11. In addition, 1st Lt. Ned Heintz, 23, from De Graff, was wounded that day and died five days later.

Among the nearly four dozen soldiers that died on May 12 were two Ohio soldiers: Army servicemen Cpl. Charles Koon from Piqua, and 1st Lt. Kenneth Rogers from Cincinnati. Koon, who would have celebrated his twentieth birthday in eight days, died in Cambodia from his wounds. Rogers, 23, died in a helicopter crash in Pleiku Province. Fifteen days before his death, he wrote his parents, saying,

> *"...well another sat. night. It is 10:00 o'clock here and everyone is ready for bed. One thing here is that we don't keep late hours. Not much has happened here out of the ordinary this week. I did receive Bert's package last Tuesday, thank her for the cookies..."* (post, Wall of Faces).

Army SP4 Robert Lemons is also counted among the May 12 list of dead. He was killed by a booby trap while on patrol in Quang Ngai Province. Ironically, he was from War, West Virginia.

In the following two days, the list of casualties would include Air Force Capt. Alan Trent, from Wadsworth, and Army David Winder of Mansfield, who died on May 13. Trent, 29, whose plane was shot down in Ratanakiri Province, Cambodia, was a graduate of the Air Force Academy. He is one of four graduates from the academy who remains MIA. Winder, 23, was a medical corpsman who died from small arms fire while serving in Quang Ngai Province. According to records:

> *"...responding instantly to the cries of his wounded comrades Private Winder began maneuvering across 100 meters of open, bullet-swept terrain toward the nearest casualty. Unarmed and crawling most of the distance, he was wounded by the enemy before reaching his comrades. Despite his wounds...Private Winder reached the first casualty and administered medical aid. As he continued to crawl across the open terrain toward a second wounded soldier he was forced to stop when wounded a second time. Aroused by the cries of an injured comrade for aid, Private Winder's great determination and sense of duty impelled him to move forward once again, despite his wounds, in a courageous attempt to reach and assist the injured man. After struggling to within ten meters of the man, Private Winder was mortally wounded."*
> *(Coffelt Database of Vietnam Casualties)*

Two additional Ohio servicemen would die on the following day, May 14. This list includes Army Capt. Thomas Larkin, 23, from Steubenville, and Sgt. Robert Lowe, 21, from Ostrader, a population of less than 400. During a storm, Larkin's helicopter crashed in Tay Ninh Province; all seven aboard were killed. Lowe, the son of a minister and Navy veteran, died in Thua Thien Province from his wounds. He died three days before his twenty-second birthday. Army Sgt. Jerry Eaton, 22, from Clermont, was injured on February 14 in Bien Hoa Province when he was shot by another soldier. Eaton died on May 17 at Walter Reed Hospital.

Between May 15 and the last day of the month, the location and causes of death varied for many of the twenty-one Ohio soldiers that lost their lives in Southeast Asia. Moreover, the decrease in fatalities would see a downward trend that would continue throughout the remainder of the year.

On May 16, two Ohio soldiers died, including:

Marine Pvt. George Beal, from Cincinnati, and Army SP4 Harry Cotterman from Piqua. Beal, 18, who arrived in Vietnam just before Christmas 1969, died in Quang Nam Province when he reportedly jumped from a bridge to save another soldier's life. Unfortunately, he was swept away by the river's swift current and drowned. His body was recovered four days later. Cotterman was electrocuted when a high-voltage wire fell on his truck in Quang Tin Province. He was nineteen.

Less than twenty-four hours later, two more soldiers from Ohio would die. Records indicate that Army Staff Sgt. Alan Martin, 22, from Maple Heights, died from wounds he received while serving at FSB Ready in Cambodia. He began his tour of duty on Christmas Eve 1969 and was thirty-two days away from his 23rd birthday. Army helicopter door gunner Sgt. Roy Petty was among five soldiers killed when their helicopter was hit by enemy ground fire and crashed in Quang Tri Province. Petty, 21, from Akron, had replaced a crew member who had come down with a high fever.

Army SP4 Robert Urbassik, 19, was the lone Ohio soldier among over two dozen soldiers to die in Southeast Asia on May 19. Prior to entering military service, Urbassik, the only son of a veteran, worked for the Bell Telephone Company. He was killed from mortar fire in Cambodia and had a 1965 GT Mustang waiting for him back home in Cleveland.

On May 20, Army Cpl. Roy Carter, 23, died in Thua Thien Province from an accidental grenade explosion. He was from Circleville and had been in Vietnam for twenty days. The same day, Army Sgt. Kenneth Vore, from Casstown, died in Cambodia when his unit was ambushed. He was 25 and had a wife and three daughters.

Two Ohio Marines, both lance corporals, died on May 22: Lance Cpl. Lawrence Theis from New Riegel and Lance Cpl. Robert Beaver from Ashtabula. Additionally, both soldiers had completed their eight weeks of basic training at Parris Island. They were then sent to Camp Lejeune for advanced instruction. Theis, 22, was killed in Thua Thien Province during Operation Hickory when his vehicle was fired on by enemy troops. He held a degree from Ohio Technical College in Columbus and worked at Western Electric Company before enlisting in the Marines. Lance Cpl. Beaver, 19, had three sisters and three brothers: one was in the Air Force, and another was in the Marines. In addition to a wife, he had recently become the father of a new baby girl. It is said that Beaver received pictures of his new daughter the day he was killed from friendly fire while serving in Quang Nam Province.

Except for Memorial Day, May 30, when no Ohio soldiers were killed in the Vietnam conflict, at least one Ohio soldier would die in Southeast Asia during the next eight days. Army E5 Gary Taylor, 21, from Cincinnati, died on May 24 in a helicopter crash in Tay Ninh Province. In addition to being a door gunner, he was an Army film library specialist. The following day, two Army corporals lost their lives. Cpl.

Ramon Flores, 20, from Cleveland, died in Binh Dinh Province from combat wounds. Cpl. Gregory Maynard, who died from small arms fire while in Cambodia, had been in the region for seventy-one days. Before entering the service, he played football in high school and worked for a printing company in Huntington, West Virginia. Maynard, 20, was from South Point, Ohio, and was the first casualty from Lawrence County to die in the regional struggle. He was born in West Virginia, and that's where he was buried.

Over thirty members of the U.S. military lost their lives in Vietnam on May 26, including Army *SP4 Steven Janeda of New Matamoras* and Army Cpl. Harold McCord from Lexington. Janeda, 20, a radio teletype operator, died when his vehicle was ambushed by enemy troops in Pleiku Province. He was the ninth soldier from Monroe County, Ohio's second least populated county, to die in Vietnam. Army Cpl. Harold McCord, 21, known as Butch by family and friends, was on guard duty at a base camp in Binh Dinh/Long Khanh Province when the camp came under enemy mortar attack around 10pm. He died from his wounds. McCord, whose father was a WWII veteran, came from a family of seven and had three brothers and one sister back home in Lexington. Moreover, Cpl. McCord was forty-four days away from completing his one-year tour.

Over the next five days, no less than six Ohio soldiers lost their lives. The first was Army SP4 Donald Baker, 21, from Harrison, who died from his wounds on May 27 while in Quang Tin Province. He was an only child and was buried in Kentucky. Army E4 David Maze, 20, Pataskala, died in Tay Ninh Province when FSB Jamie was attacked. Also killed on May 28 was Army Cpl. Robert Roshon from Canton. He died in Cambodia when he stepped on a mine planted by other U.S. Army members. Roshon, who celebrated his 21st birthday on May 4, was an only child and was buried in the same cemetery plot as his parents. Finally, Army 1st Lt. Dale Reising, 25, from Dayton, died from wounds on May 29 while in Go Cong Province. Reising, who spoke Vietnamese, was less than one month away from celebrating his sixth wedding anniversary. He was buried in New Mexico, in the same national cemetery as his father, retired Air Force Lt. Col. Albert Reising, who, according to his tombstone, served in WWII, Korea, and Vietnam.

The last day of the month saw the passing of Marines Pvt. Hilario Perez from Deshler, and Army Sgt. Douglas Simpson from Heath. Perez, 20, was fatally wounded in Quang Tri Province when another U.S. soldier encountered Perez in the dark and mistook him for one of the enemy and shot him. He was described by fellow soldiers as an avid reader of the Bible and a ladies' man. Sgt. Simpson, who stood six feet tall, was slim, and had blonde hair, died in Thua Thien Province when his vehicle overturned. Growing up, he attended Central Christian Church, Disciples of Christ, in Newark and lettered in track while in high school. He was drafted in March 1969 and had celebrated his 21st birthday less than a month earlier. More, his father was retired from the Navy. While serving at FSB Veghel, he received a pass to see the 1969 Bob Hope Christmas Show at Camp Eagle (Hue). Joining Hope on stage that day was actress Ursula Andress and the Cincinnati Reds' catcher, Johnny Bench.

With the rainy season over, the number of deaths among Ohio soldiers stationed in Southeast Asia decreased dramatically between June and December 1970, as did all U.S. deaths in the region. The last seven months of the year saw just over one hundred and twenty-five deaths among members of the Ohio armed forces involved in the Vietnam conflict. This number stands in stark contrast to the over 2,100 U.S. soldiers killed in May 1968 and the nearly two hundred and fifty that died on January 31, 1968. While there was a temporary increase in deaths in June to thirty-eight, the number of Ohio soldiers to die in the conflict each month after that would not exceed twenty-five. The least number of deaths among Ohio soldiers came in October when thirteen were killed. Still, the backstory of some of these Ohioans needs to be told because *Everyone Has a Story.*

The first death among the nearly forty Ohio soldier casualties in June occurred on June 2. SP4 James Gibson, from Columbus, died from wounds he received when a booby trap went off near him. Over the next two weeks, no less than eighteen Ohio soldiers would die in Southeast Asia, including fifteen from the Army and three Marines. Of these numbers, four soldiers were killed in Cambodia; four in Quang Tin, three in Binh Dinh and Quang Nam provinces; two in Quang Ngai Province; and one in Chau Doc and Kontum provinces. Additionally, eight were killed by small arms fire, five by an explosive device (booby trap, etc.), three by mortar fire, and one each from a vehicle crash and disease (pneumonia). Of the eighteen soldiers that died between June 3 and June 16, seven were sergeants, four were corporals, four were ranked SP4, two were private first class, and one was a lance corporal. Finally, the average age of those killed during those two weeks was twenty. This includes eight that were twenty, seven soldiers that were nineteen, one that was twenty-one, one that was twenty-two, and one that was forty-two.

Of the eighteen soldiers killed between June 3 and June 16, Army Pfc. Michael Chase, from Cleaves, and Army Sgt. Carl Ealy, from Cleveland, had been in Vietnam less than three months, while Army Sgt. Daniel McMahan, also from Cleveland, had been in-country just over two months. More,

Army Staff Sgt. Jerry Hurley, from New Concord, and Staff Sgt. Dale Williams, from Attica, were the only soldiers from their towns to die in Vietnam. Combined, the two towns had a population of around 3,000. Finally, the bodies of four soldiers killed during those fourteen days, including Cpl. Michael Chase, from Cleaves; SP4 Orla Hammack, from Columbus; Sgt. Carl Ealy, from Cleveland; Sgt. Daniel McMahan, also from Cleveland, are buried out of state.

As for the last two weeks of June, an additional seventeen soldiers from Ohio died in Southeast Asia. This includes eight who died between June 17 and June 23 and the nine who died during the last week of the month. Three Ohio soldiers…Air Force Major Carl Drake, from Roseville; Army Cpl. Ralph Triplett; from Portland; and Army Sgt. Frank Zonar, from Cleveland…died on June 18. The first two died while serving in Cambodia, and the last in Tay Ninh Province. Additionally, three other Ohioans…Army Staff Sgt. Charles Hann, from Northfield; Army Pfc. Robert Gumbert, from New Richmond; and Army Cpl. Thomas Schalk, from Cincinnati…died on June 22. Finally, four soldiers from the Buckeye State died on June 26. Both Army Pfc. Gary Fleck, 20, from Niles, who had been in-country for twenty-seven days, and Marine Cpl. Forest Highland, 21, from Massillon, died in Cambodia. Army Sgt. Wallace Roberts, from Piketon, died after being wounded on June 3, while Army Sgt. William Endress, from Geneva, died from wounds he received on June 22.

The last Ohio casualty to die during the month was Army Pfc. Lester Parker, 20, who was killed in Quang Tri Province. He was the second soldier from Urbana to die in three weeks. A longtime friend and school classmate posted on *Faces on the Wall* that he will never forget the time Parker and he urinated in their second-grade teacher's trash can.

The last six months of the year would record the death of one hundred and five Ohio soldiers. This includes twenty during July, twenty-four in August, sixteen in September, fourteen in October and December, and seventeen in November.

Among the eleven soldiers killed during the first two weeks of July was Army Pfc. Walter Puchalski from Cleveland. He had just returned from fighting in Cambodia the day before. Puchalski, 19, a paper boy for the *Cleveland Plain Dealer* and a gifted musician who could play five different horn instruments, was scheduled to fly to Hawaii in August to meet his fiancé and get married. Puchalski, who died on July 2 from a firearms accident in Binh Duong Province, was survived by his parents and six siblings.

The lone Air Force member to die during those first fourteen days of the month was Capt. William Justice, 28, from Columbus. A crossing guard in elementary school and later a commander with the Ohio State University Air Force Drill Team before his deployment to Southeast Asia, he died on July 3 when his plane went down during a mission over Cambodia. On July 12, Army SP4 Kenneth Hinds, from Cincinnati, died in Darlac Province. He had celebrated his 20th birthday five days before and was one of seven siblings.

The regional fighting in Southeast Asia during the last two weeks of July claimed the lives of nine Ohio soldiers, including seven members of the U.S. Army, one Marine, and one member of the Air Force. Among the seven members of the Army were SP4 Christopher Schaeffer, 20, from Lancaster, who was born on Veterans Day; Cpl. George Kelly, 20, who died on July 22; and Pfc. Ronald Jones from Toledo. Kelly would be the last of six soldiers from Bellaire to die in the conflict. Jones had celebrated his nineteen birthday precisely one month before his accidental death on July 29 in Binh Dinh Province. On July 21, Air Force Sgt. Richard Pearl, 32, from Lorain, was killed when an enemy rocket hit near him as he walked across the base parking lot. In addition to being an excellent card player, he was a telephone cable antenna specialist and oversaw the alert system at his base. He enlisted in 1960 and spent four years in the Air Force. Pearl reenlisted in 1966 and was told he would not be sent to Vietnam. In a letter sent to his parents the week before his death, he said he was scheduled to leave Vietnam in a few days. Marine Pvt. Darwin Brandon, 20, from Columbus, was injured on July 25 in a vehicle crash in Quang Nam Province. He died the next day from his injuries.

During August, nearly two dozen soldiers from Ohio lost their lives in the Vietnam conflict, including eighteen members of the Army, four Marines, and one each from the Air Force and Navy. The deadliest day of the month came on August 25, when three soldiers died. That day's list of casualties was Army SP4 John Jasso from Rudolph, Army Carl Dunn from Chillicothe, and Marine Lance Cpl. Richard Savieo from Fostoria. Jasso, 19, died from a booby trap while serving in Binh Dinh Province, while Cpl. Dunn, 27, the oldest of the three casualties that day, was killed while in Quang Ngai Province. Marine Savieo, 21, died from wounds he received while in combat in Quang Nam Province. Finally, Cpl. Dunn's body arrived in the states the same day his daughter was born.

Air Force Capt. John Powell, 30, from Dayton, was scheduled to complete his duty tour in less than forty-five days. However, he was killed when his plane went down over Quang Tri Province on August 13. His twin sister, who had never been to a funeral or visited a cemetery, was placed in charge of all her brother's funeral arrangements, including the choice of a casket. She chose a bronze one.

The lone Navy man to die during August was Hospital Corpsman Second Class Michael Kempel from Cuyahoga Falls. He died in the Arizona Territory in Quang Nam Province while serving with the Marines. Kempel, a Boy Scout, was wounded when he stepped on a mine while running to the aid of a wounded soldier and died as he attempted to crawl toward the hurt soldier. Following his death, fellow medics took up a collection, purchased Kempel's son a savings bond, and sent flowers to his funeral. He celebrated his twenty-second birthday on July 22.

Army Cpl. David Amheiser was nineteen when he was killed in combat from small arms fire on August 29. He had been in Vietnam less than two months and was from Lodi. A medic serving with Amheiser's unit in Phuoc Long Province wrote in a post on *Faces on the Wall* that Amheiser "*...did his duty without complaint. A man who allowed himself to be placed at the very forefront of battle, and gave his life as a warning of the insueing (sp.) battle....*" Among Cpl. Amheiser's awards include the Oak Leaf Cluster, a Purple Heart, and two Bronze Stars.

Sixteen Ohio soldiers lost their lives during September. The number includes ten members of the Army, five Marines, and one member of the Navy. Additionally, four members of the military died on consecutive days...September 18–21.

The list included Army 1st Lt. James DuPont, 23, who died from small arms fire when his platoon was ambushed while on patrol in Binh Thuy Province. A thirteen-year-old student from Steubenville, Ohio, began corresponding with DuPont as part of a class project. The two remained regular pen pals throughout his time in-country. Among DuPont's prize possessions was his boat that was waiting for him back in Westerville. He carried a picture of the boat while he was in Vietnam.

The following day, September 19, fighting claimed the life of Army Cpl. Frank Miller, 18, from Athens. He had been in Vietnam for thirty-five days and would have turned nineteen in less than two months. Cpl. Miller, killed in Binh Dinh

Province from small arms fire, surprised many of his family and friends by enlisting in the Army.

Marine Lance Cpl. Michael McVey, 19, from Cleveland, died in Quang Nam Province on September 20 from non-combat injuries. He had been in the Marines for less than one year and had been in Vietnam for eighty-eight days.

Navy First Class Petty Officer Kenna Taylor, a twenty-two-year military veteran from Shadyside, died from a heart attack while stationed in Quang Tin Province. He was sixty-two years old and had also served in WWII and Korea. Taylor was the oldest Ohio soldier to die in Vietnam and the oldest U.S. soldier to die in the conflict.

———

Despite the low number of Ohio military casualties in Southeast Asia in some time, around fourteen, the number of reported deaths during October may have been overshadowed by the airplane crash involving a college football team.

On October 2, buses carrying Wichita State University football team members, coaches, staff, and boosters departed the school for the twenty-minute ride to Eisenhower National Airport. They were going to Logan, Utah, for a Saturday football game against Utah State. Upon arrival at the airport, they found two planes waiting on them. However, these were not the planes the athletic department had contracted to fly the group to the game. The contract was for the players, coaches, and others to fly to Logan and back to Kansas in two DC-6B planes. Instead, everyone going to the game would be transported by two other aircraft of different make and model. The two planes, one nicknamed the "Gold" and the other "Black" for the school's colors, departed the airport shortly after arriving. The submitted flight plan would take them from Eisenhower Airport to the Denver Stapleton Airport, where the two planes would be refueled, and then on to Utah for the game.

The "Gold" aircraft carried forty passengers, including the twenty starters on the football team, coaches, their wives, and a crew of five. The "Black" plane carried the reserve players, assistant coaches, boosters, etc.

At some point following the Denver stop, the pilot of the "Gold" plane deviated from the original flight plan to give his passengers a more scenic route over the Rocky Mountains. The second plane stayed on its original course, taking them over southern Wyoming. Not long into the second leg of the flight, the pilots of the "Gold" plane determined that they were flying too low to make it over the Colorado mountains. They decided to make a U-turn and head east toward Denver. By then, it was too late. Investigators later determined the "Gold" plane crashed into Mt. Bethel in the Arapaho National Forest just after 1:00pm. The crash killed twenty-nine at the scene, including fourteen on the football team.

Meanwhile, as the nation was reeling from the loss of lives from this tragedy and investigators sought answers to why this event happened, fourteen Ohio soldiers died between October 4 and the end of the month. The number of military lives lost in Southeast Asia during that time includes ten from the U.S. Army, two from the Air Force, and one from the Marines and the Navy.

Among those killed during the first two weeks of the month was Army Capt. Warren Kindsvatter, 27, from Cincinnati. An intelligence officer, he died in a vehicle accident in Vinh Long Province on October 4. Capt. Kindsvatter was buried in the Gate of Heaven Cemetery in Montgomery. Five days later, the conflict in Southeast Asia claimed the lives of two Ohio soldiers: Sgt. Raymond Moore from Cincinnati, and SP5 James Turner from Columbus.

On October 9, Moore, Turner, and three other soldiers were being extracted along the banks of the Dong Nai River in Long Khanh Province when their helicopter's blades clipped a bamboo thicket and crashed into the river's swift waters. Army personnel searched for ten days for the soldiers onboard the downed aircraft. Unfortunately, the bodies of Sgt. Moore, SP5 Turner, and three others were never recovered and remain missing in action.

On Columbus Day, October 12, President Nixon announced that troop levels in Vietnam would be reduced from the current level of over 385,000 to under 350,000 by the end of the year. The number would be substantially less than in April 1969, when troops in the region numbered over 540,000. The same day, Marine Staff Sgt. Theodore Rowley lost his life in Quang Nam Province from a booby trap. Rowley, 27, enlisted in the Marines in 1960 at age seventeen and had served four tours of overseas duty. He had a brother that was killed in action during WWII. Sgt. Rowley was buried in New Bern National Cemetery in New Bern, North Carolina.

The remaining weeks of the month would record the deaths of at least eight more Ohio soldiers, including five members of the Army, two from the Air Force, and one from the Navy. Airman First Class John Thayer, 19, from Toledo, died from his injuries after he was hit by a truck at Qui Nhon Airbase in Binh Dinh Province on October 17. At the time of his death, Thayer had a brother in the Air Force that was stationed in Japan. The second member of the Air Force to die during October was Capt. Craig Schiele, 27, from Steubenville. He died when his helicopter was shot down on October 24 in Khammouan Province, Laos, while attempting to rescue Laotian troops from approaching North Vietnamese troops. Growing up, he was in the scouts, while his father was a Scoutmaster and his mother was a Den Mother. Following graduation from Steubenville High School, the younger Schiele went on to graduate from MIT (Massachusetts Institute of Technology) with a degree in Chemical Engineering. Wanting to choose his own path in life, he enlisted in the Air Force after receiving a high draft number, which meant he would likely be called into the military. Capt.

Schiele, who was scheduled to return to the states around Thanksgiving, was buried at Arlington National Cemetery with full military honors.

The lone Navy member to die during October was Petty Officer Second Class Frederick Nutter, 24, from Zanesville. A radarman, he was killed on October 18 from a booby trap while serving in Quang Nam Province. A fellow member of the Navy wrote that Nutter…

> *"…was the type of individual that always left an impression on all who served with him in the Navy. He brought humor, a deep sense of commitment, and in CIC was one of the best radio operater's (sp.) and navigational plotters I've known…." (post, Faces on the Wall).*

Born in Peru, Indiana, he was buried less than thirty minutes away in Burlington.

Despite registering the lowest casualty rate of the conflict in five years and the fifth consecutive week the death toll for American soldiers was below fifty, there were Ohioans still dying in Southeast Asia. The first twelve days of November saw the number of Ohio soldiers killed increase by three.

On November 4, Marine Lance Corporal Ray Arnett from Dayton was killed by small arms fire while on patrol in Quang Nam Province. Arnett, 19, arrived in Vietnam in March, and his monthly pay included a base salary of $167, hostile fire pay of $65, and an additional $9 foreign duty pay. Two days later, on November 6, a second U.S. Marine from Ohio died in Vietnam. Sgt. Meredith Barnett, from Belpre, was killed in Quang Nam Province from friendly fire when a reconnaissance team called in artillery fire, believing they had encountered an enemy patrol. He was one of two Marines killed that day in the accident. According to the report,

177

"...Sergeant Barnett's platoon came under artillery attack, the first round which detonated approximately two hundred yards distant. As more rounds were heard coming in, and with members of the platoon unable to reach covered positions, Sergeant Barnett rushed to the Marine nearest him and threw himself on top of the man seconds before another round detonated only ten feet away. Although mortally wounded by this explosion, Sergeant Barnett succeeded in protecting his companion." (Coffelt Database of Vietnam Casualties)

As a result of his actions that day, Sgt. Barnett was awarded the Silver Star. He would have celebrated his twenty-first birthday in fifteen days.

Fellow Ohio soldiers Army Cpl. William Reed, 19, from Hamilton, and SP4 John Conrad, 22, from Fremont, died two days apart. Cpl. Reed died on November 12 in Quang Ngai Province when his truck, the third in a column, hit a mine placed in the road. The convoy was on its way to deliver supplies to a forward firebase. The mine, which left a crater four feet wide and eight feet deep, killed a total of seven American soldiers. Cpl. Reed had been in Vietnam for twenty-nine days. SP4 Conrad, one of fifteen members of the Army killed on November 14, died in Phu Yen Province. Like Reed, Conrad was part of a resupply convoy to deliver supplies to troops when a command-detonated mine went off in the road.

However tragic, the deaths of these last two soldiers may have been overshadowed when a second airplane crash involving a college football team happened less than six weeks after the WSU crash.

Following a game on November 14 against East Carolina University in which the visiting team lost by three points, a DC-9 plane left a Kinston, North Carolina, airport, headed for Tri-State Airport in Huntington, West Virginia. Onboard the aircraft were seventy-five people, including thirty-seven Marshall University Thundering Herd football team players, over two dozen boosters, eight members of the coaching staff, and a crew of five. This was the team's only flight scheduled that year since most away games were within driving distance.

Around 7:20pm, the crew contacted air traffic controllers at the Huntington Airport. The pilots were told to descend to 5,000 feet and that there was rain, fog, and smoke in the area. Not long after 7:30pm, the crew reported to the tower they had passed the airport's outer marker and were continuing their descent, despite not seeing the airport's runway or lights. At 7:34pm, the plane clipped the tops of several trees on a hillside, causing the aircraft to flip and land nose-first in a nearby ravine. The plane, engulfed in flames from burning jet fuel, came to rest around three-quarters of a mile short of the runway. All seventy-five aboard the aircraft died. The crash remains one of the deadliest sports-related tragedies in American history.

Between November 14 and the end of the month, an additional twelve Ohio soldiers would die in Southeast Asia, including ten members of the U.S. Army, one of the Marines, and one from the Air Force. The last week of the month saw the death of no less than ten Army soldiers. This includes two Army soldiers killed on November 24. Pfc. David Bryan, 20, from North Canton, was killed from a booby trap while serving in Quang Ngai Province. SP4 Norman Paley, 20, a helicopter door gunner from Mentor, died in a helicopter crash over Laos while attempting to extract soldiers from the enemy. Not long before his death, he had the chance to visit with his brother aboard a ship anchored off Da Nang. SP4 Paley was buried in All Souls Cemetery in Chardon.

Two days later, there was a total of six soldiers that lost their lives in the conflict, and one-third of those were from Ohio. One of the soldiers killed was Army Pfc. David Killian, 19, from Toledo, who died in Quang Nam Province. Before joining the Army, he worked on the railroad. Also passing on that day was Chief Warrant Officer Philip Richard, 21, from South

Euclid. A helicopter pilot, he had recently returned from R&R in Hawaii and died when his aircraft experienced engine failure during take-off and crashed in Quang Ngai Province. It is believed that the family, including Richard's father, a retired lieutenant colonel, and former POW, had just sat down for their Thanksgiving meal when a green Army vehicle pulled up to the house. After answering the door, he motioned the officers in. Then, without saying a word, the elder Richard immediately saluted the two officers. WO Richard's father knew why the officers had come. The younger Richard, whose older brother had recently returned from Vietnam because of injuries, was scheduled to go home to Ohio in two weeks to get married.

A third major airplane crash in two months made national headlines the day after Thanksgiving. This time, however, those that perished would not be football players but mostly military personnel on their way to serve in Southeast Asia.

A chartered flight carrying two hundred and nineteen passengers and a crew of ten departed McChord Field in Tacoma, Washington, on Friday, November 27, 1970. The passengers were mostly Army and Air Force personnel headed for duty in Southeast Asia as replacements. The final destination for the DC-9 was Cam Ranh Bay, South Vietnam, following stopovers for fuel in Anchorage, Alaska, and Yokota, Japan.

After taking on fuel in Anchorage, the aircraft began its trek down the runway just after dark in cold temperatures and drizzling rain. Before long, the pilots noticed the plane had not reached a sufficient speed and aborted the takeoff. Unfortunately, it was too late to safely stop the aircraft, and it crashed and began burning. Forty-seven individuals died, including twenty-five members of the Air Force and twenty-one from the Army. Among the deceased was Air Force Tech

Sgt. Earl Halley from Vienna, West Virginia. It was later determined that the unintentional braking of the aircraft caused the tragedy.

———————

Less than twenty-four hours later, no fewer than forty-nine soldiers, twenty-seven from the Army, seventeen from the Air Force, four Marines, and one from the Navy lost their lives in regional fighting. Among the casualties were three from Ohio who died on November 28. Cpl. Robert Koly, 21, from Parma, died in Quang Tin Province from a booby trap. Also passing was Pfc. Albert Hall, 21, from Cleveland, and Marine Lance Corporal Craig Ward, from Dayton. Pfc. Hall died in Gia Dinh Province, while Ward, also twenty-one, was killed from small arms fire while serving in Quang Nam Province.

The following day, November 29, three more Ohio soldiers died. Army SP4 George Beedy, 19, was among thirty U.S. troops killed when their plane crashed into a mountain range outside of Cam Ranh Bay in Ninh Thuan Province in bad weather. He was twenty-one and from Springfield. Also killed in the same flight was Air Force 1st Lt. Elmon Caudill from Berea. While attending the USAF Academy in Colorado Springs, Colorado, he was on the Pistol Team and the Dean's List. According to a post on his *Findagrave* page, *"...He was on his way to Cam Ranh Bay to catch the freedom bird home...."* The only personal item recovered at the crash site was his class ring. 1st Lt. Caudill was 25. The last Ohio soldier casualty, and the third to die on the next to the last day of November, was Army SP5 Phelbon Green from Toledo. SP5 Green, 21, died when the truck he was driving was suddenly caught in a flash flood in Thua Thien Province.

———————

During the closing month of 1970, no less than fourteen "Sons of Ohio" died in Southeast Asia. The number includes one soldier that lost his life during the first week, Army Sgt. Bruce Spring of Wadsworth. Born on Valentine's Day, he died on December 5 in a land mine accident at FSB Buttons in Phuoc Long Province. Among his awards were the Silver Star, the Purple Heart, and two Bronze Stars. A fellow soldier wrote on *Faces on the Wall* that Spring *"...was a solid man of character. A gentleman. A Father. And a proud American. And so much more...."*

Spring would be the third soldier from Wadsworth to die in 1970 and the thirteenth overall from the city of thirteen thousand residents.

Over the next two weeks, seven Ohio soldiers would be killed in Vietnam. On December 11, Army Staff Sgt. Bernard Swiger died in Binh Thuy Province when his helicopter was brought down by enemy fire. He was thirty and from Madison. Two days later, two more Ohioans were killed while fighting in Vietnam. Marine Lance Cpl. Donald Jenkins was from Cleveland and died in Quang Nam Province from friendly fire. He died one week after celebrating his twenty-third birthday. Army NCO Medic and SP4 Timothy Thompson, 20, from Norwalk, was killed in Quang Ngai Province after stepping off a helicopter and onto a booby trap. The explosion shattered the glass vials he was carrying, making it impossible for him to receive morphine for his fatal wounds. He had a daughter that was born while he was in Vietnam.

Four Ohio soldiers died between December 16 and December 19, including Army soldier SP4 Robert Callan from Youngstown, who was fatally wounded in Thua Thien Province on December 16 from ground fire while a door gunner on a helicopter. He was twenty. 1st Lt. Raymond Flynn, 24, a helicopter pilot from Toledo, died on December 17 from wounds he received on December 2. Pfc. Elwood Baker, 20, from Toronto, died the following day when his boat capsized in Long Khanh Province. Navy Chief Petty Officer Johnny Ratliff was from Washington Court House. He died on December 19 when his helicopter suddenly went down in An Xugen Province. His body, along with the bodies of three others onboard the aircraft, was found three days later by a seven-year-old Vietnamese girl. Ratliff was thirty-two.

The list of Ohio casualties killed in the last week of December included four members of the Army, one Marine, and one from the Navy. Among the list was Army Cpl. Finley Rice, 19, from Athens, died in a rocket attack while serving at FSB Apache in Binh Duong Province. Two soldiers, one member of the Army and one Marine, were killed on Christmas Eve, 1970. Pfc. William McLean, 18, from Glouster, died while clearing mines in Phuoc Long Province. He was the only boy of five children and had been in Vietnam for fourteen days. After arriving for basic training at Fort Dix, his local newspaper, the *Athens Messenger*, ran his military address so friends and local townspeople could write him. Marine Lance Cpl. Michael Tecco was from Cleveland and was accidentally killed in Quang Nam Province. He was 21 and had four brothers and a sister.

Army Pfc. Richard Knickerbocker, from Youngstown, was hospitalized on December 14 when he stepped on a Claymore mine and was seriously wounded in Thua Thien Province. Over the next eleven days while in a hospital, he celebrated his twentieth birthday on December 16, and his wife, unbeknownst to Pfc. Knickerbocker, gave birth to a baby girl on December 22. Marine Knickerbocker, whose parents were officers in the local Salvation Army, had six brothers, one in the military in Pennsylvania, and four sisters. He passed away on Christmas Day.

On December 29, Army Sgt. Robert Curtis from Springfield died in Quang Nam Province. He was forty-one and was buried at Fort Bragg Main Post Cemetery in North Carolina.

Among the sixteen Army and five Navy members that died on the last day of the year was Navy E3 Wayne Rushton, 21, from Eastlake. He was a Seabee and had arrived in Vietnam on November 6. E3 Rushton, who was headed for R&R, was among six individuals in a boat. However, the vessel's regular operator, who typically took the soldiers to their departure point, was on leave himself, so getting the sailors to their pick-up point was placed on the shoulders of a substitute unfamiliar with the route. When the vessel did not show up at its arrival point for several hours, a search team was dispatched to find them. The small boat was later found with all onboard dead. It is believed that the boat's driver got lost when he took a wrong turn on one of the countless dead-end canals in Bien Hoa Province. As the group was trying to exit the canal, they were ambushed by Viet Cong in a sampan. The only weapons on the U.S. vessel afterward were three rifles and a pistol. This tragedy is believed to be the deadliest loss of Seabees since WWII.

1971

The first soldier casualty from Ohio in the new year died on January 3. Army Chief Warrant Officer Kenneth Powers, 32, from Cincinnati, died in Phuoc Tuy Province. He had been in Vietnam for forty-seven days. WO Powers was married and had two sons.

Army SP4 Gerald Hill and SP4 Robert Michalk were among fourteen soldiers, twelve Army personnel and two members of the Navy, to lose their lives in Southeast Asia on January 7. SP4 Hill, 20, from Milford, was most likely killed in an ambush in Binh Dinh Province as he and members of his unit were returning to LZ Uplift following a three-day mission in the jungle. SP4 Michalk, also 20, died from an explosion while investigating an ammunition dump in Quang Nam Province that had killed five Koreans and two civilians earlier. The accident was said to be the worst ammunition explosion in South Vietnam in two years. His sister posted on *Faces on the Wall* that…

> *"…He was the best kind of brother. He had my dad sign a permission form so he could join the Army early so he could send my parents most of his pay for his six sisters and one brother. He sacrificed everything for us…"*

Michalk, from Alliance, was on his third tour of duty and had been in Vietnam for around seventeen days.

Less than one week later, on January 12, a fourth soldier from Ohio was killed in the region. Army SP4 Billy Price, a radio operator, was killed in Thua Thien Province from a booby trap. He had celebrated his nineteen birthday forty-three days earlier.

Over the next two weeks, seven soldiers from Ohio would be killed in the regional conflict, including two soldiers on January 16 and two more eleven days later. The first two soldier casualties were Army Sgt. Herbert Hinson, 23, from Cincinnati, and Army Pfc. Bruce from Marietta. Sgt. Hinson, known by many nicknames including Blue, Earnie, and Monger, was active in his high school band, the Camera Club, the Spanish Club, and ran track. He was twenty-three and was killed from a booby trap in Quang Ngai Province. Army Pfc. Bruce Shover, 20, from Marietta, had been in Vietnam for less than forty days when he was killed in Binh Dinh Province. He was one of three soldiers killed on patrol when a landmine exploded nearby. A fourth soldier, running to offer aid to his fellow soldiers, tripped a booby trap and was killed. Pfc. Shover enlisted nine months before his passing.

Killed on consecutive days was Army Pfc. Ronald Garrison and Staff Sgt. Kenneth Lovelace. Pfc. Garrison, 19, from Canton, died on January 21 from small arms fire while serving in Long Khanh Province. Sgt. Lovelace, 27, was from Bellefontaine. He volunteered to go into an enemy zone in Bien Hoa Province to look for survivors of a downed helicopter. As part of the mission, his helicopter hovered over an open field, and a rope ladder was being dropped. As he descended the ladder, the aircraft began receiving enemy ground fire and crashed. There are no less than six accounts from fellow soldiers who were either part of the mission and survived or were in other helicopters and saw the crash of Sgt. Lovelace's aircraft. He is remembered by one high school classmate as one who *"...always dressed to nines loafers, buttondown shirts tan back buckle pants or pressed jeans (sp.)...." (Faces on the Wall)*. Sgt. Lovelace is buried in Highland Memorial Cemetery in West Liberty, Ohio.

Three additional Ohio soldiers would die before the month was out in the conflict. Army Cpl. Roberto was from Toledo and died from small arms fire while serving in Phuoc Long Province. He was twenty-one and had been in Vietnam for seventeen days. Also killed on January 27 was Air Force Capt. John Neill from Hiram. He was a fighter jet pilot and was shot down over Cambodia seven days before his twenty-eighth birthday.

On the last day of the month, SP4 Larry Pepper died from wounds he received in Quang Tin Province four months earlier. According to a post on *Faces on the Wall*, SP4 Pepper

> *"...was the fourth person in a line behind the point man, a scout dog and its handler, and a newly in-country soldier on possibly his first mission. At some point during the patrol, the point man stepped over a booby trap without detonating it. The scout dog in the slack position, however, alerted and his handler signaled for the column to stop. Reportedly, the new soldier didn't understand the signal or didn't see it and moved past the scout dog team triggering the explosion. Shrapnel from the blast hit SP4 Pepper...."*

He was helicoptered first to a nearby military hospital and then to a medical facility in Japan. Finally, when he was well enough to be transported to the states, he was admitted to a

Veterans Administration Hospital in Chillicothe, less than forty miles from the family home in Jeffersonville. He died from his wounds on January 31 at age twenty-one.

———————

No less than eighteen soldiers from the Buckeye State died in February, including six during the first fourteen days and twelve during the last two weeks of the month. On February 3, Army Sgt. Terrence Weldon, from Cincinnati, was killed from small arms fire during an enemy attack on FSB Bandit II in Bien Hoa Province. He enlisted on Valentine's Day, 1969. Moreover, he was twenty-two days from celebrating his twenty-fourth birthday. Four days later, Army Cpl. Douglas Schmaltz would be killed during night combat from small arms fire while serving in Quang Tri Province. He was twenty.

During the next six days, eighty-six U.S. soldiers, including four from Ohio, would lose their lives in the region. Army Sgt. Joseph Pietrzak, 26, was part of a two-person crew onboard a helicopter conducting visual surveillance when it was brought down from enemy ground fire in Thua Thien Province, near the Laotian border. He died on February 10 and was buried in Arlington National Cemetery. Sgt. Pietrzak, 26, was the third soldier from Roseville to die in the conflict and the second soldier from the town of less than 1,800 in the last eight months. The following day, Army SP4 George Huston, from Cleveland, died from rocket/mortar fire while serving at Ca Lu Airfield in Quang Tri Province. SP4 Hutson, 21, was one of three American soldiers killed in the attack. Army SP4 Michael Adkins and Army Capt. Kenneth Price died on February 13 in separate episodes. SP4 Adkins, 19, from Jamestown, died while serving in Quang Nam Province, while Capt. Price, from Windsor, drown at the mouth of the Da Rang River in Phu Yen Province. He was twenty-nine and had been in-country for thirty-seven days.

Most of the eighteen Ohio soldiers to die in Southeast Asia during the last two weeks of February, including seventeen members of the Army and one Marine, would pass away between February 15 and February 28. Army Pfc. James Brobst, who had celebrated his twenty-first birthday on February 11, died in Quang Tri Province four days later when another soldier accidentally shot him. Pfc. Brobst graduated from Southeast High School and worked for Republic Steel before enlisting in 1968. Additionally, he had been in Vietnam for less than two months, was on his second tour of duty, and was scheduled to return home to Newton Falls in October. He was the third soldier from the city to die in the last eleven months. Three days later, the conflict in Vietnam would claim the lives of Army Pfc. Early Grace from Cincinnati and Marine Allen McElfresh from Zanesville. Pfc. Grace, 19, a tall and lean man who loved to sing, died in Khanh Hoa Province from drowning. He was a member of the Military Police. Sgt. McElfresh, 21, known by his family as Buzzy, was aboard a helicopter with eight other soldiers when the aircraft experienced sudden mechanical issues and crashed in Thua Thien Province.

Over the next five days, between February 20 and 24, no less than seven Ohio soldiers would be recorded as casualties. Army soldiers Cpl. Daniel Hohman, from Caldwell, and 1St Lt. John Hunter, from New Philadelphia, would die on the third Friday in February. Pfc. Hohman, 20, was killed in Quang Tin Province by a booby trap. Capt. Hunter attended Ohio University and was a member of the Sigma Chi fraternity. After two years at school in Athens, he enlisted in the Army in 1967. Hunter was described by a fellow soldier who roomed with him at Ft. Rucker as quiet and reflective. While in Vietnam, Capt. Hunter, a helicopter pilot, made a deal with a fellow soldier that if the other soldier died first, Hunter would get the soldier's air conditioner. The other soldier would get his mattress and box spring if Hunter died first. Capt. Hunter, who celebrated his twenty-fourth birthday thirteen days before, was shot while flying a mission over Quang Tri Province. The mattress and box spring were delivered on February 21. A female wrote that Capt. Hunter *"...was so handsome and tall..."* and *"...didn't have a mean bone in his body and was kind to everyone. I can't imagine him with a gun in his hand...." (Faces on the Wall)*

Two soldiers from Cleveland, Army SP4 Edward Downey, 21, and SP4 Richard Martin, 20, were killed on February 21. A high school classmate's post on *Faces on the Wall* proclaimed that *"...You and I were without doubt the fastest runners at the school and I guess that was good because we avoided the gangs that way...."* After graduating in 1968, SP4 Downey worked for the Erie Railroad and attended Youngstown State University. He died from small arms fire while in Quang Tri Province, three hundred and sixty-two days after joining the military. SP4 Martin is a 1969 graduate of Hempfield High School and was a star on the football team. While engaged in combat in Thua Thien Province, he was killed by U.S. planes as they were firing on the enemy. On February 22, Cpl. Edward Scott was killed from small arms fire while in combat in Binh Dinh Province. He was the second soldier from Parma to be killed in Vietnam in the past two weeks.

February 23 and 24 recorded the deaths of two Army soldiers from Akron. Early in the morning of February 23, the Viet Cong attacked FSB Blue in Tay Ninh Province near the Cambodian border. Five soldiers, all crew members on the same anti-aircraft vehicle, were killed when an explosive was thrown into their quarters. The list of those killed included Pfc. Ronald Fisher, 22. He is buried next to his parents at a cemetery in his hometown of Akron.

The day before Halloween, 1970, Army Capt. Dennis Smith volunteered to fly his helicopter to assist in evacuating approximately seven hundred South Vietnamese citizens from rising flood waters in Thua Thien Province. In pitch darkness, he landed his helicopter, jumped into the swift waters, and proceeded to swim toward a nearby pagoda where a group of civilians were hold up. He made five trips back and forth to the stranded civilians, bringing back a total of four adults and three children to his helicopter. For his heroism, he was awarded a citation. Less than four months later, on February 24, Capt. Smith, 27, would die from wounds he received when a booby trap went off near him while in a combat operation…in Thua Thien Province.

On the next to last day of the month, the Vietnam conflict would claim the lives of Army Sgt. Fred Mooney and SP4 Kevin Thorne. Sgt. Mooney, 36, from Northrup, was a door gunner aboard a helicopter that went down over Laos during Operation Dewey Canyon II on February 27. Reports are that "*…he was not required to fly, but volunteered to show the younger draftees that old lifers could be as tough as they were…" (Faces on the Wall)*. It is believed that Sgt. Mooney and the pilot survived the initial crash but were killed by small arms fire when they exited the aircraft. The two bodies were never recovered. Army SP4 Kevin Thorne, 20, was from Englewood and played center on his high school football team. He was killed from small arms fire near Highway QL-19 while serving in Pleiku Province. SP4 Thorne, who was awarded two Bronze Stars, had turned twenty-two on February 3. He was buried in Seneca, South Carolina.

With twenty-four recorded military casualties from Ohio, March would become the costliest month for Buckeye soldiers since August 1970. The twenty-four would include twenty members of the U.S. Army, two from the Air Force, and two from the Navy. During the first seven days, an average of one Ohio soldier would die each day.

Air Force Airman First Class Karl Gantz was the first Ohio

soldier to die during the month. A native of Louisville, in Stark County, Gantz, 19, was a member of a loading crew stationed at Phu Cat Air Base in Binh Dinh Province. While performing a routine check on one of the aircraft, the plane's guns inadvertently discharged several rounds into Airman Gantz, killing him. He was covering the shift for another airman that had become sick. Airman Gantz had around ninety days left on his tour and was looking forward to returning to the states and seeing his wife and new baby.

One day later, Army Medical Officer Paul Bright and Navy Petty Officer First Class Andrew Toth were killed in separate incidents. NCO Bright, 26, from Columbus, died from injuries received on Valentine's Day when his vehicle was hit with a rifle-propelled grenade while traveling in Quang Tri Province. In addition to a wife and son, he had five brothers. PO Toth, 45, was born on Memorial Day, 1925, and had spent twenty-five years in the military, including active deployment in the Korean War. A native of Lorain, he died in Quang Nam Province and was buried in Martins Ferry.

At least one Ohio soldier would die every other day between March 3 and March 9. The first Ohio casualty was

Army SP4 Paul Sgambati from Girard. Born on Veterans Day 1950, he attended Rider High School. SP4 Sgambati, 20, was helicopter crew chief and was wounded by small arms fire on March 3, when his aircraft was attempting to land during a mission in Laos. He was flown to a hospital in Quang Tri Province, where he later died.

Army Capt. Ralph Ward, 28, was among seventeen soldiers from across the U.S. killed on March 5. He graduated from OCS (Officer Candidate School) in September 1968 and had further training as a helicopter pilot. While attempting to land at an airfield in Binh Dinh Province, a Korean observation aircraft clipped Ward's Chinook helicopter causing it to crash to the ground and burn. Capt. Ward and all four of his passengers onboard his aircraft died. He was from

Hamden in Vinton County, the state's least populated county.

Forty-eight hours later, Army *SP4 Phillip Brandon*, 19, from Beallsville, died in Thua Thien Province from small arms fire. His vehicle was ambushed while traveling on Highway QL-1. SP4 Brandon was the tenth soldier from Monroe County to die in the Vietnam conflict.

On March 9, Army Cpl. Robert Schoenhoff, 23, died from small arms fire while on search and rescue operations in Quang Tri Province. He began his tour of duty on Halloween 1970 and was an only child.

Between March 12 and 29, no less than sixteen Ohio soldiers would die in regional fighting in Southeast Asia. The first of the fourteen members of the Army from the state to die was Army Sgt. Jerry Kuney. He was a member of the 73rd Signal Battalion and died while serving in Ninh Thuan/Khanh Hoa Province at age twenty-eight. Sgt. Kuney was on his second tour of duty. He had five sisters and three brothers, one of which had recently returned home from his second tour in the military. At the time of his passing, his hometown of Fayette had less than twelve hundred residents. Over the next four days, four more Ohio soldiers were killed in Vietnam, including one from Cincinnati, Huron, Cambridge, and Marietta.

Army Pfc. Ronald Jackson, 20, from Cincinnati, died in Thua Thien Province on March 14. Before deploying to Vietnam, he completed his basic training at Ft. Leonard Wood and advanced training at Ft. Ord in California. Pfc. Jackson, who was returning after a night mission and was fatally wounded after being mistaken for the enemy, had been in-country for twenty-six days. On March 15, Sgt. David Sexton, 22, from Huron, was a member of a cannon crew and lost his life in Quang Tri Province. Sgt. Sexton's wife was told of his passing not long before she gave birth to their firstborn, a son. The elder Sexton was due to return home in two weeks, and his remains have yet to be recovered. One day later, SP4 Clifford Bench, 18, from Cambridge, died from small arms fire while serving in Binh Dinh Province. A

1970 graduate of Cambridge High School, he was awarded the Silver Star. The last of the four Ohio soldiers to pass away between March 14 and 17 was Air Force Capt. Douglas Seely from Marietta. He was the pilot of an aircraft hit by enemy ground fire over Laos and went down on March 17. Like SP4 Sexton, his remains have yet to be located.

During the last ten days of March, no less than ten U.S. soldiers from Ohio were killed in the conflict. Army Cpl. Thomas Kingsley, from Toledo, was on a mission in Bien Hoa Province with three other soldiers when an explosive device, placed there by friendly forces, detonated. In high school, he was an outstanding wrestler and went on to attend Ohio University. In a letter written two months before his death, he wrote to a friend back home in the states, saying…

"I firmly believe that I will not leave here without being shot or injured first. And it seems no one gives a damn besides us grunts in the bush. You people in the world don't know what's happening because the Army won't let you know…as long as the death count is reasonable-say under 40 a week…Don't tell Mom or Dad or Mary about this letter because they think everything is ok." (Harper's Magazine, June 1974)

Cpl. Kingsley died on March 20, two weeks after celebrating his 24th birthday.

Meanwhile, two Army soldiers and one Marine would die during the following three days. Army Pfc. William Glenn was twenty-two when he died from small arms fire in Quang Tri Province on the first full day of spring 1971. He was nineteen, married, and from Toledo. Army Cpl. Jeffrey Keetle, 22, from Akron, was killed the day after in an early morning attack at his base at Khe Sanh in Quang Tri Province. He was one of four soldiers killed during the attack and was on guard duty when the enemy attack began around 2:30am. Cpl. Kettle was cremated. Some of his remains are interred at a mausoleum in his hometown of Ashland, and the rest are scattered in the Gila Wilderness in New Mexico. The last Ohio soldier to die during those four days in March was Marine 1st Lt. Ronald Yale from Cuyahoga Falls. He was a pilot and was scheduled to leave Vietnam for redeployment in the Philippines. Instead, he drowned when his aircraft malfunctioned on the way to his new base and was forced to eject into the South China Sea off Quang Tri Province. Capt. Yale, twenty-five, was the only Marine among twenty members of the Army to die on March 24.

The next four days would be extremely costly for Ohio soldiers as seven "native sons" would die in regional fighting in Vietnam. Army Cpl. Albert Vencel, from Warren, was killed in Binh Dinh Province on March 26 from a booby trap. He had turned twenty on February 26. Less than forty-eight hours later would mark the single costliest day for U.S. soldiers in some time.

During the early morning of March 28, over four dozen enemy soldiers began an assault on FSB Mary Ann in Quang Tin Province. After breaking through the outer perimeter of the camp, the enemy then began firing mortars. This was followed by enemy soldiers tossing explosives into buildings and bunkers. After nearly ninety minutes of close combat, almost three dozen American soldiers, including four from Ohio, were dead. Among the dead U.S. soldiers was Army Sgt. Ronald Becksted, from Cleveland, and Sgt. Larry McKee, from nearby Delaware, Ohio. Also killed in the surprise attack was Cpl. Donald Bennett from New Lexington, and SP4 Victor Bennett from Haskins. Sgt. Becksted was less than sixty days from completing his tour of duty. A teenage friend from his hometown, who remembers playing pool with Sgt. McKee at the local recreation center, commented on *Faces on the Wall* that the friend *"...can only hope they have pool tables wherever you (McKee) are...."* Cpl. Bennett, whose father served in the Navy in WWII, was a lifeguard at the local pool in his younger days. SP4 Bennett, whose father also served in WWII, had three sisters and four brothers. He was the only one of the four Ohio soldiers that was married. Moreover, all four soldiers were twenty and were born within ten months of each other. Sgt. Becksted was born in February 1950, Sp4 Bennett in August, and Cpl. Bennett in November. Sgt. McKee, the youngest of the group, was born in December. Finally, all four Ohio soldiers began their tour of duty within six months of each other: Sgt. Becksted in May 1970, Cpl. Bennett in June, SP4 Bennett in July, and Sgt. McKee in November.

The last of the two dozen Ohio soldiers to die in March was Army Staff Sgt. Andrew Steward, from Columbus. He died on March 29 when his vehicle ran off the road and plunged into a river in Quang Tri Province, drowning the twenty-five-year-old serviceman.

Six Ohio soldiers would die in Vietnam during the first seven days of April. Army SP4 George Youngerman began his tour of duty on July 4, 1970. SP4 Youngerman, the last of three soldiers from Vandalia to die in the conflict, was killed from small arms fire at the age of twenty-one in Quang Tri Province. He was an only child. His older cousin by eighteen months, Pfc. Michael Youngerman, 22, was killed the following day, April 2, in Binh Dinh Province by small arms fire. Pfc. Youngerman was on his second tour of duty and had been in Vietnam for thirty-seven days. His father served in WWII. Pfc. Youngerman's name appears on the Vietnam Memorial…one line below his cousin's.

On April 2, two Ohio soldiers were among the thirteen U.S. service members that lost their lives that day in Southeast Asia. Army 1st Lt. Noel Laplante, 24, from Toledo, died when the helicopter he was piloting was shot down over Vinh Binh Province. He was born on Christmas Day, 1946, and laid to rest in Calvary Cemetery in Toledo. A friend posted on *Faces on the Wall* that 1st Lt. Laplante was *"...Always with a smile, always determined to do the right thing, and always a man of unquestionable honor, determination, and courage...."* Army SP4 Harvey Reynolds, 19, from Cincinnati, was less than two months from completing his tour of duty when his helicopter was shot down. He was a crewman aboard the same aircraft as 1st Lt. Laplante.

The first Wednesday of April brought the death of three Ohio soldiers. SP4 Grover Pierson died in Quang Tri Province when an explosion occurred inside his vehicle. He was twenty-one, from Cincinnati, and had been in Vietnam less than three months. Army Cpl. Richard Morgan, 21, was killed in Quang Tin Province when his vehicle hit a mine on the road. His father served in WWII. Not only born on the same day but died on the same day as Cpl. Mogan was Army *Medical Corpsman Pfc. Dale Hood*, 20, from Lewisville. He died when an explosion happened inside his vehicle. Pfc. Hood, who was buried in Noble County, was the last of eleven soldiers from Monroe County to die in the Vietnam conflict.

As we stand on the threshold of learning the backstory of the eleven sons of Monroe County that lost their lives in Southeast Asia between November 17, 1965, and April 7, 1971, it would serve us well to look back to where we've been in this work. After all, *Everyone Has a Story,* and those stories deserve...no, they need...to be told.

In the first chapter, we learned about the early settlement of one of Ohio's oldest counties, Monroe County, and how many early settlers were German and Swiss immigrants looking for a better life than they had in Europe. Using the Ohio River as their primary mode of travel, many settled along the river's west bank between Wheeling (West) Virginia and

Ohio's first organized settlement, Marietta.

As settlements grew into towns and towns into counties in the Northwest Territory, the counties would adopt the names of recognized leaders and political figures. Among the list was Washington County, Ohio's first county, Adams County, located in the far southcentral part of the territory, and Hamilton County, situated in the southwestern corner of the new region, along the banks of the Ohio River.

As time progressed and the territory became the nation's thirty-third state, land was taken from the older counties to form new ones. On January 29, 1813, with land from neighboring Belmont, Guernsey, and Washington counties, Monroe County was formed. The coming years would see the county of 450 square miles divided into eighteen townships, including Benton, Center, Lee, Salem, Sunbury, and Switzerland. The eleven sons of Monroe that would die in the Vietnam conflict would come from one or more of these six townships. In Sunbury township, the village of Beallsville alone would lose five young men in the Vietnam conflict.

In the second chapter, we traced the history of conscription...the draft...from its pre-biblical time to its acceptance and practice in the U.S., beginning with the American Revolutionary War and ending with the Vietnam conflict. A significant portion of the pages that followed examined the organization and structure of the Selective Service System and the role that state and local boards played in the organization. The middle section of the chapter focused on the composition of local boards, examples of their devotion and commitment to their "no salary and long hours" position, and the heavy burden placed on local board members to decide who was classified I-A, who received deferments, and which draftees were rejected outright for military service because of physical issues. The concluding pages of the chapter took a concentrated look at the draft process, beginning with a young man's registration for the draft at age eighteen, through his physical and induction, concluding with details of the first peacetime draft since WWII on December 1, 1969.

In the most recent chapter, we learned the backstory of some of the 58,000 names that appear on the Vietnam Memorial...*The Wall*...including the story of the Edison 64, the dozen soldiers from Our Lady of Guadalupe Catholic Church in Chicago, and the brotherhood of the Morenci 9 and the Midvale three. Additionally, the pages recorded the backstory of the twelve chaplains that died in the Vietnam conflict, the eight female nurses, and the Donut Dollies. And in between, there were countless stories of the young men killed from booby traps, ambushes, small arms fire, and friendly fire. Likewise, the pages told the story of the countless young men, most in their late teens and early twenties, that died a few days before their birthday, on their birthday, or shortly thereafter. More, there were the stories, all tragic, of soldiers that left behind parents, spouses, and children. Above all, there were the stories of soldiers losing their lives because they lost in a coin flip, they took over a fellow soldier's duty because the other guy had gotten sick, or the countless young men that lost their lives in airplane or helicopter crashes.

And now, we turn our attention to those eleven sons of Monroe County who died in Southeast Asia. One by one, we will hear about their lives growing up, their lives before they found themselves in Vietnam, and how they died. Like those mentioned in the preceding pages and those mainly remembered only by family and close friends, their stories need to be told for their example of patriotism and sacrifice. *Everyone Has a Story*, and now we focus on theirs.

Chapter IV

Glenn Eugene McCammon was born on February 20, 1933, in Woodsfield, Ohio, to Charles Thomas and Mildred Irene Thomas. At the time of Glenn's birth, Thomas was twenty-three, while Mildred was twenty. She would turn twenty-one in late July. Although both Thomas and Mildred lived in Woodsfield, the couple was married in Wetzel County, West Virginia, in 1932.

According to the 1940 census, the McCammon family lived on a farm and rented/owned a home on Route 1 in Woodsfield, Center Township, valued at $1,200. Beyond recording Thomas' occupation as a water pumper employed by the City of Woodsfield, the census noted Mrs. McCammon's occupation as a housewife. Additionally, the census listed that a second son lived in the home at the time, Roy, age three. In the 1950 census, the McCammon homeplace was chronicled as not being a farm, less than three acres, and was located one mile from Ohio State Route 78. Moreover, the same census would note the addition of three daughters since the 1940 census, including Nancy, 8, Janice, 4, and Susan, age 1. Finally, the 1950 census stated that Mr. McCammon worked forty-eight hours a week in 1949, and his income that year was $2,000.

Glenn attended elementary and high school in Woodsfield. He was conscripted/drafted into the Army in 1953 and completed his basic training at Fort Knox and advanced training at Fort Devens, Massachusetts. At some point during his tours of duty in Korea and Japan, he re-enlisted. In the November 5, 1963 issue of the *Daily Jeffersonian*, a brief article appeared stating that *"...S-Sgt. Glenn McCammon and Mrs. McCammon, Columbus, Ga,...were recent guests of Mr. and Mrs. J. E. Morris and Virginia Lee" (pg. 15).* It was while he was stationed at Fort Benning, Georgia, that he received his deployment orders for Vietnam.

On August 14, 1965, over 1,000 members of the U.S. Army, including Staff Sgt. McCammon, departed Fort Benning. Upon arriving at Warner-Robins Air Force Base near Macon, the soldiers boarded C-130 planes that would take them first to Travis Air Force Base in California, then Hickman Field in Hawaii, Clark Air Force Base in the Philippines, and eventually Vietnam. The group arrived two days later, on August 16, at Nha Trang Air Base in Khanh Hoa Province.

Upon arriving, Staff Sgt. McCammon and the others of Company A, 2nd Battalion, 7th Cavalry, 1st Cavalry Division boarded trucks headed for a temporary base near An Khe, in the central highlands of Binh Dinh Province, approximately forty miles inland from the city of Qui Nhon. Within weeks, McCammon and others from his battalion would be involved in Operation Shiny Bayonet. Among the early casualties of the operation was 17-year-old Army Pfc. Terry Wright of Ft. Wayne, Indiana, who died on October 10.

During the next several weeks, the fighting increased between U.S. troops and PAVN (People's Army of Vietnam). The most intense came when American forces were called to reinforce U.S. and ARVN troops under siege at an outpost near Plei Mei in Pleiku Province. Little did Allied forces know that the PAVN troops were waiting to ambush the reinforcements. However, ARVN forces intercepted radio messages, and Allied soldiers were able to initiate a surprise attack of their own, driving the PAVN from the immediate area.

In the last week of October, orders came down for the American troops to pursue the enemy into the rugged jungle terrain of the central highlands. Around November 2, intelligence was received that additional PAVN troops were congregating near the Chu Pong mountains and the Ia Drang Valley. Within two weeks, plans were underway to helicopter forces into the area. Two landing sites were chosen.

The first was LZ X-Ray, a flat and tree-lined area bordered on the east by a mountain and on the west by a dry river bed. However, because the landing zone was only around one hundred yards wide, only eight or ten helicopters could land simultaneously. Transporting soldiers to the landing zone, returning to pick up more soldiers, and then flying them to the landing zone would take around one hour. Consequently, it would take 16 helicopters around four hours to land a whole battalion (300-1,200 soldiers). The second landing zone, LZ Albany, was located five miles northeast.

On November 14, a heavy bombardment of artillery and air strikes hit the enemy area. Soon after, the first wave of helicopters, each carrying less than a dozen soldiers, began landing at LZ X-Ray. Immediately upon arriving, the first troops, around seventy-five, fan out to create a perimeter around the landing zone. Little did the U.S. and ARVN soldiers know they were less than one thousand feet from two regiments of PAVN. After depositing the troops, the helicopters returned to a nearby base, around thirty minutes away, to bring in additional troops. Within an hour, the second wave of U.S. soldiers arrived by helicopter. It is believed that Staff Sgt. McCammon was among the group, arriving at LZ X-Ray in the early afternoon.

Before long, the U.S. troops captured two prisoners. During the interrogation, intelligence officers learned that not only were PAVN troops lying in wait just beyond the perimeter of the LZ X-Ray, but the enemy troops numbered as many as 2,000. A reconnaissance group was deployed to check the accuracy of the information.

In short time, the small platoon of fewer than thirty soldiers began chasing a lone enemy soldier into the thick brush of the jungle. Suddenly, the soldiers were surrounded by the enemy and cut off from the American and ARVN troops. Sadly, there were not enough American troops on the ground at the time to provide support for the trapped troops and still guard the landing zone perimeter. Any further call for artillery and air support was risky because the enemy remained too close to Allied troops.

The fighting around LZ X-Ray continued for nearly seventy-two hours, including some hand-to-hand combat. Repeated efforts to get help to the remote platoon failed, resulting in mass casualties on the American side. Eventually, what was left of the lost platoon was rescued.

Among the dead from the deadly 3-day and 2-night battle, November 14-16, are two Ohio soldiers: Army SP4 Thomas Burlile from London and Army Sgt. Travis Poss, 23, of Brook Park. Burlile had celebrated his 23rd birthday four days earlier. In addition, three soldiers from neighboring West Virginia died in the battle, including 2nd Lt. Timothy Blake, 24, from Charleston, Army Sgt. Herman Hostuttler, 25, from Terra Alta, and Sgt. James Riley, 30, of Vienna. Riley, who had seven siblings, was a door gunner on one of the helicopters transporting soldiers into the Ia Drang Valley. He died when his helicopter was hit by enemy fire and crashed.

———————

During the early morning of November 17, troops left LZ X-Ray and headed for LZ Albany. As they neared the second landing zone, the American forces were ambushed with mortar and sniper fire. Over the next six hours, the fighting claimed over one hundred and fifty-five dead or missing

American lives, nearly twice the number of casualties at LZ X-Ray. Among the dead or missing were no less than twelve soldiers from Georgia, ten from Pennsylvania, seven from California, six from Tennessee, and five from Florida. Included among the soldiers from California was Pfc. Robert Moreno of Los Angeles. He would be the last of the seventeen-year-old soldiers to die in 1965.

The list of West Virginia soldiers killed at LZ Albany on November 17 includes Army Sgt. Cecil Kittle, 25, from Huttonsville, and Army Staff Sgt. Martin Knapp from Wheeling. Kittle was a machine gunner on one of the helicopters that transported soldiers in and out of LZ Albany. Knapp, 33, had been in the Army for sixteen years and had been in Vietnam less than ninety days.

Eleven Ohio soldiers also died in the battle. Among them was Army Pfc. Ellwood Davis, 25, who was recently engaged to be married, Jack Lynn, 19, from Hilliard, and David Mendoza, 24, who had been in the military less than one year and whose monthly pay at the time of his death was $163.50. Among the other Ohio soldiers to be killed around LZ Albany on November 17 was Army Pfc. Thomas Pizzino, 20, of Hopedale, Army Pfc. Matthew Shelton, 20, from Cincinnati, and Army Staff Sgt. Robert Wright, 29, from Youngstown. The family of Pfc. Pizzino received the news of his passing on Thanksgiving Day. In addition to being the first soldier from Harrison County to die in Vietnam, Pizzino's funeral service was held at the same church where he had served as an altar boy. Wright had been in the military for over a decade, and his base pay was almost $350 a month.

Also killed during the LZ Albany battle was Staff Sgt. McCammon. According to the Army-issued death certificate, Staff Sgt. McCammon died *"...as the result of metal fragment wound to head received in hostile ground action." (Coffelt Database of Vietnam Casualties)*

In addition to his parents, one brother, and four sisters,

Staff Sgt. McCammon, 32, left behind three children: Lori, Kirk Douglass, and Beth Ann, all under the age of ten. The Monday, November 22, issue of the *Daily Jeffersonian* noted that McCammon's wife *"...who resides in Perry, Fla. entered a hospital there the same day her husband was killed to await the birth of the couple's first child" (pg. 21).* Mrs. McCammon later gave birth to a girl, and named Glennis Elaine. In the same article, the newspaper also reported, "*...the McCammon family received regular letters from their son, the last having been received two days before his death."* Ironically, an article in the same newspaper two days after his death reported that Staff Sgt. McCammon had *"...recently arrived in Viet Nam (sp.) where he is serving with the U.S. Army..." (Daily Jeffersonian, November 19, 1965, pg. 17).*

On November 23, the Department of Defense released the names of over eighty U.S. military members killed in Vietnam. The list...

"...was the longest list issued in a single day since the United States became involved in the war...." Additionally, the *"...daily casualty lists issued by the Pentagon have been growing by leaps and bounds as the United States has increased its involvement and the size of its forces in Vietnam" (Panama City News, November 23, 1965, pg. 1).*

The funeral for McCammon was held the following year, on his birthday...February 20. An Army honor guard from Fort Hayes, Columbus, participated in Staff Sgt. McCammon's funeral service. He is buried in Oaklawn Cemetery in Woodsfield, and his name is etched on The Wall: Panel 03, Line 087.

Not much is known about the LZ Albany battle because the...

"...daily journal for the period 16 through 22

November has itself vanished. That key piece of evidence, missing at least since September 1967, would have allowed a more accurate and authoritative understanding of the tragic events to emerge and would have answered many of the questions raised. In addition, official reports prepared in the aftermath of Albany either disassembled the facts or avoided the battle altogether." (Combat Operations: Stemming the Tide: May 1965–October 1966, John M. Carland, 2015, pg. 145)

Nevertheless, the epic battle in the Ia Drang Valley in November 1965 and its after-effects should be noted for several reasons. First, it is considered the first significant confrontation involving U.S. and ARVN forces and troops from the PAVN. Secondly, it became a blueprint of battle tactics for both armies. The Americans learned the value of air mobility from helicopters and airplanes (reconnaissance, troop support, and bombing) and long-range artillery. Meanwhile, the North Vietnamese learned they could neutralize the American firepower by engaging U.S. troops quickly and at close range. The battle also instituted changes domestically regarding how families were notified of a soldier's death.

Instead of the family being notified of their loved one's death in a letter from the Department of Defense that commonly began with the words "I wish to extend to you my deepest and profound sympathy." Also included in the letter, commonly delivered by a taxi driver, were details about how and where the soldier died. The letter would be signed by an officer, usually a 1st lieutenant or captain, who knew the deceased soldier and was familiar with the details. It all changed following the battle in the Ia Drang Valley.

Now, mainly because the military did not want the families to learn of their loved ones passing secondhand, two officers, commonly a chaplain and an officer, would arrive at the family's home in a green military-issued car. Upon arriving, and with the utmost sympathy and compassion, the officers would share the details of the soldier's passing as the officers understood them. Additionally, the officers would explain how and when the soldier's body would return to the U.S. and any other questions the family needed to be answered.

Jack Pittman was born on St. Patrick's Day (March 17), 1946, in Bellaire, Belmont County, Ohio. At birth, his father, Earl "Peanut" Pittman, was around twenty-five, and Maegene Adams Pittman, Jack's mother, was twenty-three. The couple were married in Belmont County eleven months earlier, on April 9, 1945.

According to the 1950 census, the family of three lived about three and one-half miles outside the village of Beallsville on Ohio State Route 556. The next closest town was Clarington, around ten miles away. Additionally, the census listed Earl's occupation as a farmhand, working around sixty hours a week on a private fruit farm, and his wife as a housewife. When he was not working on the farm, some records say that Earl also worked a regular afternoon or midnight shift at the Ormet aluminum plant in Hannibal, Ohio.

Surrounded by over three hundred acres of peach trees, the family's white house sat at the end of the lane. They operated a seasonal fruit stand at the head of the lane, where it met Route 556. Naturally, they were well-known for their peaches. During the off-season, they would preserve and eat what they did not sell at the vegetable stand. The family was active in the Captina Church of Christ on Route 556, near their home.

Growing up, Jack was well-known in the Beallsville sports community and Monroe County. As a sophomore at Beallsville High School, he was among a list of football players that attended the school's all-sports banquet in March 1962. The Daily Jeffersonian reports that Jack played an outstanding game against neighboring Byesville High School the following year, saying....

> *"The 'big one' for Beallsville came in the second period when quarterback Kenneth Darby hit the ozone with a five-yard pass to left end Jack Pittman good for a touchdown and a 6-0 lead...Offensively, Darby and Pittman turned in the best performance...."*

The article goes on to say that…

*"At halftime, Senior Linda Laubert was crowned 1963
homecoming queen by Jack Pittman, captain of the
Beallsville gridders…" (October 5, 1963, pg. 9).*

In December, he was named to the first team, All Pioneer
Football Team. During his senior year in high school, 1963-
1964, he was the captain of the school's football and
basketball teams. Called quiet and shy, Jack was among the
approximately sixty or seventy students who graduated from
Beallsville High School in 1964. Besides being a part of the
wedding party when his cousin married in June 1964, it is said
that in the months that followed, Jack not only worked at
Ormet but found time to coach an eighth-grade boys'
basketball team.

Not long after his eighteen birthday, Jack registered with
the local Selective Service board in Woodsfield and received
his draft card. His SS number: 33 86 46 24. It is said that Jack
was encouraged by others to join the reserves. He told his
family and friends he wanted to get his two years of military
service over. Further, he told others that upon completing his
obligation, he wanted to return and work on the family farm
and build a house on the property.

On September 24, 1964, he was one of eleven sons of
Monroe County who traveled to Fort Hayes in Columbus for
their military physical. He would be officially inducted into
the Army on November 4, 1965, at 19.

In short time, several soldiers from the Beallsville area
boarded a bus to begin their military training. The list included
Randy Ray, Terry Hickman, and Jack, all three were headed
to basic training at Fort Jackson, South Carolina. Hickman
would go on to advanced training at Fort Gordon.

The day before Thanksgiving 1965, an article appeared in

the *Daily Jeffersonian* announcing the engagement of Ms. Judith Blakely, of Alledonia, Monroe County, to Jack. The announcement stated that the bride and groom were graduates of Beallsville High School and that Ms. Blakely was employed at First National Bank in Powhatan. *"Mr. Pittman...was formerly employed by Ormet Aluminum Plant, Hannibal, and is now with the U.S. Army at Ft. Jackson, S.S."* *(November 24, pg. 6)*. The same article would appear in the same newspaper less than six weeks later *(January 6, pg. 16)*.

On April 7, 1966, Pfc. Jack Pittman began his tour of duty in Vietnam. He was assigned to Company HHC (Headquarters and Headquarters Company), 1st Battalion, 2nd Infantry, 1st Infantry Division, and stationed near Phu/Phou Vinh in An Giang Province. His MOS (Military Occupational Specialty) listed him as an Infantry Direct Fire Crewman. According to one source, Pfc. Pittman wrote a letter home around a month after arriving. In the letter, he stated that he was confused because they had given him a machine gun and a pistol, and he was merely a radio operator *(Heroes, John Pilger, 1986, pg. 110)*.

Just over one hundred days after arriving in Vietnam, Pfc. Pittman was riding in an armored personal carrier along highway QL-13, known by American troops as Thunder Road. The highway, a main artery that began on the northern outskirts of Saigon, ran nearly sixty miles through several provinces, including Binh Duong and Binh Phuoc, and terminated at the Cambodian border. Keeping the highway open was vital because it transported troops and supplies to firebases along the route. Knowing this, the road was heavily mined, and enemy troops commonly ambushed convoys. The enemy's approach was to destroy, or at least stall, the U.S. convoys and was calculated.

First, the PAVN and Viet Cong would plant land mines in

the road, more commonly, Claymore mines. According to one newspaper article, the mine…

"…is a football-sized container of sharp steel fragments which, when detonated, sends its mutilation over an area the size of Yankee Stadium…The mines are normally exploded by electrical impulse. A simple process…two attached wires, strung as much as a thousand yards from the bomb, are stripped of insulation and touched together…For the soldiers from Someplace, U.S.A, it's a hell of a way to live" (Daily Jeffersonian, March 10, 1966, pg. 14).

After detonating the mines, usually under the first vehicle of the convoy, the other vehicles would be forced to stop. Consequently, this would allow the enemy to ambush the American and ARVN troops on the road. An entire convoy could be halted with one mine, cutting off much-needed troops and supplies to firebases along the highway.

And when mines were detected in the road, extracting or removing them was a slow and tedious process. The convoy would be forced to stop, providing the enemy another opportunity to ambush troops.

————————

On Monday, July 18, Pfc. Pittman and several other soldiers were riding in a personnel carrier near Binh Duong Province when a Claymore mine exploded nearby. He was hit in the neck, chest, and back with shrapnel. According to the casualty report…

"He was bleeding profusely and having difficulty breathing when Specialist Four Dennis Graham from Milwaukee, Wisconsin reached him. He sent word back to the battalion aid station of the seriousness of the wounded soldier and immediately applied first aid treatment and began mouth to mouth (sp.) resuscitation

to keep the soldier alive. Nearby Captain Donald Masler, Minneapolis, Minnesota, the battalion surgeon stood by to receive the injured soldier. When Pittman was evacuated to the aid station, Masler performed a tracheotomy...He then inserted a plastic hose through the opening, and had five other medical personnel assist him in 'breathing' through the hose to keep Pittman alive. A 'dust off' ship arrived in a matter of minutes and the wounded man was air lifted (sp.) out of the jungle...It was the first time since the 1st Battalion, 2nd Infantry arrived in Vietnam, that such an operation was necessary" (Coffelt Database of Vietnam Casualties).

SP5 Patrick Dwyer, a twenty-three-year-old platoon leader from Philadelphia, and Pfc Donald Priest, also twenty-three, from Monroe County, New York, were killed in the attack. According to the *Coffelt Database*, Dwyer and Priest are buried in a cemetery bearing the same name. Dwyer is buried in Holy Sepulchre Cemetery in Cheltenham, Pennsylvania, beside his father, while Priest is buried in Holy Sepulchre Cemetery in Rochester, New York. Both of the soldier's fathers served in WWII.

Pfc. Pittman, later transported to Letterman Army Hospital in San Francisco, was one of over seven hundred and fifty Army soldiers evacuated from Vietnam in July 1966. Sadly, his family did not know his whereabouts for about a week. When his mother called the Pentagon to find out her son's whereabouts, the response from the person at the other end of the phone was unexpected. *"Listen lady,"* the person said, *"what's happened to your boy is an every day (sp.) account. I can't trace every kid who got hisself (sp.) hurt out there"* (*Heroes, pg. 110*). Pfc. Pittman died from his wounds on July 25, 1966; no less than seven area newspapers reported his passing. His monthly pay at his death was $121.50. Moreover, Pfc. Pittman would be one of over fifty-two hundred soldiers injured in combat in Southeast Asia and later die.

The funeral service for Pfc. Pittman drew a standing-room-only crowd, forcing many mourners to stand outside the building. His parents, who refused a military funeral, buried their son in his high school graduation suit on the last day of July 1966. The cemetery where Pfc. Pittman is buried overlooks the high school football field. Jack's name is etched on The Wall: Panel 9E, Line 076.

Duane Theodore Greenlee was born on April 30, 1947, to Duane F. and Mary Margaret Greenlee. He was named after his father and possibly his maternal grandfather, Theodore Crall. The younger Greenlee and Jack Pittman are related as both are the great-grandsons of Obediah Pittman. When the younger Greenlee was born, his father had recently turned twenty-two on January 11, while his mother had turned twenty in October of the previous year. The two were married in Glencoe, Belmont County, by Rev. C.E. Simms on July 27, 1945. The marriage license noted that Mr. Greenlee was in the U.S. Army at the time of the marriage. He enlisted in the Army on April 21, 1943, at his local SS office, number 3, in Belmont County.

The 1950 census lists five in the home, including the mother and father; Duane; a younger brother, Jackie, age 1; and a newborn daughter, born in January, named Diana. Additionally, the census lists Mr. Greenlee's occupation as a machine man in the coal mine. Finally, the same census lists the last name as Greenler rather than Greenlee *(FamilySearch.org)*.

Duane graduated from Beallsville High School in 1965. Just under six foot tall, he was thin and described as quiet when he enlisted in the Marines in the late winter of 1966, a few months before his eighteenth birthday. It is said that his mother was not happy about his enlistment. The number on his draft card read: 33 7 47 299. At that time, Duane was the oldest of nine children living in the home on a farm located on Route 1 (Clover Ridge) in the Captiva Creek area. The list included brothers Jack, James, Johnny, George, and sisters Dianna, Barbara, Brenda, and Marijo. The youngest, George, was born on February 19, 1964, in the same hospital as his brother, Duane. It is said that it was not uncommon for Duane to ride horseback in the dark to visit a cheerleader girlfriend who lived several miles away.

213

Between graduation and his enlistment, Duane worked at the Ohio Boxboard Company in Rittman, Ohio. While working at Ohio Boxboard, later, the Packaging Corporation of America, Duane lived with his great aunt and uncle, Mr. and Mrs. Ralph Christy (Mrs. Christy was Duane's mother's sister). The Christy's had a son, James, who was around nine years older than Duane and had recently been conscripted/drafted into the Army. It may have been while he was making the one-hundred-and-thirty-mile trip from Rittman to Beallsville that Duane was ticketed for speeding on September 1965. After appearing in district court and paying the $15 fine, he was released *(Dover Daily Reporter, September 8, 1965, pg. 2)*.

Duane completed his basic training at Parris Island, South Carolina, and his advanced training as an Infantry Rifleman at Camp Lejeune, North Carolina. Pvt. Greenlee reported to Camp Pendleton, California, around July 11, 1966, and arrived in Vietnam within a few days. Upon arriving, he was assigned to E (Echo) Company, 2nd Battalion, 3rd Marine Regiment, 3rd Marine Division. The 3rd Marine Division was one of the first Marine units to arrive in South Vietnam in early 1965 to provide security for the air base at Da Nang. The 3rd Marine Division would be involved in nearly fifty military operations during the conflict. Among the 1966 operations was Operation Double Eagle in Quang Ngai and Quang Tri provinces during January and February and Operation Macon in Quang Nam Province, which began in July.

According to one source, a build-up of PAVN and Viet Cong troops around thirteen miles southwest of Da Nang, in Quang Nam Province, caught the attention of U.S. and ARVN intelligence in mid-August 1966. A platoon of four American soldiers, including a radioman and a Navy corpsman, volunteered to reconnaissance the area. On the third day of their operation, August 18, the platoon was ambushed, killing the radioman and injuring the corpsman. The two remaining members of the Marine platoon evacuated the injured soldier while deciding to leave the radioman's body and return later to retrieve it. With no radio contact from the decimated platoon, a larger group went looking for the missing platoon on August 19. Before long, the missing platoon walked out of the jungle and into a nearby Marine camp. The second group was immediately contacted. However, the second group of Marines continued their search for the body of the missing radioman by retracing the route of the smaller platoon. They were unable to locate the body.

For the next two days, the search and rescue mission, now termed Operation Allegheny, continued to search for the missing soldier, now identified as Lance Cpl. Edward Rykoskey, 20, from Carlisle, Pennsylvania. On August 22, a group of Marines entered a small village to check for enemy presence while a second group of Marines set up security around the village's perimeter. Around 2:00pm, the perimeter group began receiving heavy enemy fire. After nearly two hours, the enemy disengaged. There were sporadic engagements with the enemy for the next several days. Operation Allegheny would conclude on August 29. *(Fortitudine, Vol. 34, No. 3, 2009, pg. 7-11)*

The deadliest skirmishes came on August 25 when three American Marines died. The list included Pvt. Daniel Lykins, from Willard, Ohio, and Pvt. James Dozier, from Flint, Michigan. Both were nineteen and died from small arms fire. Pvt. Lykins was a member of E Company, while Pvt. Dozier was a member of L Company. The third member to be killed on August 25 was Pvt. Duane Greenlee. He was 19 and had been in Vietnam for forty-four days.

In a letter written home prior to his death, Pvt. Greenlee said he did not know what he was fighting for in Vietnam.

215

More, he did not see any sense in it and if there's been any gain being over there. He closed the letter, stating, "I just wish it was all over."

According to the *Coffelt Database of Vietnam Casualties*, Pvt. Greenlee died as the *"...result (of) gunshot wound of the left side of his face sustained while participating in an operation against hostile forces."* A second unidentified source stated that Pvt. Greenlee was wounded in the head and unable to wear a helmet. However, he returned to the fighting and was shot by a sniper. Pvt. Greenlee's family was notified of their son's death on August 26 when a green military vehicle came down the lane to the family's home, and two Marine officers exited the car. It is believed that Mrs. Greenlee, who was holding one of her children in her arms, immediately dropped to her knees when she was told the news of her son's death. Several days before receiving the bad news of her son's passing, Mrs. Greenlee sent her son a letter, sharing with him the news of the death of Jack Pittman. The letter was returned several weeks later...unopened. At the time of his passing, Pvt. Greenlee, who was receiving a monthly pay of $100.50, had a brother, Jack, serving in the Army in Okinawa.

The announcement of Pvt. Greenlee's death appeared in several newspapers around the area on August 30. The *Willoughby News-Herald* announced Pvt. Greenlee's passing on page 12; the *Washington Court House Record-Herald* noted his death on page 8, just above a grocery store proclaiming it had the freshest bread in town; and in the *Elyria Chronicle-Telegram* on page 3, immediately below an article stating that the Alabama legislature was firmly behind Gov. George Wallace's efforts at segregating the state's public schools.

Pvt. Greenlee's passing was not the only bad news for his extended family. A little over a week before Pvt. Greenlee's passing, the Ralph Christy family, whom Greenlee had lived with while working at Ohio Boxboard in Rittman, received word that their son, Army SP5 James Christy, 27, had lost his life in South Vietnam on August 17. While pursuing a sniper near a rice paddy, SP5 Christy, a combat engineer, and twelve-year veteran, slipped off the trail, fell into a hole in the paddy, and drowned. He had been in-country less than three weeks.

The body of Pvt. Greenlee did not have far to travel since the Da Nang airbase, where the bodies of deceased soldiers were prepared for transport to the states, was a short distance away. When his body arrived in the U.S. several days later, the words "Unviewable" and "This side up" appeared on the side of his casket. *(Heroes, pg. 110)*

Pvt. Greenlee's funeral was held on September 14, at Toothman Funeral Home, in Jacobsburg, Ohio, with Rev. Don Ake officiating. The burial was at Belmont Memorial Park in St. Clairsville. In addition to being buried with full military honors, he received the Purple Heart. Pvt. Greenlee is among the nearly 10,000 Marines to lose their lives in Quang Nam Province during the conflict, and his name is engraved on The Wall: Panel 10E, Line 39.

Charles Glenn Schnegg was born at home on Saturday, September 20, 1947, to Ernest and Esther Schnegg. The same day as one of the Edison 64: Joseph Mieczkowski. When Charles was born, his father was thirty-six, and his mother was thirty-three. Another son, William, age seven, was waiting at home to welcome his younger brother. Located on Clover Ridge, about halfway between the villages of Beallsville and Powhatan Point, the family lived on a 162-acre farm split between two counties and three townships. Part of the farm was located in Washington and York townships in Belmont County. The remainder of the farm lay in Switzerland Township in Monroe County. Moreover, most of the half-mile lane leading to the family house was in Washington Township, while the Schnegg home was in York Township. The nearest neighbor was a half-mile away.

The 1950 census lists five in the household, including the parents, George, Charles, and a one-year-old daughter, Georgiann, born in December 1948. Later on, Mr. Schnegg's occupation would be listed as a construction worker. His wife was known to have worked in nearby Barnesville as a nurse's aide, even as Mr. Schnegg and her raised several children.

According to Roger Schnegg, one of Charles' younger siblings, the bus that would take kids that lived on Clover Ridge to school in Beallsville would fill up fast. The third stop on the route to school would see no less than six Schnegg children get on the bus. Three stops later, no less than five children from the Greenlee family, including Duane, would board the bus for the ten-mile, forty-minute ride to school. The typical school day would begin around 9:00am and last until 3:00pm. With the elementary school located about a half-mile from the high school, it is said that Charles would work during the school lunch hour by delivering hot food from the high school, where it was prepared, to the elementary school. With the village of Beallsville around ten miles from the family farm, socializing with classmates and participating in high school sports was challenging for most teens living on Clover Ridge. Subsequently, it was not uncommon for boys in the area to work on a neighbor's farm for a few hours following the school day or after graduation...and Charles was no exception. He began working on the farm of a nearby neighbor, Emery Walters, when he was 13. Charles remained working there until he graduated from Beallsville High School in 1965.

Following the lead of his brother, Fred, who had already registered for conscription/draft, Charles registered with the local Selective Service board in Belmont County not long after his eighteenth birthday. Because of the location of the family farm, along with attending high school in another county, Schnegg may have been on the list of possible draftees of two local draft boards: Belmont and Monroe counties.

The summer following graduation, Charles worked with his brother, Fred, at the DEK Manufacturing Plant, a fiberglass plant, in Orrville, Ohio. When Fred left for military service in December 1965, Charles stayed on working at DEK. The following year, Charles would begin working with another brother, Bill, at Timken Roller-Bearing in Canton. It is believed that Charles worked in the plant while Bill worked outside, driving a truck for the company. Before long, Charles would receive his draft notice. He began his military service on December 4, 1966.

Upon completion of his basic and advanced training, Pfc. Schnegg was sent to Vietnam. He reported for duty on May 11, 1967, and was assigned as a member of the infantry of A Company, 3rd Battalion, 47th Infantry Regiment, 9th Infantry Division.

As battles continued to increase between Allied troops and the PAVN and the Viet Cong in the Mekong Delta in the second half of the 1960s, the U.S. command was reluctant to order troops there for several reasons. First, despite the area containing over one-third country's population and a central food-growing region, Allied leaders felt that troops were needed more in other parts of the country. Next, the topography made establishing any military bases next to impossible. Finally, the countless canals and rivers which dissected the region restricted ground troop movement. However, that all changed in 1966 when enemy troop strength increased dramatically in the area.

In the late spring of the year, a joint venture between the U.S. Army and the Navy produced the Mekong Delta Mobile Afloat Force (MDMAF). The two-fold task of the soldier and sailor unit was to regularly patrol and assess the waters of the delta for an enemy presence and to transport combat troops to the area when needed. Specifically, the joint unit was tasked with searching local boats and junkets (sampans) for enemy supplies and keeping the waterways free of water mines.

The combined military force was based on a large naval ship. The force includes several smaller vessels capable of navigating the narrow rivers and streams of the delta. Known by most as the "brown water navy," the smaller crafts were manned by members of the U.S. Army, including many from the 9th Infantry Division. Because of its flexibility and mobility, it is said that the MDMAF could transport over five hundred soldiers anywhere in the delta in less than twenty-four hours. In May 1967, the joint force was renamed the Mobile Riverine Force, or the MRF.

A series of eleven water operations involving American and ARVN troops began among the twenty provinces in the Mekong Delta in the early summer of 1967. Following the conclusion of Operation Coronado I in Long An Province in the northern part of the delta, operations moved south into the waterways of Dinh Tuong Province. The four-day battle, termed Operation Coronado II, continued the Allied assault on enemy troops in the region. Operation Coronado III disrupted

Viet Cong operations in Gia Binh Province. During Operation Coronado IV in mid-August and early September, Allied troops moved into Go Kong and Kien Hoa provinces. American losses numbered around sixty. In Operation(s) Coronado V, VI, VII, and VIII, U.S. and ARVN troops continued battling the Viet Cong as the Allied forces continued their push into the southern provinces. Thirty-five U.S. soldiers were lost in Operation Coronado V.

Around 4:00am on December 4, a contingent of around forty vessels of the Marine Riverine Force began making their way north on the Mekong River. Three hours and approximately forty miles later, a bridge spanning the entrance to the Rach Ruong Canal was blown up by engineers. This allowed the contingent vessels with armored troop carriers (ATC) and a regiment of ARVN Marines onboard to access the narrow canal.

After traveling a short distance up the canal, the caravan of vessels encountered several large cables strung between opposite banks of the river. This caused the flotilla to come to a stop. As the boats try to break the cables, first by firing machine guns into the water and then ramming the restraints, those onboard the vessels suddenly begin taking small arms fire from the shorelines. This was followed by rockets and mortar fire from point-blank range.

In short time, several of the vessels transporting the ARVN Marines were able to free themselves from the ambush and land north of the enemy's position. Once onshore, the ARVN Marines began moving south toward their attackers. Shortly after, a second group of soldiers landed south of the ambush and began moving north toward the Viet Cong. A third group of forces was dropped to the west of the enemy by helicopter. At the same time, several more American soldiers from the flotilla landed and made a frontal assault on the well-fortified enemy bunkers. In addition to machine guns mounted on the MRF vessels returning fire, a flame thrower aboard one of the flotilla's boats was directed toward the enemy's position.

It is believed that it was during the last stage of the assault, while he was taking a radio to an officer, that Pfc. Schnegg was shot and killed by small arms fire. He died on a Monday, in Kien Phong Province, along the banks of the Rach Ruong Canal. According to the casualty report, Pfc. Schnegg, who was seeing his first action since returning from R & R in November, *"...died from gunshot wound received while on a combat operation when unit engaged a hostile force in a firefight"* (Coffelt Database of Vietnam Casualties). In addition to dying a day before the anniversary of entering the service, Pfc. Schnegg was the fourth soldier from Monroe County to die in the conflict, and the third member of Beallsville High School, the Class of 1965, to lose his life in Vietnam in the past eighteen months.

––––––––––

It is said that the first of Pfc. Schnegg's family to receive the call about his death were his brothers, Don and Fred. Ironically, Fred, a radio operator in the Army who had recently returned from deployment in Germany, had been in the states less than one week before receiving the news of his brother's death. The phone call came from Army personnel in Pittsburgh on December 5. The same day the two brothers received the dreadful call, a green military vehicle made its way up the family's lane on Clover Ridge. It is said that when Pfc. Schnegg's father spotted the car making its way toward the family home, Mr. Schnegg ran into a nearby cornfield.

Of the eleven regional newspapers that posted Pfc. Schnegg's passing, nearly half ran the same headline: *"2 Ohio servicemen killed in Viet action."* Several newspapers placed the notice not far from an article announcing that USC star running back O.J. Simpson was college football's Player of the Year, while other newspapers listed Pfc. Schnegg's death among the last few pages of the issue. One newspaper listed the passing of the 20-year-old not far from a dental health section and another near a large ad for a washer and dryer.

The body of Pfc. Schnegg arrived in Monroe County around the second week of the month and was taken to the Harper-Campbell Funeral Home in Beallsville. This was the same funeral home that took care of the arrangements of Pfc. Jack Pittman. The funeral service for Pfc. Schnegg was held on December 16, with Evangelist Richard Pryor officiating, and included full military honors. In addition to his brothers, Don and William, Pfc. Schnegg was survived by two other brothers, Fred and Roger, and three sisters, Georgiann, Shirley, and Carol.

On April 3, 1969, the *Albuquerque Tribune* printed a half-page article noting the loss of a fourth soldier from Monroe County. Commenting on the death of her son as he took the radio to an officer, Mrs. Schnegg spoke, saying, *"...He literally served as a decoy in enemy gunfire to save other members of his company...I'm proud of what he did...but I'd rather have my son" (pg. 4)*.

In addition to receiving the Silver Star and the Bronze Star, Pfc. Schnegg, one of nearly 9,400 soldiers that lost their lives in Southeast Asia in 1967, was awarded a Purple Heart and was posthumously promoted to Corporal. His name is etched on The Wall: Panel 31E, Line 37.

Richard Lee Rucker was born to Kenneth and Dorothy Rucker on September 28, 1947. Records indicate that Richard's mother and father were married in Monroe County, and their ceremony was officiated by Rev. J.V. Armstrong Traylor of Woodsfield. The documents also show that Kenneth, a veteran of WWII, was twenty-one. At the same time, Dorothy was a few years younger when they exchanged vows. Their marriage license shows Kenneth was born in Beallsville, Ohio, and was a steelworker. Dorothy was born in nearby Clarington. The 1940 census indicates that Kenneth's family lived along Ohio State Route 556 in Switzerland Township and Dorothy's on Sykes Ridge in Salem Township.

Richard would be joined by a sister, Donna, born in August 1950.

———————

Like most of those around him, Richard attended elementary school in Beallsville and was a member of the Class of 1965 from Beallsville High School. Following the path of many of his classmates, including Jack Pittman, and Richard's best friend, Duane Greenlee, Richard registered with the Selective Service when he reached eighteen.

Soon after, Richard began attending drafting school in Cleveland, Ohio. When not attending class, he worked at May Company Department Store, later Macy's. Probably from the drafting classes that required him to print, it is believed that Richard soon abandoned writing in script!

Although it was said that he was small-framed and weighed between 150 and 175 pounds when he entered the Army and left for basic training at Fort Jackson, South Carolina, in May 1967, Richard was described as physically and emotionally strong from working during his teenage years. He may have followed up his basic training with advanced training at Fort Lewis, near Tacoma, Washington.

He departed for Vietnam in October 1967.

Upon arriving in Southeast Asia as a U.S. Army rifleman, he was assigned to Company A, 4ᵗʰ battalion, 199ᵗʰ LIB (light infantry brigade), and stationed in Long Binh, in Binh Phuoc Province. As one of the U.S. Army's largest military installations in South Vietnam, the Long Bien base was around fifteen miles northeast of Saigon, in Dong Nai Province. Beyond being a military logistics center during the conflict, the base was a virtual city. It housed an evacuation hospital, dental clinic, restaurants, a bowling alley, and nightclubs. In addition, the installation had several swimming pools, tennis and basketball courts, and a driving range for golfers. Consequently, the base became a prime target for surprise enemy attacks.

The first came a few months before Pfc. Rucker arrived in-country when the Viet Cong destroyed munitions and bombs. However, the heaviest attacks on the base and the surrounding areas would come during the TET offensive.

———————

Begun in late January 1968, the first TET offensive caught Allied commanders by complete surprise. The coordinated attacks were launched against several major military installations in South Vietnam, including Kha Sanh, Da Nang, and Pleiku, and symbolic civilian sites like Hue and Saigon. The first "wave" of the TET offensive involved PAVN and Viet Cong troops attacking no less than thirty-five provincial capitals and over one hundred towns and cities south of the DMZ.

It is said that the attacks followed a similar pattern. First, mortars and rockets were fired into the targets. Enemy ground troops would then follow. Finally, the locals, well-acquainted with the layout of the bases and cities, would lead enemy troops toward command headquarters and significant buildings. In addition, enemy forces shelled airfields and supply depots. The offensive reached as far south as Bac Lieu in the Mekong Delta. When the initial phase by the enemy ended in early spring, the numbers indicated that over fifteen hundred Allied troops had been killed.

In late April, the enemy began a second wave of attacks. Termed mini-TET by military historians, the wave would continue through late May, with PAVN and Viet Cong troops targeting over one hundred towns and cities, including Saigon. On May 5, enemy troops invaded the South Vietnam capital from three directions, north, south, and west. The initial phase of the attacks ended around a week later. U.S. losses during the week-long series of battles were over seventy-five.

In a letter to his parents dated May 8, the mild-mannered Pfc. Rucker, who neither smoked nor drank, wrote, saying,…

"…hello everyone. Well this shit is really happening here. I didn't want to tell you but I'm torn up bad mentally. My buddy Frank got zapped the other day right next to me. He was all over me. He had 13 days to go."

A second letter to his family dated May 21 read…

"got ambush patrol tonight. Ugh! They won't let you out of this field until you drop. I haven't had a real break since I got here, wherever here is. The leeches got all my blood now. Covered with sores and mud…."

Following a brief retreat in which enemy troops departed Saigon, they returned in late May to resume their planned take-over of the city with an assault on the city's police headquarters, several bridges, and radio and tv stations. The second surge began on May 25, with PAVN and Viet Cong troops entering the city from the north and south. They made their northern entrance into Saigon through Gia Dinh Province, specifically, the suburb of Gia Dinh City.

A third letter to his family eight days later communicated a common theme of desperation and frustration in Pfc. Rucker's words.

"some of us were thinking of refusing to go in tonight,

but they'll only send us to jail. Hell, why am I here?
Do you know? Yes all I can do is go for broke and kill
as many...groups as I can...Hope you got a good price
for my car."

For the next several days, most of the fighting occurred in the urban parts of South Vietnam's capital city, as enemy troops occupied countless buildings. With enemy snipers firing on allied troops from inside concrete structures, air support was called in by American commanders on the ground, despite the closeness of the fighting.

Regarding the building-to-building fighting between American and enemy troops near Gia Dinh City on May 30, the Duty Officer's log dated May 31 states...

"...come in contact approx. 1230 hrs...w/unk size
enemy force firing from houses...At 1420 LTC Mastoris
gave permission to fire artillery into housing area...At
1520 Airstrike put into area of contact. Second
airstrike at 1600...A Co sweeping south spotted 1 sqd
VC moving SW out of Saigon...At 1835 in contact
w/unk size force...At 1950 3 US KIA...from short rkt
rnd from gunship...." (Coffelt Database of Vietnam
Casualties)

The three soldiers were killed from A Company by "friendly fire" were Army Pfc. Ernest Molzon, 20, from Chardon, Ohio, and Pfc. Herbert Snell, 18, from New Milford, Pennsylvania. Pfc. Molzon had been in Vietnam for thirty-seven days. Pfc. Snell died one day before his nineteenth birthday.

The third soldier killed was twenty-year-old Pfc. Richard Rucker. According to the casualty report, Pfc. Rucker *"...died from wound received while on combat operation when hit by a fragment from a friendly rocket fired at hostile forces."* (*Coffelt Database of Vietnam Casualties*)

The parents of Pfc. Rucker, Kenneth and Dorothy Rucker, received the news of their son's death shortly after that. The telegram was brought to the family via a local gas station operator. Pfc. Rucker died five days after his mother celebrated her birthday. Meanwhile, only two newspapers in the area carried the news of the soldier's passing: the *Daily Jeffersonian* and the *Zanesville Times Recorder*. Moreover, the *Daily Jeffersonian* reports in its June 4 edition that Pfc. Rucker's sister, Donna, graduated from Beallsville High School the same week her brother was killed. *(pg. 1)*

One day after the death of Pfc. Rucker, May 31, would record the second deadliest day for American troops since the U.S. troops first arrived in Vietnam in 1965. The deadliest day was January 31, during the early stages of the TET offensive. May 1968 was the deadliest month of the conflict when nearly 2,500 U.S. soldiers lost their lives.

The body of Army Pfc. Rucker arrived in Monroe County on June 15 and was taken to Harper-Campbell Funeral Home in Beallsville. This would be the same funeral home that took care of the arrangements of Pfc. Pittman and Pfc. Schnegg. The funeral for Pfc. Rucker took place on Monday, June 17, at the funeral home. Following, he was buried at Beallsville Cemetery with full military honors. Rev. J.V. Armstrong Traylor officiated. Oddly, he was the same minister that married Pfc. Rucker's parents twenty-one years earlier.

Commenting several months after his son's passing, Kenneth said that Pfc. Rucker had a job waiting on him when he returned from serving in Vietnam, adding…

> *"There wouldn't have been any problem there. He was a hard worker and able. Everybody he ever worked for liked him. I think he would have made four something an hour to start. But he'd have went up real fast. He was a damn good worker, remember. If he'd a got back, hell, no tell where a kid like him woulda (sp.)*

went." (Wilson Daily Times, Wilson, North Carolina, September 6, 1969, pg. 14)

Later on, Kenneth Rucker was instrumental in founding the American Legion Post 768 in Beallsville.

Among the no less than seven medals awarded to Pfc. Rucker was the Purple Heart and the Bronze Star. His name is etched on The Wall: Panel W62, Line 1.

James Alvin Ravencraft, Jr. was born on Tuesday, February 20, 1945, in Bellaire, Ohio, to James Alvin Ravencraft and Elizabeth Brown Ravencraft. At the time, the elder Ravencraft, a veteran of WWII, was ten days away from celebrating his twenty-fifth birthday, while Elizabeth was twenty-three. Both were born in Belmont County, Ohio: James in Stewartsville and Elizabeth in Jacobsburg. Their marriage license application indicates that Elizabeth, 21, was living on RFD #1 in Jacobsburg, while James, 22, a coal miner at the time, was living in Powhatan Point, Belmont County. Further, the marriage application states that neither had a living spouse, are *"...not nearer than second cousins...and that neither are...under the influence of any intoxicating liquor or narcotic drug at the time of making this application."* The couple were married on June 9, 1942, in Shadyside, Ohio, by Justice of the Peace James L. Fry.

James Jr. was the couple's second child. Waiting at home for his new brother was Paul, age 2.

The 1950 census records that the family may have lived along Township Road 157, near Clarington, Salem Township. Additionally, the census shows that the family lived on a farm, that the elder Ravencraft worked as a Joy Operator in the coal mine, earned over $3,200 the previous year, and that Mrs. Ravencraft's occupation is listed as a housewife. The census also reveals that a fifth person, a daughter, Phyllis, age 2, also lived in the home at the time.

———————

James, Jr. attended River High School in Hannibal, Ohio, and followed his brother, Paul, into the Army. His military record indicates that on October 30, 1967, Pfc. Ravencraft was a member of the Brigade Combat Team at Fort Jackson, South Carolina, specifically, Company A, 2nd Battalion, 1st Brigade. Nine weeks later, Army Pfc. Ravencraft received advanced infantry training at Fort Jackson as part of Company B, 14th

Battalion, 1ˢᵗ Training Brigade. On January 19, 1968, he was re-assigned to Company A, 11ᵗʰ Battalion, 1ˢᵗ Training Brigade.

On April 5, 1968, Pfc. Ravencraft and Brenda Cool applied for a marriage license. The application stated that Ravencraft was twenty-three and was in the U.S. Army at the time, while Ms. Cool was nineteen, born in Barberton, Ohio, and a student. The couple listed a home on Briner Street in Akron as their residence. It is believed that the two met while the future Mrs. Ravencraft was a student at Ellet High School in Akron. They were married eight days later, on April 13, with the Rev. Frederick Harrold of Akron officiating.

Within a month, Pfc. Ravencraft would ship out for Vietnam.

Upon arriving in Vietnam on May 7, Pfc. Ravencraft was assigned as a Rifleman to Company E, 3ʳᵈ Battalion, 4ᵗʰ Infantry, 9ᵗʰ Infantry Division, stationed in Phong Dinh Province.

———————

On June 18, forty-nine days after arriving in Vietnam and sixty-six days after getting married, Pfc. Ravencraft was a member of a reconnaissance patrol when the group came under ambush. According to the *Coffelt Database of Vietnam Casualties*, two soldiers acted as point men for the platoon. The two were *"...approximately 50 feet ahead of the platoon. When they approached to approximately 30 feet of a trip-line the four men received hostile fire from the front...."* Two of the soldiers escaped and later told commanders that Pfc. Ravencraft and Pfc. (Jerry) Fleming, 20, from Chicago...

"...were hit. The platoon was forced to evacuate before the SUBJECT (name Ravencraft added) and Fleming could be evacuated from the area. A search of the area on 19 June 1968, recovered Fleming's body. However, no trace of Ravencraft or HIS (sp.) equipment could be

found."

Later, the two platoon members that survived the ambush reported that they…

*"…saw when SUBJECT was hit and wounded by
hostile fire (location and extent of HIS wounds
unknown) both felt that SUBJECT had been captured.
SUBJECT was carrying an M-79 Grenade Launcher
and during the time the unit was pinned down, members
of the squad could hear M-79s being fired. Also a
green smoke grenade was fired from the vicinity of
where SUBJECT was wounded."*

In addition to the deaths of Pfc. Ravencraft and Pfc. Fleming, who had been in Vietnam for thirty-seven days, there were over seventy other members of the U.S. military killed that day in South Vietnam. Among the list was Marine Sgt. Jose Roberto Moncayo, who was killed in Quang Tri Province from small arms fire. He was 22 and was the sixth member of the Morenci 9 to die in the conflict.

On June 22, the *Oxnard* (California) *Press-Courier* printed a list of eleven soldiers that the U.S. Department of Defense classified as missing in action in Vietnam. Included among the list are eight Marines and three members of the Army…1st Lt. Charles Bedsole, 20, from Severna Park, Maryland, and 2nd Lt. David Bolton, 22, from Marysville, California. The third name on the list was Pfc. Ravencraft *(pg. 2)*. While the bodies of 1st Lt. Bedsole and 2nd Lt. Bolton were eventually recovered, the remains of Pfc. Ravencraft were not. In March 1975, search teams returned to the area where Pfc. Ravencraft was last seen and recovered his remains, which were then transferred to the Central Identification Laboratory in Thailand, where they were positively identified.

Pfc. Ravencraft, one of nearly one hundred and fifty fellow Ohioans killed in Vietnam who were members of the 9th Infantry, was posthumously promoted to Staff Sergeant and awarded America's oldest military award…the Purple Heart.

The award, given to those wounded or killed in combat, was presented to his family.

He is buried near his father and mother in the Powhatan Cemetery, Powhatan Point, Ohio. In addition, his name is etched on The Wall: Panel 56W, Line 27.

William Robert Lucas was born in Barnesville, Belmont County, on October 9, 1948. Known to family and friends as Bobby, he was the first child of Robert Elmer and Betty Lee Lucas.

According to the 1950 census taken in April, the family lived on New Castle Ridge, near the Malaga and Sunsbury Township border in northern Monroe County. Four people lived in the home then, including Mr. Lucas, 19, Mrs. Lucas, 17, a sister-in-law, Barbara Davis, 15, and Bobby, eighteen months. The census also indicates that Mr. Lucas, a farmer, worked around sixty hours a week the previous year while Mrs. Lucas worked at home. As expected, the neighbors on both sides of the Lucas' on New Castle Ridge were farmers. Beyond farming, family members say that Mr. Lucas also cut timber. Mrs. Lucas was known to help around the farm, including feeding farm animals and milking cows. Mrs. Lucas began driving a school bus when the couple had more children. With no less than five children in elementary school through high school, and since the bus was commonly parked near their home, the Lucas were usually the first ones on the bus in the mornings and the last ones off the bus in the afternoons.

It is said that Robert and Betty Lucas purchased the farm from Betty's mother. When a piece of land adjoining theirs went up for sale, it was purchased by Bobby's parents. At one point, the family possessed over four hundred acres, with some of the land located across the Belmont County line, in Wayne Township.

In the family for three generations, the front of the Lucas faced County Road 92. Interestingly, one side house of looked out on Crum Road.

Mr. Lucas was known as a hard-nosed, strict disciplinarian. Moreover, he had no gray areas…it was either black or white…and truthfulness was important. The family was churchgoers. Most assuredly, Mrs. Lucas, who worshipped at the Jerusalem Methodist Church.

By most reports, Bobby was a good student. He was on the eighth-grade honor roll in 1962 while attending Beallsville High School. In high school, he was enrolled in several college prep classes. This included Math class with Mr. Haudenschield, which had only five students, English with Mrs. Pritchard, and Physics with Mr. Thomas. Besides being a student in Miss Morris' Music class, Bobby was a member of the school's Glee Club.

Classes at BHS began at 8:00am and lasted until 3:00pm; however, the long days and classroom demands did not stop Bobby from participating in sports. Despite his slight frame, barely 5' 9'' and 150 pounds, the speedy Bobby played running back and linebacker on the school's football team in the fall and ran track in the spring. His specialty was the 100-yard dash and the 220. More, he was chosen prom king in his senior year.

Bobby had an interest in the medical field. In particular, he wanted to be a doctor. His high school guidance counselor suggested that Bobby enlist in the military, become a corpsman to receive valuable training, and then return from the service to attend college on the GI Bill. Around the time he turned eighteen, he registered with the Selective Service. The number on his draft card...33 7 48 595...said it all. Bobby was from Ohio (33), the number of his local draft board in St. Clairsville (7), the year of his birth (48), and his line in sequence of others born that year (595). However, after graduating from Beallsville High School in 1966 with the other fifty-one class members, he set his career plan in motion by joining the Navy. Here, he could choose his own MOS (military occupational specialty). Bobby chose the route of becoming a hospital corpsman (HM). He knew that although he was in the Navy, a medic would commonly accompany

Marine infantry units on patrol, search and destroy missions, and large-scale military operations. A medic was viewed by fellow soldiers as having the same importance as a radioman. Consequently, medics were a prime target for the enemy, which explains why around 2,000 lost their lives in the Vietnam conflict.

Although the elder Lucas was not in the military service, mainly because he was underage and his parents refused to sign the necessary papers, Bobby came from a deep military pedigree. His maternal grandfather served during WWI, and his great-grandfather fought in Civil War on the side of the North.

Bobby enlisted in August 1966 and was inducted into the military on March 7, 1967, in Pittsburgh, Pennsylvania. He did his basic training at the Navy's largest and only boot camp: Naval Station Great Lakes, located in North Chicago, Illinois. Following his completion, he was sent to Camp Lejeune, North Carolina, where he was trained in all areas of medical care, from post-op to ob-gyn. It is said that while stationed at Camp Lejeune, Bobby would hitch a ride with fellow soldiers to New Stanton, Pennsylvania. His family would then meet him there and drive him back to Monroe County for his visit. When his visit ended, his family would drive him back to New Stanton so he could meet his ride back to North Carolina.

At the end of the hospital training, the military would choose the top six candidates from each class to go to Vietnam. Bobby was one of the six from his class chosen.

He deployed to Vietnam the day after Thanksgiving, 1968. The journey took him to Honolulu, Hawaii, then to Okinawa, Japan, and finally to Da Nang. The military records show that he officially began his tour of duty in Vietnam on December 8. Upon arriving, he was assigned to H&S (Headquarters and

Service Company), 3rd Battalion, 26th Marines, 1st Marine Division, III MAF (Marine Amphibious Force). The 1st Marine Division, nicknamed the "Old Breed," was the Marines' oldest and largest combat unit. In addition, the 3/26th is best known as the unit that raised the flag on Iwo Jima on February 23, 1945. Now referred to as HM3 Lucas, the rank was the equivalent of a lance corporal in the Marines. However, soldiers in the unit referred to him as simply "Doc." In short time, HM3 Lucas found himself among a unit of Marines in Quang Nam Province.

Operation Taylor Common was a joint operation of the 1st Marine Division and ARVN troops. The three-phase operation, instituted around the time HM3 Lucas was arriving in Southeast Asia, was developed to address the build-up of PAVN and Viet Cong troops southwest of Da Nang. The first Marines arrived in the area on December 6.

Known as the Arizona Territory or Dodge City because it reminded soldiers of the American Wild West of the 1850s, the area was a free-fire zone where enemy ambushes could come at any moment and from any direction. Furthermore, the area, three miles long and five miles wide, was home to countless Vietnamese villagers that were hostile to American forces and showed that anger by riddling the area with enemy booby traps and mines.

The second phase of the operation took place during the last two weeks of the month. It involved the establishment of a landing zone and several firebases, around seventy-five miles south of An Hoa Airbase, in Quang Nam Province. During the final phase of the operation, January thru March 1969, the plans called for soldiers to use the firebases to attack enemy operations. Nonetheless, the plans were scaled back when Allied troops were called to confront a build-up of

PAVN troops immediately south of the DMZ.

In late February, the remaining troops from Operation Taylor Common were hit with a barrage of mortar and rocket fire. When the Allied forces could no longer hold onto the firebases in the area, a decision was made to abandon the operation. It is believed that as many as two hundred Marines died during the final phase. During the final phase of fighting on March 9, as HM3 Lucas responded to the call of "medic," he was killed by an enemy sniper.

According to the casualty report, HM3 Lucas died *"...as a result of gunshot wounds while on a search and clear mission" (Coffelt Database of Vietnam Casualties).* Ironically, it is said that HM3 Lucas did not want a gun because he didn't want to shoot anyone.

Also killed that day in Quang Nam Province from the 3/26 Marine unit was Pfc. Elijah Herring from Leslie, Georgia. Pfc. Herring, 19, had been in Vietnam for sixty-six days. A third Marine, Lance Corporal Randall Shackelford, 20, from Coggan, Iowa, population around 620, was wounded and would later die. Quang Nam Province was not only the same place where Marine Pvt. Duane Greenlee lost his life two years and two days earlier, but in the same province where Marine Pvt. Dan Bullock, the youngest soldier to be killed in Vietnam, would lose his life in less than a month.

The news of HM3 Lucas' death came quickly to his family and the Beallsville area. When the green-colored Army vehicle approached the house, his mother knew it was bad news. Mrs. Lucas was holding the youngest of the Lucas children in her arms, Jodi, eighteen months, when the officers told her of her son's death. Afterward, the officers left to tell Bobby's siblings the news, including Nancy, a senior at BHS; Toni, a junior; Tim, a seventh-grader, and Clint and Wade, who were in elementary school.

Toni was looking out the window during Health Class when the military car pulled into the school parking lot. Within minutes, a teacher was knocking on the classroom door. The teacher quietly asked Toni to gather her books and follow her to the school office. It was the same for the other siblings since they were all in the same school building. Toni was the last of her siblings to arrive.

As the military officer told the children the bad news about their brother, one of the children remembers Toni saying that "Bobby's only wounded." The officer corrected her and then repeated the sad news that their oldest brother was dead. A boyfriend of Bobby's sister, Nancy, and the son of the local funeral director, was in the office when the news was shared with the Lucas children. The friend, Bob Harper, offered to go to Toni's locker and get her purse.

Supposedly, all the children rode home in the military car. However, most do not remember doing so because they were in shock. Mr. Lucas, now 38, and Mrs. Lucas, 37, waited anxiously for the children to arrive home.

Across town, the announcement of Bobby's death came to the local funeral home via phone. After hearing the news, the funeral director's wife turned to her husband and spoke, saying, "My God. Now it's Bobby Lucas."

Before long, the grim news that another BHS graduate had died in Vietnam, the fourth in three years, began circulating in the village of less than five hundred and among the residents of the state's second least-populated county. The news of HM3 Lucas' death brought added attention to the fact that a high number of Beallsville's graduates were going off to serve in Vietnam.

Regarding the large numbers, Monroe County Treasurer

Raymond Starkey spoke to Ohio Congressman Clarence Miller in a phone conversation on March 17, telling the congressman that *"...Beallsville High graduates have more exposure to the 'draft' than most graduating students from other schools...Is it fair,"* Starkey asked Miller, that *"...such a large percentage of our young men should be exposed to the war simply because they do not have the money to go on to college?"*

Starkey continued...

"...it's not that our boys are not college material, but they just do not have the money to further their education....as few as 20 percent of boys in some recent Beallsville high graduation classes have gone on to college while the percentage of boys graduating from other schools and continuing their education is 60 to 70 percent." (Cambridge Daily Jeffersonian, March 20, 1969. pg. 12).

Echoing Starkey's words of concern, the local funeral home director, Keith Harper, remarked that...

"...we have a right to think the way we do. We felt that way after the first three died. Officials should know about this because they are the only ones who can help." (The Daily Jeffersonian, March 17, 1969, pg. 11).

Other newspapers around the U.S. were quick to circulate the story, including an article in the *Cedar Rapids Gazette (pg. 11)* and the *Albuquerque Tribune (pg. 8)* in their March 22 issues, and on page three of the March 23 edition of the Oxnard, California, *Press Courier (pg. 3)*. In neighboring West Virginia, the news from Beallsville caught the attention of around four state newspapers. The limited attention is understandable since the state was dealing with an exceedingly high number of soldier deaths, quickly approaching 475, at the time of HM3 Lucas' dearth. One Tennessee newspaper noted that...

*"...Of the 24 young men in Lucas' class, 19 others are
in various military branches, with six in the Vietnam
combat zone. (Kingsport Times-News, March 23, 1969,
pg. 4).*

Responding to the words of Starkey, Harper, and most of
Beallsville's citizens, Congressman Miller agreed that the
community...

*"...has given more of their youth than they should have
been asked. It's certainly out of proportion to what
other communities have sacrificed." (The Salem News,
Ohio, March 24, 1969, pg. 7).*

In a matter of days, Congressman Miller sent a formal
letter to Secretary of Defense Melvin Laid at the Pentagon.
Before long, the letter was returned with a response that
denied the request, with an explanation that read, in part, that
the...

*"Danger is personal to the individual, not the
community from which he comes. If one individual
should be excused because of his geographic origin, the
risk he is spared...would have to be assumed by some
other young man whose family and community would
be equally solicitious (sp.) of his welfare."
Guantanamo Gazette, April 1, 1969, pg. 4)*

———————

The body of HM3 Lucas arrived in Beallsville during the
third week of March. His funeral was set to take place on
Sunday, March 22. Although he was a patient at the
Barnesville hospital after suffering a heart attack, Mr. Lucas'
doctors allowed him to attend the viewing on Thursday, March
20.

Two days later, on a cold and windy March day with chilly
temperatures, several hundred people gathered for Bobby
Lucas' service at the Beallsville Cemetery. Except for one gas

station which serviced no customers, it is said that every business in the village was closed for the funeral. The number of mourners included Naval reservists from nearby Wheeling and Steubenville who acted as pallbearers and honor guard, along with the mothers of Pfc. Pittman, Pvt. Greenlee, and Pfc. Schnegg. In addition, there was Mrs. Lucas with five of the six children. The only immediate family members not attending were the youngest child, Jodi, and Mr. Lucas, who remained in the hospital.

Following readings from Psalm 23 and 90, Rev. Richard Perkins, from the Methodist Church, began his eulogy by saying that...

> *"...He had gone to the hill cemetery four times*
> *before for the burial of recent graduates, and I*
> *will be coming again if this war does not stop*
> *and man does not change...."*

And as he pointed to his heart, he continued, saying that...

> *"man must change in here...this is a sick, sick world.*
> *We have to change this world." (Sandusky Register,*
> *March 24, 1969, pg. 14)*

The service concluded with a classmate of Nancy Lucas' playing Taps. Little did Rev. Perkins know that he would be officiating at the funeral of another Beallsville soldier in twenty-five months.

———————

The body of HM3 Lucas is interred beneath a headstone in the village cemetery that reads "Our Dear Bobby." The name of HM3 Lucas is etched on The Wall: Panel 30, Line 91.

Dwight Herbert Ball was born on May 26, 1949, to Howard Monroe Ball and Clarice Odessa Jones Ball. At the time of Dwight's birth, Mr. Ball, nicknamed Baggie, was thirty-eight, while Mrs. Ball was thirty-six. Waiting for Dwight's arrival at the family's two-story gray house, located on Ohio State Route 7 (Main Street), in Sardis, Lee Township, Ohio, was his sister Mary, age 12; brother Duane, 5; and another sister, Patti, 2.

According to their marriage application, Mr. and Mrs. Ball were married in Sardis, Ohio, on September 29, 1934. W.H. Deaton, Justice of the Peace, presided over the ceremony. At the time, the elder Ball, who was born in Ravenswood, West Virginia, was twenty-four, and his occupation was listed as a truck driver, while his wife, born in Sardis, was twenty-one. Their marriage license shows her occupation as "domestic work." The 1950 census records Mr. Ball's occupation as a farmer and Mrs. Ball's as a housewife.

———————

Beginning in the third grade at Sardis Elementary, Dwight had been assigned to the same homeroom as his cousin, Bryan Beisel. When the two entered high school at River High School, just up the road in nearby Hannibal, Ohio, they were assigned the same homeroom teacher: Mr. Forni, Room 148. Although they would begin each day in the same classroom, this would change following daily announcements and the pledge of allegiance.

Dwight's classes included English, Math with Mr. Rich, History/Civics with Mr. Repco, mechanical drawing, and shop class. Meantime, Bryan took other courses. In addition, Dwight, who stood around six-feet tall and weighed 170 pounds, played on the boys' basketball team at River for the first two years of high school. Consequently, Dwight and Bryan may not see each other until the end of the school day

243

and sometimes not until the next day in homeroom! Nevertheless, it is said that the two were nearly inseparable, and it was not uncommon to find them fishing or swimming together in the Ohio River.

As with most of those his age, Dwight, who had grown into a handsome young man with light brown hair and was particular in his clothes and how he dressed, worked in the area during the summer months. At one point in his teen years, it is said that he bought a record album of Paul Revere and the Raiders from his work earnings and presented it to his sister, Helen.

It was during the time he was working at his sister Mary's (Valentine) greenhouse and store in nearby New Matamoras, Ohio, that he met Debbie Montgomery. At the time, she was approaching her sixteenth birthday. Dwight and Debbie hit it off and soon began dating.

It is said that during the two years they saw each other, the couple did numerous things together. If they were not seeing a movie at the Sardis Drive-in, they were sitting in his 1956 two-tone, turquoise and white Chevrolet Bellaire, listening to the Beatles or the Rolling Stones on the car radio. Dwight, who at one time during their dating also worked in a gravel pit, was known to travel over to Debbie's school, pick her up, and take her out to lunch. One thing for sure throughout their two years of dating was Dwight's "go-to" snack: a cold glass of milk and a maple twist roll. It is said he ate it nearly every day.

In 1967, Dwight took his place among the other forty-eight boys and forty-four girls to graduate from River High School. Within a matter of months, he began working beside Debbie's brother, Keith, at Republic Steel in Canton, Ohio. In a letter written to Debbie from Canton in the early months of 1968, he wrote about his job, saying…

"…I'll have a pretty good pay check in three weeks.
I've been pushing a broom every day now. It doesn't

pay so good only $2.86 an hour but I'll get a better
paying job soon. Me and my boss have set (sp.) and
shot-the-bull everyday. I like him. He said he'd try to
get me a better job...."

In a lengthy letter sent to Debbie sometime later, Dwight
shares that he and Keith are living together on *"...Second*
Street, NE in Canton...." He also tells her he's having car
trouble and has decided to...

"...put a for sale sign on are (sp.) Chevy. I got it fixed
the other day. It cost me $9.00. It wasn't bad but I had
about $5.00 worth of labor that day. I'm going to sell it
before something else happens to it. I had to walk to
work Sunday & Monday. It's about a mile to the plant.
My feet were so sore I couldn't get in my work shoes. I
carried my work shoes to work the second day...."

He goes on to say that he's...

"...got a pretty good chance to work all summer
because they need a lot of guys now. And then the ones
working now will be taken (sp.) their vacations. I'd be
moving up from laborer to third helper that pays $2.96
an hour plus incentive...."

About halfway through the seven-page letter, Dwight gets
very personal with Debbie, saying...

"...I love you so much honey. I don't think I could live
without you. 'I love you' to (sp.). You're so nice.
You're one of a kind and I'm glad you're mine...."

His time at Republic Steel would be interrupted in late
March 1969 when he received notice to report for *"...armed*
forces examination..." (Daily Jeffersonian, March 21, 1969,
pg. 20). His name was among eleven other males from Monroe
County to receive the same letter. The article also listed the
names of around a dozen other males from the county who
were to report for induction on March 20 to meet the county's
March induction quota.

By June 1968, Dwight had moved from laborer to working

around the steel furnaces at Republic. In a letter dated June 15, he writes to Debbie, saying,…

> "…there must be an easier way to earn a living than working in a dirty old factory. Why couldn't I be a writer or a poet or an artist, etc., jobs like that don't take much effort in the way of physical movement. I hate to think that working in a place like this all my life. I wouldn't mind being a farmer. That way I'd be my own boss and I could work when I felt like it…."

At the age of twenty years, Dwight officially began his military service in the U.S. Army on July 23, 1969. He would do his basic training at Fort Dix, New Jersey. As with all soldiers in basic training, they were not allowed to call home. Instead, they were given note paper to write to family or friends.

In one of his first letters to Debbie since arriving at Fort Dix, Dwight wrote on paper given to him by the Army…the paper was made all the more impressive by the Army symbol at the top of the page…he wrote that he to "…shine a pair of boots. Our company is marching in the VFW National Convention parade in Philadelphia Tuesday night, so we have to have everything shining…." In the same letter written between August 13 and August 20, he shares that he "…had physical training yesterday morning. I scored 391 out of 500 which was pretty good…" He later adds that he's…

> "…got six more weeks of this. Time is starting to go slow. I wish I were out of the Army. I don't like it at all. I don't know anymore (sp.) now than when I did when I first went in…."

Pfc. Ball followed that with a one-page letter dated August 20, saying…

> "…Here it is Tuesday night 11:00. We just got back from the parade in Philadelphia. It was sort of interesting. We got to see the astronauts and the Sec of Defense & a "four" star General…I was supposed to

*be a squad leader for about a week but I guess I'll be
on all 8 weeks. No big thing...."*

One week later, he followed with a five-page letter to
Debbie, writing, among other things, that...

*"...we just got through qualifying with our M-14 rifles
today. I qualified as a sharpshooter...I'll be home in
about 3 months. I hope...Most guys are outnumbered
by Ohio. There's 20 guys from Ohio here in the
barracks so we pretty much control the place...I want
you to send me Bryan's address...."*

Pfc. Ball closes by asking Debbie, *"...how's everything
back in the Village?"* The "Bryan" he mentions in the letter is
his cousin, Bryan Beisel, who was serving in the U.S. Army
in Vietnam, and the "Village" was his hometown of Sardis.

Following a short visit around the Thanksgiving holiday,
Pfc. Ball deployed to Vietnam on December 12, 1969.

Not long after arriving in Vietnam, Pfc. Ball sent Debbie
a letter. In it, he said that he had been assigned to the *"...25th
Division, 27th Infantry, 2nd Battalion better known as the
Wolfhounds..."* adding that he's got *"...one heck of a sun
tan....and that the cookies she sent were good but they were
crumbled...."*

It seems that between letters, Debbie has discovered that
she's pregnant. In a letter from Dwight to Debbie dated January
15, he apologizes for the situation he's put her in and that...

*"...Getting married doesn't seem to pose such an awful
problem. I can get a 30 day (sp.) leave...In order for
me to get a leave you must contact the nearest chapter
of the American Red Cross. They will take care of all
the formalities. They are the only ones you can
contact...."*

In a follow-up letter written over a month later on February

18, Pfc. Ball writes to Debbie saying that he is having difficulty getting leave. After being denied a trip back to Sardis twice by his superiors, he tells her that he's…

"…*got one more choice on getting a leave & that's re-inlisting (sp.). I'd have to re-up for 3 years. That's a long time but if it comes to the last straw (and with your consent) I'll do it…*" He closes his letter, saying, "…*I'll be home one way or the other.*"

Within a month of the February letter, Pfc. Ball had returned to Sardis to marry Debbie.

———————

After receiving a pass, Pfc. Dwight Ball and Debbie Montgomery were married on March 22, 1970, in the home of Rev. Frank Conley in Washington Township. Witnesses included Debbie's brother and his wife. It is said that Pfc. Ball spent the remainder of his leave celebrating his marriage and visiting family and friends, including his cousin, Bill Beisel, who had recently returned from a tour of duty in Vietnam. On the last day of March, Bill drove his cousin to the Canton/Akron Airport for his return trip to Vietnam.

Upon arriving, Pfc. Ball rejoined his unit, which had been in Tay Ninh Province since March 31. Allied commanders were acting on intelligence about a possible build-up of PAVN and Viet Cong forces near the Cambodian border in an area known as Renegade Woods. As a reconnaissance unit made their way into the area of thick vines and deep elephant grass in the early morning hours of April 2, they were ambushed by much larger enemy forces. The reconnaissance quickly became a full-fledged battle. The initial encounter cost the lives of no less than ten U.S. soldiers, six from the 2nd Battalion, 27th Infantry.

The following day, April 3, several other companies from the 2nd Battalion, Pfc. Ball's battalion, were sent into

Renegade Woods to reinforce any remaining U.S. soldiers and retrieve any fallen troops. Little did the second group know that the first group of soldiers that had survived the battle had already been removed from the area by helicopter. Immediately upon entering the site, the second group came under enemy fire. The fighting on Friday, April 3, cost the life of one American soldier from Company A, 2ⁿᵈ Battalion, 27ᵗʰ Infantry: Pfc. Dwight Ball.

According to the casualty report, Pfc. Ball *"...was killed while on a combat operation when an artillery round directed at a hostile force landed in the area"* *(Coffelt Database of Vietnam Casualties)*. A post on *Faces on the Wall* from someone who was close to Pfc. Ball during the fighting, wrote that...

> *"...We were moving forward into renegade woods*
> *(sp.). There were bombs coming down into the area.*
> *You and I were sitting around chatting. A bomb came*
> *close (sp.) a piece of shrapnel went into your chest and*
> *you went asleep."*

Debbie Ball had just returned from church on April 5 when a green military vehicle pulled up to her parent's home on Grandview Avenue in New Matamoras, Ohio. The two officers had come to tell Debbie that her husband of twelve days had been killed in a friendly-fire incident when a bomb from an American aircraft fell short of its target. Also told the sad news were Pfc. Ball's parents: Howard, who had become crippled by arthritis, and Clarice.

On April 5, Pfc. Ball's body was delivered to the Bien Hoa Airbase, where his cousin, Bryan Beisel, who was in-country at the time, identified it. Bryan accompanied the body from Vietnam to Alaska and then to the airport in Pittsburgh, Pennsylvania. Pfc. Ball's body arrived in Sardis around 1:00am. Robert Beisel, a brother of Bill and Bryan, was called to help unload Dwight's body and place it under the care of

Rush Funeral Home, who was taking care of arrangements. No less than six area newspapers announced Pfc. Ball's death.

The open casket funeral was officiated by Rev. Frank Conley, the minister who officiated at the wedding of Dwight and Debbie. A close friend of Dwight's family also participated in the funeral service. Debbie remembers her husband's hair being parted to one side to cover his head wound. The elder Ball attended the funeral while seated in a wheelchair. Pallbearers at the service were Bryan and Bill Beisel and fellow friends of Dwight's: Steve Grimes and Dave Richey. After the graveside service, which included full military honors and a twenty-one-gun salute, the American flag was presented to Debbie. She remembers the painful words spoken to her by an officer: "On behalf of the President of the United States, the United States Army, and a grateful nation...." Several years later, Debbie gave the flag to their son, who would follow in his father's footsteps and serve in the military.

In addition to being posthumously promoted to corporal, Dwight was awarded two bronze stars, one for bravery and one for merit, and a Purple Heart. Pfc. Ball was buried in Mount Olive Cemetery in Sardis, and his name is etched on The Wall: Panel 12W, Line 86.

Steven Michael Janeda was born in Pittsburgh, Pennsylvania, on Monday, August 6, 1949. At the time of Steven's birth, his father, Joseph Valentine Janeda, was 39, and his mother, Sarah Ellen Musrage, was two years older. The elder Janeda was born in Allegheny County, Pennsylvania, while his wife was born in Ohio. Both were of Polish descent. They were married a few days before Christmas 1928 in Pennsylvania. Most likely waiting on the family farm, located approximately twelve miles west of New Matamoras, to welcome Steven were no less than seven siblings, including five brothers. The children ranged in age from the late teens to three years old. As the youngest child then, it is no surprise that the family had a nickname for Steven. They called him Munchkin. Also waiting on the newest addition to the Janeda household to arrive was the family dog, Skippy.

According to the 1950 census, the family lived in Pittsburgh, and the records indicate their name was spelled Janida. More, the census listed the children in the home as William, 16; Joseph, 13; Robert, 10; Ellen, 8; James, 4; and Steven, eight months. Finally, the census shows that Mr. Janeda, a towboat pilot on the Ohio River, worked around fifty hours a week. There is no occupation listed for Mrs. Janeda. It is said that the name of Mr. Janeda's towboat was the Capt. Joe.

In 1954, Mr. Janeda traveled to the Monroe County area to assist the daughter and son-in-law with some building construction on their farm. The elder Janeda liked Monroe County so much that he purchased a farm there. The family moved from Pittsburgh to Monroe County the following year. Although their mailing address was listed as New Matamoras in Washington County, it is said that the family farm, and possibly the home, was located along County Route 12 in Benton Township in Monroe County. One son, Robert, chose to stay in Pittsburgh.

Prior to the move to Ohio, the school-age kids in the family attended a private Catholic school in Pittsburgh. The school was near where the family worshipped: St. Peters Catholic

Church. Undoubtedly, the move from an urban school in Pittsburgh to a rural, 2-room school in Brownsville, Ohio, may have shocked the Janeda children.

Following the same path as some of his older siblings, Steven went from attending the school in Brownsville to the Midway School on Ohio Route 800, near Antioch, in Perry Township. In the ninth grade, he began attending River High School. The driver of the school bus that took Steven and the other students to the high school in Hannibal was Rev. Frank Conley, the minister at Mt. Olive Baptist Church in New Matamoras. Joining his family at St. Paul's Evangelical Church, Steven became a church member in 1963.

Possibly because his mother was a strict disciplinarian, his family says that Steven was an outstanding student in the classroom. Described by his brothers as a quiet kid, some of his fellow students remember Steven as having a great personality. Beyond playing the trumpet in his high school's marching band, Steven's 5'10' and 160-pound frame made him an excellent competitor in track. Beyond running, he was also a high jumper during his four years of participating in sports at his high school. He graduated from River High School in the Class of 1967 along with ninety-two others, including Dwight Ball and Bryan Beisel.

In the December 11, 1967, issue of the *Dover Daily Reporter*, the newspaper notes that Steven was pulled over by a local patrolman and ticketed $15 for speeding *(pg. 9)*. This may have been around the same time that he wrecked his brother Robert's 1952, blue and white, Chevrolet.

Following graduation, Steven went on to attend technical school.

In 1969, Steven followed his four brothers into the military. Three brothers, William, Joseph, and James, served in the Army, while the fourth, Robert, was in the U.S. Coast Guard. Steven chose to enlist in the U.S. Army.

He completed his basic training at Fort Knox, Kentucky. Steven then went to advanced training at Fort Bragg, beginning in the summer of 1969. During his six months at Fort Bragg, learning to be a radio operator, he met another radio operator, Roel Montalvo, from Texas. Moreover, the two would become bunkmates, with Steven on the top bunk and Roel on the bottom. In a phone interview with Montalvo, he described SP4 Janeda as one of the least racial and prejudiced individuals he had ever known. Sadly, during his advanced training at Fort Bragg, SP4 Janeda received word that his mother had passed away. Mrs. Janeda died on February 5 at the age of 62/63. Little did the family know that her death would be the first of three deaths in the immediate family over the next eleven months.

After completing their advanced training in early Winter 1970, the two soldiers made a pact as they awaited their deployment orders. They agreed to keep in touch through Steven's girlfriend, a baton twirler in the RHS band. Roel would write to the girlfriend and tell her where he was stationed. In turn, the girlfriend would relay Roel's address to Steven...and vice-versa. Reportedly, Stephen told Roel that he hoped he would be sent to Vietnam. It seems Steven was given his wish.

On St. Patrick's Day, March 17, 1970, SP4 Janeda began his tour of duty in Vietnam. Meanwhile, SP4 Montalvo was sent to Germany. Upon arriving, SP4 Janeda was assigned to the 146th Signal Company, 43rd Signal Battalion, 21st Signal Group, 1st Signal Brigade. Before long, he found himself in Pleiku Province as a radio teletypewriter operator, or simply, a radio man.

As a radio operator, SP4 Janeda had one of the most dangerous military specialties during the Vietnam conflict. With an average life expectancy of around five seconds, a radio operator had a great deal going against them.

First, there was the weight issue. The average weight of a basic radio unit was around fifteen pounds. However, this did not include other elements, like batteries for the unit and backup batteries. It is said that even the most common radio units used by field operators in combat could weigh over fifty pounds. Next, the antenna to the radio proved to be a negative in combat situations. Most radio units used an antenna measuring three to ten feet long, and that drew attention to the operator. A third issue that made the radio operator's military specialty a challenge was that the operator was often unable to control the volume or the chatter on the radio because the volume control was located on the soldier's back. Last but not least, the radio operator was usually near a platoon leader or unit officer who used the radio to call in coordinates for air or artillery support, pinpoint troop location, or ask for reinforcements.

Consequently, these issues combined to make a radio operator a prime target in combat. All the enemy had to do was shoot their small arms or send their mortars or rockets near the sound or the antennae. If the helicopter or radio were critical entities in battle, the radio operator was the next in line of importance

―――――――――

On May 26, around 6:30pm, SP4 Janeda was part of a vehicle convoy traveling near Kontum City in the central highlands of Pleiku Province when they were ambushed. The enemy used a similar tactic throughout the conflict: take out the first and last vehicles in the convoy, halting the remaining trucks from going frontward or in reverse. The remaining vehicles and their passengers became sitting ducks. SP4 Janeda was in the last truck. The *Coffelt Database of Vietnam Casualties* notes that SP4 Janeda was *"...killed while a passenger on a military vehicle on a military mission when a hostile force was encountered."* His military death certificate records that he was shot in the head, and his death was immediate. His passing came on Memorial Day, 1970.

Before long, a khaki-colored military vehicle arrived at the Janeda home near New Matamoras with two military officers inside. After introducing themselves, Mr. Janeda opened the front door to their home. Then he led the two men into the living room. As he sat in his chair with daughter Ellen nearby, the family was told the heartbreaking news that Steven had been killed in Vietnam. Almost as if to verify what he was hearing, it is said that Mr. Janeda immediately turned to his daughter, Ellen, the youngest of the children and the only other person in the home at the time, and asked her to repeat what the officers had said. "Steven has been killed," she told her father. No less than six newspapers in the area noted his passing, but only two reported his death on the front page. Meanwhile, Steven's girlfriend shared the news with Roel Montalvo. SP4 Janeda would become the third soldier from River High School to die in Vietnam and the second to be killed in the past two months.

After his body left Vietnam, it arrived at an airport across the Ohio River in West Virginia and eventually at McCullers Funeral Home in Marietta. SP4 Janeda's funeral service was officiated by Rev. Frank Conley...the same person who drove the school bus that took Steven and many of his family and friends to school. He received full military rites, including a twenty-one-gun salute at his burial. He was interred at Valley Cemetery, later East Lawn, in Reno, Washington County, Ohio, next to his mother. Mr. Janeda passed away on January 19, 1971, from a heart attack while sitting on his front porch. His body was placed in the same cemetery plot with his youngest son next to him.

SP4 Janeda was awarded a Bronze Star and a Purple Heart. His name appears on The Wall: Panel 10W, Line 104.

Phillip Michael Brandon was born on Monday, November 19, 1951, to Stanley Robert Branson and Bertha Isabelle Riley Brandon. At the time of Phillip's birth, Mr. Branson, an Army veteran of WWII, had recently turned 25, while Mrs. Brandon was two months away from celebrating her twenty-fourth birthday. Beyond listing on their marriage application that he was living in Newcomerstown, Ohio, and employed as a truck driver, and she was born in Beallsville and unemployed, the February 10, 1951, application indicates that the local probate judge waived the standard waiting period of five days so the couple could get married sooner. The Brandons exchanged marriage vows later that day, with the ceremony officiated by Rev. G.H. Farmer of Clarington. Their marriage abstract further lists Mr. Branson's birthplace as Tuscarawas County.

At the time of Phillip's birth, the couple had been married nine months and nine days. The family is believed to have lived between Beallsville and Clarington along Ohio State Route 556 in Switzerland Township.

Like many other students from around Monroe County, Phillip attended high school in Beallsville and was a member of the Class of 1969. One of his classmates was Shirley Schnegg, the sister of Pfc. Charles Schnegg. In the Spring of his senior year at BHS, about the same time that one of his sisters, Phyllis, was making the Honor Roll at the school, Phillip enlisted in the U.S. Army. It could have been that he wanted to choose his own MOS (military occupational specialty) that he decided to go that route. Otherwise, as part of the 1971 draft lottery, he had a slim chance of being called for military service.

As part of the second draft lottery on July 1, 1970, involving males born in 1951, Phillip's APN (administrative processing number) was 295 of 365. This meant that Phillip and the other males born in the U.S. on November 19 would be called to military service only after the other 291 groups of males were called. The first lottery capsule chosen was July 9, and the highest number called that year for the military was 125…August 9. Except for those males born on July 4, 1951, who were called in the forty-second group, males born on other major American holidays were safe, including those born on Easter (March 25), who would be called in the two hundred and ninety-eighth group; Thanksgiving (November 22), in group two hundred and fifty-three, and Christmas in group three hundred and sixty-one.

Following basic training, Army Specialist SP-4 Brandon arrived for his tour of duty in Vietnam on October 29, 1970, as a Heavy Vehicle Driver. He was assigned to the 805th Transportation Company, 39th Transportation Battalion, 26th General Support Group, Army Support Command Da Nang, 1st Logistical Command.

On March 7, 1971, SP-4 Brandon was driving an Army truck on Highway QL-1 in Thua Thien Province when his vehicle was ambushed while crossing a bridge over the Song Bo River, around ten miles northwest of Hue. The records indicate that SP4 Brandon was the only soldier killed in the ambush on March 7. It wasn't until two days later, on March 9, that the family learned of his death.

According to the Department of Defense, SP4 Phillip Brandon *"…was killed while the driver of a military vehicle on a military mission when the area came under attack by a hostile force "* (*Coffelt Database of Vietnam Casualties*). The *Virtual Wall* says that Brandon was killed by small arms fire.

The first Ohio newspaper to report his death may have been the *Daily Jeffersonian* in its March 11, 1971, edition. The eleven-paragraph article entitled "Another Beallsville GI

257

Killed in Vietnam Action" begins by writing that...

> *"...Two years ago the U.S. Secretary of Defense turned down a request from this small Monroe County town to have its servicemen removed from combat in Vietnam...Today the community is mourning another death...SP-4 Phillip Michael Brandon, Beallsville, R.D. 1, was killed when a truck he was driving in Vietnam, was ambushed."*

The article goes on to say that *"...Beallsville's war dead includes three members of its 1965 graduating class, one from 1964, and one from its 1966 class...."* This includes Pfc. Jack Pittman (1964), Pvt. Duane Greenlee, Pfc. Charles Schnegg, Pfc. Richard Rucker (1965), and HM3 William "Bobby" Lucas (1966). The article adds that *"...Contributions received from the nationwide press coverage were used to build a memorial here..." (pgs. 1, 13)*. Another newspaper in the area ran an article adding to the details, including the fact that SP4 Brandon was a member of the United Methodist Church and his funeral arrangements were being taken care of by Harper-Campbell Funeral Home in Beallsville *(Zanesville Times Recorder, March 11, pg. 1)*. This is the same funeral home that served the families of several other Beallsville residents that lost a loved one in the Vietnam conflict. The *East Liverpool Evening Review* of March 11 noted that since the death of HM3 Bobby Lucas, another *"...two villagers have been killed in the war and two returned Vietnam veterans have died in auto accidents" (pg. 33)*.

In the following days, the story of Beallsville's pain reached other parts of the U.S. The *Charleston Gazette* (West Virginia) added that *"...The people of this community are exhausted from the flood of visitors who do not feel the grief..."* as do the citizens of Beallsville *(March 12, pg. 11)*. The *Sarasota Herald Tribune's* (Florida) March 16 edition stated at Brandon's funeral the citizens of Beallsville *"...chased NBC out of town and told all other news media to stay away" (pg. 7).* However, most powerful may have been the article in *Defiance Crescent News* (Ohio) which contrasted the large number of Beallsville soldiers killed in Vietnam and the village's relative population in ratio to New York City. The reporting shared that *"...With a population of 8 million, New York City would have to lose 160,000 men in the war to equal the percentage of the tiny Beallsville's toll – population now 393...."* The article added that while *"...Two percent of 8 million doesn't seem so big, but out of 400, it is devasting... (March 16, pg. 1).* Finally, the *Logan Daily News* (Ohio) reported that *"...with the death of SP4 Michael Brandon, 19, (Ohio Congressman Clarence) Miller has again written to (Sec. of Defense Melvin) Laird and sent a special plea to President Nixon on behalf of the families of young men in Beallsville...."* (March 25, pg. 2).

The funeral for SP4 Phillip Brandon was held in the chapel of the Harper-Campbell Funeral Home on Monday, March 15, with the Rev. Richard Perkins officiating. The burial took place at Holly Memorial Gardens in Mount Pleasant, Jefferson County, and included full military rites.

SP4 Brandon was awarded the Purple Heart. His name is etched on The Wall: Panel 4W, Line 30.

Dale Robert Hood was born on September 5, 1950, to Emmett and Opal Marie Leasure Hood. At the time of Dale's birth, Mr. Hood, a veteran who had served three years in the military during WWII, was in his fourth decade of living, while Mrs. Hood was sixteen years younger. Their marriage application, dated June 20, 1946, indicates that the elder Hood was thirty-five, from Lewisville in Summit Township, and was a farmer. The application also records that the wife-to-be was from Summerfield, Marion Township, Noble County, and lists her occupation as a houseworker. Because she was under twenty-one, her parents had to sign a court document granting their daughter permission to marry. Beyond stating that neither the bride nor the groom had been married before, the application records that the couple petitioned the local judge to waive the time between the marriage application and the marriage license issuance. The waiver was granted, and the couple married two days later, on June 22, 1946, with Justice of the Peace L.A. Massie from Woodsfield performing the ceremony. The 1950 census listed Mr. Hood's occupation as a farmer and his wife as a farm helper.

Two other Hood children were waiting at the family home on R.D. 1, Morris Hill Road, in Lewisville, for the new addition to arrive: Shirley Ann, 2, and Connie Marie, 1.

Lastly, it's worth noting that Dale was born on the same day as another of the "Edison 64" from Edison High School in Philadelphia, Pennsylvania. In this case, it was Samuel Nurrell Burton.

Like most other children in the township, Dale attended Lewisville Elementary School near his home. It is believed that Dale remained at the school until it consolidated with schools from Graysville and Bethel in 1958 to form Skyvue High School in Stafford, in Franklin Township. He was a sophomore when the new Skyvue High School, located on Hartshorn Ridge in Washington Township, opened in 1966.

While attending Skyvue, Dale ran track his senior year. His specialty was the 880 and the mile. He was a member of the Class of 1969 at Skyvue.

Most likely, it was around the time of his last year in high school that he registered with the Selective Service. A few months afterward, the first draft lottery was held on December 1, 1969, for all males born between 1944 and 1950. The first number drawn was September 1, and the last number, 366, was July 8. With draft number eighty-two, Dale entered the Army as a Medical Corpsman on March 30, 1970.

Pfc. Hood did his basic training at Fort Bragg and additional training at Fort Sam Houston in Texas. He began his tour of duty in Southeast Asia on October 22, 1970, as a member of HHT (Headquarters and Headquarters Troop), 3rd Squad, Company, 5th Calvary, 5th Infantry Division, stationed in Laos.

On April 7, 1971, exactly one month after the death of SP4 Phillip Brandon, an explosion happened inside an armored personnel carrier traveling along a road near the DMZ in Quang Tri Province. The blast killed E3 Dale Hood and two other U.S. servicemen. According to the casualty list, E3 Hood was killed *"...while a passenger on a military vehicle on a military mission when an explosion of unknown origin occurred inside the vehicle" (Coffelt Database of Vietnam Casualties).* Also killed in the explosion were another passenger, E4 Earl King, 20, from Ft. Walton Beach, FL, and the driver of the personnel carrier, E4 Grover Pierson, 21, from Cincinnati.

As expected, the death of E3 Hood was reported in several

area newspapers. The first to report may have been the *Daily Jeffersonian* in their April 14 edition. In the April 15 issue of the *Hamilton Daily News*, the newspaper noted that E3 Hood *"...died of a cause other than battle wounds" (pg. 14)*. As for the *Findlay Republican Courier*, their article of April 15 read E3 Hood was *"...previously listed as missing, but changed to dead of nonhostile actions" (pg. 5)*.

The funeral for E3 Hood was held on April 17, at Mt. Tabor United Methodist Church in Stock Township, Noble County, with the Rev. Starling Perkins officiating. E3 Hood was buried in the church cemetery on Crum Ridge Road with full military rites. He is the last of the eleven sons of Monroe County to be killed in the conflict...thank God!

The name of E3 Dale Robert Hood is etched on The Wall: Panel W4, Line 111.

Chapter V

"Who were they?" This is the question that writer Ray Abbott seeks to answer in his article in the June 1993 edition of *Vietnam* magazine. More, he is spot-on when he writes…*"One wants to know more about these Americans."*

Generally speaking, Abbott writes that over 58,000 Americans lost their lives as a result of the conflict in Southeast Asia. Of this number, the Army suffered the most casualties, nearly 38,200. Similarly, Marine casualties numbered almost 15,000, the Navy about 2,600, and the Air Force about the same. The Coast Guard lists around ten of its personnel killed during the conflict. Additionally, there were eight females that never came home, along with sixteen chaplains.

Next, Abbott writes that nearly ninety percent of those that lost their lives were privates or corporals, with a rank of E-1 to E-4, and that almost one in four were teenagers between the ages of 17 and 19. If one increases the perimeters to include those ages 17-21, the number jumps to three of every four casualties. The author continues, saying…

"…These young men were trained quickly and shipped to Vietnam quickly. They also died quickly, many within a few weeks or months of arriving in Vietnam. But given the draft policies, the hard-sell recruitment, the severe escalation from month to month and the refusal by President Lyndon Johnson to call up the older reserves and National Guard, it could not have been otherwise. The burden of combat fell on the very available non-college-bound young…."

Abbott goes on to say that those in the seventeen to twenty-one age category were the best suited for military combat. Among the reasons offered were that these young men were at the age to accept military discipline and were single. More, they were nearing or had reached the peak of their physicality and were less likely to be afraid of combat because they had not reached the point of recognizing their own mortality.

Moreover, the author writes that nearly six in ten casualties of the conflict were not enlisted but volunteers and did so under the belief that a volunteer…

"…could enlist as early as 17 (with parental consent); that he was allowed to select his branch of service; that he would receive specialized training if he qualified; that he could request a specific overseas assignment; and that his three year enlistment followed by three years in the inactive reserves satisfied his military obligation immediately. Sad to say, many of these recruitment promises were fudged in one way or another, and many of these young men found themselves shipped directly to Vietnam after basic training."

The influence of a relative such as a father, grandfather, uncle, or sibling also played heavily into a soldier's decision to join the military. Any attempt to avoid one's obligation to country, including seeking a deferment, dodging, or joining the reserves, was seen as unpatriotic and un-American.

Abbott also points out that nearly three in four American enlisted casualties…

"…were of English/Scottish/Welsh, German, Irish and Scandinavian-American ancestries, more from the South and Midwest than the other regions, many from small towns with a family military tradition."

Furthermore, it should not be surprising *"…that West Virginia, Montana, and Oklahoma had a casualty rate (per 100,000) almost twice that of New York, New Jersey and Connecticut…."* This may be related to the fact that there was…

*"...better employment opportunities in the Northeast
reduced the number of volunteers; greater college
matriculation in the Northeast increased the number of
status deferments for the region's 17-to 24-year
olds...and more anti-war sentiment in the media and on
college campuses in the Northeast."*

Another factor that Abbott highlights in the article is the
high number of casualties and the educational levels of the
soldiers. The records indicate that between sixty and sixty-five
percent of all deaths were high school graduates, and

*"...those who could have qualified for college probably
did not have the funds...A more precise equation would
be that the college bound stayed home while the non-
college bound served and died. The idea that American
enlisted dead were made up largely of society's poverty
stricken misfits is a terrible slander to their memory
and to the solid working-class and middle-class
families of this country who provided the vast majority
of our casualties. Certainly, some who died did come
from poor and broken homes...And more's the pity,
because many of them were trying to escape this
background and didn't make it."*

No truer words could have been written, especially
considering the eleven young men from Monroe County who
lost their lives in the conflict.

For starters, nine of the eleven young men killed in the
Vietnam conflict were members of the U.S. Army. This
includes Staff Sgt. Glenn McCammon, Pfc. Jack Pittman, Cpl.
Charles Schnegg, SP4 Richard Rucker, Staff Sgt. James
Ravencraft, Cpl. Dwight Ball, SP4 Steven Janeda, SP4 Phillip
Brandon, and Pfc. and Army Medic Dale Hood. The lone
Marine from Monroe County to be killed in Vietnam was Pvt.
Duane Greenlee and the sole Navy serviceman was HM3

William "Bobby" Lucas.

The rank of these eleven sons at the time of their deaths includes one at the rank of E2 (Greenlee), five at E3 (Pittman, Schnegg, Ravencraft, Ball, and Hood), four at E4 (Lucas, Rucker, Janeda, and Brandon), and one at the rank of E6 (McCammon). Posthumously, five soldiers would be promoted: McCammon to Staff Sergeant, Ravencraft to Staff Sergeant, and Schnegg, Lucas, and Ball to Corporal(s).

As for the soldier's mortal wound/death location, two of the eleven would die in Quang Nam Province (Greenlee and Lucas) and two others in Pleiku Province (McCammon and Janeda). The other Monroe County soldiers would be killed in **Binh Duong Province** (Pittman), **Kien Phong Province** (Schnegg), Gia Dinh Province (Rucker), Phong Dinh Province (Ravencraft), and Tay Ninh Province (Ball). As for Hood, he would be killed in Quang Tri Province and Brandon in Thua Thien Province.

Nearly one in three soldiers killed in Southeast Asia died by small arms fire, with the *Virtual Wall* citing no less than seven from Monroe County. Here, the list of soldier deaths included Pittman, Greenlee, Lucas, Schnegg, McCammon, Janeda, and Brandon. Friendly fire would claim the life of Rucker and Ball. A vehicle accident was listed as the cause of death of one of the soldiers (Hood). There is no cause of death listed for Ravencraft.

Among the over 58,000 names appearing on *The Wall*, nearly thirty to thirty-five thousand were under twenty-two. The number includes two nineteen-year-olds from Monroe County (Greenlee and Brandon) and seven twenty-year-olds (Pittman, Schnegg, Rucker, Lucas, Ball, Janeda, and Hood). The oldest among the group to lose his life in Vietnam was thirty-two (McCammon). At the same time, the youngest (Brandon) celebrated his nineteenth birthday three months before his death. The last soldier from the list (Ravencraft) is believed to have been twenty-three at his death.

Excluding one soldier (Ravencraft), the average time spent in Vietnam for the remaining ten soldiers was around three months (approximately 105 days). Two soldiers spent less than seventy days in-country before they died (McCammon and Janeda), and two graduates from Beallsville High School (Schnegg and Rucker) had spent over two hundred days.

Last but not least, no less than eight of the eleven soldiers had a relative that served in the military (Greenlee, Schnegg, Rucker, Ravencraft, Lucas, Janeda, Brandon, and Hood), and three of the eleven soldiers from the county (McCammon, Ravencraft, and Ball) were married, two with children. Finally, at least nine of the county soldiers had siblings back home in Ohio at the time of their passing.

Currently, there are no less than 58,000 names of U.S. military personnel on *The Wall.* Near the center of the granite structure, Panel 1E, Line 1, one can find the name of Major Dale Buis. He was from Imperial Beach, California, and died on July 8, 1959, in a surprise attack by the enemy while he and several other military advisors watched a movie. And near his name, on Panel 1W, Line 132, one finds the name of 2nd Lt. Richard Vandegeer, from Columbus, Ohio. He is believed to be the last soldier killed in the conflict and died on May 15, 1975. Extending outward from each center panel are the names of those that gave the ultimate sacrifice for this country. Alaska has the least number of soldier names appearing on the wall, fifty-five. In contrast, California has the most soldier casualties on *The Wall,* over fifty-five hundred.

The seventy panels also include the names of over 3,000 soldiers from Ohio. Of this number, over twenty-five percent of all casualties came from the state's most populated cities, including Cincinnati, Cleveland, Columbus, Dayton, and Toledo. Equally striking, no less than two hundred and seventy of the state's small towns or villages lost one soldier

267

in the conflict.

But of all the places in the state that lost a native son in the conflict, one county seems to stand out: Monroe County. This county, the state's second least populated county, lost eleven soldiers between 1965 and 1971…an average of around two a year.

The first was Staff Sgt. Glenn McCammon, who grew up in the county seat of Woodsfield, and died in November 1965 at LZ Albany. The following year, the conflict would claim the life of Pfc. Jack Pittman in July, and one month later, his cousin, Pvt. Duane Greenlee. Sixteen months later, it would be Pfc. Charles Schnegg, who died during the first few days of December 1967. In 1968, two more Monroe County sons would die within three weeks of each other: Pfc. Richard Rucker in May, and Staff Sgt. James Ravencraft in June. On March 9, 1969, the seventh of the county soldiers, HM3 Bobby Lucas, lost his life in Quang Nam Province. River High School classmates Pfc. Dwight Ball and Pfc. Steven Janeda would lose their lives within fifty-three days of each other in 1970. The tenth Monroe County soldier to die in the conflict was Pfc. Phillip Brandon in March 1971, and one month later, it was Army Medic Dale Hood.

And what stands out the most of all these deaths…from the first to the last…is that *Everyone Has a Story* that needs…no, it demands…to be told. The legacy of the eleven soldiers from Monroe County, the over three thousand from Ohio, and the over 58,000 whose name appears on *The Wall* could, and should, live on by our words and in our hearts and "…On behalf of a grateful nation…."

—Dr. Michael Price